Thirty Years In The Itinerancy

by

W. G. Miller

Double9 BOOKS

Thirty Years In The Itinerancy

by W. G. Miller

ISBN: 978-93-69070-25-1

Published by

DOUBLE 9 BOOKS

2/13-B, Ansari Road
Daryaganj, New Delhi – 110002
info@double9books.com
www.double9books.com
Tel. 011-40042856

ABOUT THE AUTHOR

W.G. Miller was an American Methodist minister who served extensively within the Wisconsin Conference of the Church during the 19th century. Born in the early 19th century, Miller was initially reluctant to enter the ministry, but divine providence, as he described it, led him to serve in the church. His career as an itinerant preacher spanned decades, during which he travelled through various small communities, ministering to congregations in frontier regions. He faced many challenges typical of his time, including the difficulties of traveling across vast, unsettled landscapes and the constant need to adapt to different communities. Through his experiences, Miller witnessed significant social and religious changes in 19th-century America, particularly in the expanding frontier. His reflections, detailed in his memoir Thirty Years in the Itinerancy, offer insight into the life of a dedicated minister in the Methodist Church and highlight themes of faith, perseverance, and divine guidance. Miller's life and work significantly contributed to the Methodist movement in Wisconsin, and his writing remains a valuable account of religious life in a developing America.

CONTENTS

DEDICATION

TO THE MINISTERS AND LAYMEN
OF THE WISCONSIN CONFERENCE,
WITH WHOM THE AUTHOR HAS BEEN ASSOCIATED
IN CHRISTIAN LABOR DURING THE PAST THIRTY YEARS
ARE THESE PAGES RESPECTFULLY DEDICATED.

PREFACE

The following pages were prepared in the midst of the taxing labors of the Ministerial calling. The materials have been drawn from a multitude of sources, and, though the recollections of individuals have not been entirely harmonious in all cases, the facts and dates are believed to be mainly reliable. The general plan, it will be observed, contemplates a brief record of the Charges and Ministers of the Wisconsin Conference, rather than furnish a sketch of my own services. To place the data, however, in suitable relations, and render it acceptable to the general reader, it has been deemed advisable to let the record follow the line of my labors during the thirty years of my Itinerant life. The publication of the book at the present time, is the result of my severe illness during the past year, and the generous, appreciative action taken by the District Conferences. A record of many other Charges and Ministers had been prepared, but, to my regret, the limits of the volume would not permit its insertion. Hoping that these pages may revive many pleasant recollections, furnish interesting and profitable reading for the fireside, and preserve material for the future historian, they are committed to the generous consideration of the public.

THE AUTHOR.

CHAPTER I

The ways of Providence are mysterious. And how, to men, could they be otherwise? With their limited faculties it could not be expected that they would be able to obtain more than partial glimpses of the "goings forth of the Almighty." The Astronomer can determine the orbit of the planets that belong to our system, since they lie within the range of his vision; but not so the comets. These strange visitors locate their habitations mainly in regions so remote from the plane of human existence that his eye cannot reach them. And when they do condescend to pay us a visit, they traverse so wide a circuit that the curve they describe is too slight to furnish a basis for reliable mathematical calculations. Hence the orbit of a comet is a mystery, and the return not unfrequently a surprise. If this be true of what seem to be the unfinished or exploded worlds, that swing like airy nothings in the heavens and fringe the imperial realm of physical being, then what may not be predicated of the profounder mysteries that lie bosomed in those unexplored depths of the Universe, where the fixed stars hold high court? When our feet trip at every step of our advance to know the mysteries of nature, why need we affect surprise when the profounder domain of providence refuses to yield up its secrets? That the ways of God are mysterious is a logical necessity. The Infinite disparity between the human and the Divine intelligence involves it. Insignificant as a lady's finger ring may seem when compared to one of the mighty rings of Saturn, the human mind, in the presence of the Divine, is infinitely more so. Well hath the Scriptures said, "Far as the heavens are higher than the earth, so are my ways higher than your ways, and my thoughts than your thoughts."

The mysterious ways of Providence are, however, not unfrequently so interwoven with human events as that average intelligence may be able to understand portions of them, though much of mystery must always remain. And in no one particular do these understandable portions find a clearer illustration than in those interventions which assign individual men to given pursuits and responsibilities in life. Truly, "There is a Providence that shapes our ends, rough hew them as we will."

Nor may these special interventions be wholly appropriated by the great men of the world. On the contrary, they not unfrequently condescend to bless the very humblest. The same great thought, the same skilled hand and the same infinite power that were necessary to pile up the grandest mountain ranges and hollow the ocean's bed, were also required to create a single grain of sand and assign it its place as a part of the grand whole. So, while great and honorable men pass into the world's history as the proteges of a special providence, let it also be remembered that the humbler ones, though their names may never be chronicled, are not forgotten by the All Father. If willing to be led, they shall not want a kind hand to lead them. And even though rebellious at times, and at others shrinking from the proffered responsibilities, yet a loving Father cares for the trembling and feeble ones, as well as the brave and the strong, and kindly leads them into the paths of peace.

I have not written thus, good reader, in these opening pages, to find a starting place for the record that is to follow. On the contrary, these utterances hold a special relation to the writer and the labors of the last thirty years.

Soon after my conversion, and before I was eighteen years of age, I received an Exhorter's license. I was then engaged in teaching and found my time largely occupied by my profession. Yet, I occasionally held services on the Sabbath. During the ensuing four years I retained the same relation. I was often urged to accept a Local Preacher's license, but declined, thinking I was too much occupied in the other field to make the necessary preparation for this. And, besides, I had now reached a point of great perplexity and trial with reference to the ministerial calling as a profession. Not that I entertained a serious thought of accepting it, but, on the contrary, was wholly averse to it. But, strangely enough, while I was thus, both in feeling and convictions, opposed to the measure, every one else seemed to accept it as a matter already settled that I would enter the Itinerant field. From the good Rev. John B. Stratton, the Presiding Elder of the Prattsville District, New York Conference, within the bounds of which I then resided, and his immediate successor, Rev. Samuel D. Ferguson, down through all the ministry and laiety of my acquaintance, I was made the special subject of attack. But from what all others thought to be my duty, I shrank with a persistence that admitted of no compromise. The plan I had marked out for myself contemplated, ultimately, the position of a Local Preacher, and a life devoted largely to literature and business. On this plan I fully relied, and thought myself settled in my convictions and fixed in my purpose. Yet I am not able to say, that at times it did not require some effort of the will to keep my conscience quiet and my thought steady. A young man, from eighteen to twenty-two years of age, who was subject to so many attacks, especially in high places, and who constantly felt himself preached to and prayed at in almost every religious assembly, must be more than human, not to say less than a Christian, to bear up under such a pressure. I clearly saw that one of two things must be done, and that speedily. Either I must yield to the manifest demand of the church or "go west." I chose the latter. Nor was this decision mere obstinacy. There were several things to be considered and carefully weighed and determined before entering upon a work of such grave responsibilities as the Itinerant ministry. First of all, the question must be settled in a man's conviction of duty; then the question of one's fitness for the work; and, finally, the financial question could not be ignored. To enter the Itinerancy involved responsibilities that could only be sustained under the deepest convictions that can possibly penetrate a human soul. The minister is God's ambassador to lost men. He can only enter upon this work under the sanction of Divine authority. Having entered he is charged with the care of souls, and if these shall suffer harm, through his inefficiency or want of fidelity, he must answer in the Divine assizes for the breach of trust. Well may the best of men say, "who is sufficient for these things?" Then add to this grave responsibility, the certain and manifold trials which must come to every man who enters the Itinerancy. His very calling makes him a spectacle to men, and necessarily the subject of adverse criticism. He is the messenger of God and yet the servant of man. On the one hand, clothed with the authority of heaven, and on the other reduced to the condition of a servant. Expected to deliver the high message of the King of Kings, and yet receives his pulpit under the suffrages of man. Before he receives his appointment, he is not unfrequently the subject of a sharp canvass from one end of the Conference to the other, and after he receives it he is liable to find himself among a people, who had rejected him in the canvass, and now only acquiesce in the decision from sheer necessity. But if he escape Scylla in this particular, he is certain to drive upon Charybdis in another. Granting that his relations and labors may be acceptable, he falls upon the inevitable necessity of devoting his time and labor, during the vigor and strength of his days, for a meager compensation, and then pass into old age, and its attendant infirmities, as a dependancy, if not a pauper. And now let me submit; with such a picture hung upon the canopy of the future, and who shall say it is overdrawn? is it a matter of surprise that a young man should hesitate before accepting the position of an Itinerant?

But it will be said: "There is another side to the picture." True, and thanks to the Great Head of the church that there is. But the other side can only be seen when the beholder occupies the proper stand-point, and this position I certainly had not attained at the time of which I write. In this matter, as in most others, our mistakes arise from partial views and limited observation.

A few years since I visited Niagara Falls. Before leaving Buffalo a friend admonished me to avoid looking upon the descending floods until I should reach Table Rock, as this precaution would give me a more satisfactory impression. These instructions were more easily given than observed. I found it required no small share of nerve to pass down the near bank of the river with the eternal roar of its waters pouring into my ears, cross over Suspension Bridge, spanning the rushing tides below still tossing and foaming as though an ocean had broken from its prison, and then pass up the other bank, in full view of the cataract, and not look upon it until my feet were planted on Table Rock. But from that hour to the present, I have never regretted the effort, for therein I learned the importance of position, when face to face with any great question. The position gained, I raised my eyes upon Niagara Falls. I need not say my whole being was thrilled. There lay the great "horse shoe" full before me, and I seemed to stand upon its outer crest and look down into its deep chasm, where the angry waters wrestled with each other in their wildest frenzy. Then the floods from either side, that had seemed to sweep around the chasm and hug the shore, as if in mortal terror, despairing of escape, rushed upon each other like two storm fiends. The war of waters was most terrific. The very earth shook. Locked in deadly embrace, and writhing as if in direst agony, the mighty floods plunged the abyss, while far above floated the white plume of the presiding genius of old Niagara. The impression upon me was overwhelming. I saw Niagara Falls from the right stand-point. Whether I was equally fortunate in my early views of the Itinerancy is a question that will find solution in the following pages.

I decided, however, to go West. My father and the balance of his family had been looking enquiringly in that direction for several months, and I now agreed to accompany them.

It was our purpose to make Dubuque, Iowa, the point of destination, as the founders of that city, who were relatives, had visited us in the East and had given us glowing accounts of the city and the adjacent portions of the State. With this purpose in view we landed at Racine. The Madison, a crazy old steamer that could lay on more sides during a storm than any water craft that I had ever seen, landed us on a pier in the night, and from the pier we were taken ashore in a scow. We reached Racine in June, 1844. Racine at that time was a very small village, but, like all western towns, it was in the daily belief that, at some time in the near future, it would be a very large city. We spent the Sabbath and enjoyed the pleasure of attending religious services in a school house. The pastor of our church at the time was Rev. Milton Bourne, of the Rock River Conference. We were favorably impressed with Racine, and especially with the evidences of civilization it afforded, in the fact of a school house and the establishment of religious services.

At Racine we engaged a man to take us, six in all, with our trunks to Delavan. The roads were almost impassable. The rains had fallen so copiously that the streams overflowed their banks, the marshes were full and the prairies inundated. With a good team, however, we made an average of about fifteen miles a day. Our conveyance stuck fast in the mud eighteen times between Racine and Delavan. Sometimes we found these interesting events would occur just in the middle of a broad marsh. In such case the gentlemen would take to the water, not unfrequently up to the loins, build a chair by the crossing of hands, as they had learned to do in their school days, and give the ladies a safe passage to the prairie beyond. But woe worth the day if the wheels refused to turn, as they sometimes did, in the middle of some deep, broad mud-hole. The light prairie soil, when thoroughly saturated, is capable of very great volatility and yet of stick-to-it-iveness. While the team and wagon, buried deeply in the mud, found the soil as yielding as quicksand, the passengers, on alighting, were no more fortunate. To make the chair and wade ashore with its precious burden, at such a time, involved a very nice adjustment of balances. If the three went headlong before they reached the shore, each received a generous "coat of mail" of the most modern style.

We reached Delavan in due course of travel, where we remained several days. The Sabbath intervened. My father preached in the morning, and I held service in the afternoon. On Monday a council was held. Since our feet touched the soil of Wisconsin, our ears had been filled with the praises of the country, and especially the counties of Dodge and Fond du Lac. By the time we had spent several days at Delavan, and were ready to move on toward Iowa, this clamor had become so decided in its tone, that, as a result of the consultation, it was decided that two or three of us should go up through Dodge and Fond du Lac counties. Not with the expectation that our destination would lie in that direction, but it was thought advisable to know what had been left behind, in case we should not be pleased with Dubuque.

Leaving the balance of our company at Delavan, we started on foot on our tour of exploration. Keeping our eyes and ears open, we were ready to go in any direction in quest of the promised "Eldorado." Like all "land seekers" of those early times, a few things were deemed essential to make a location desirable. These were prairie, timber and water. But with us one additional requisite must not be ignored. We must also find a "water power." With all these objects in view, the line of travel became perplexing and described a good many angles, but the main direction lay through East Troy, Summit, Watertown, Oak Grove and Waupun. At the last named place we found a few scattered log houses, and, within a radius of five miles, perhaps a dozen families. The location was beautiful. With its prairie of from one to two miles in width, skirted on the north by groves of timber, through which ran the west branch of Rock River, and fringed on the south by extended openings, it took us captive at once. Passing up the stream two or three miles we found the looked for water-power, and abundance of unappropriated lands. By setting our stakes on the crown of the prairie, and making the lines pass down to the river and through the belt of timber, sufficient land of the right quality could be secured for the whole family, including, also, the desired water-power. To decide upon this spot as our future home, was the result of a brief consultation. All thought of going to Iowa was now abandoned. Obtaining a load of lumber, which was all that could be secured for either love or money, a shanty was immediately erected for the accommodation of the family. Was it a providential intervention that assigned us our home and field of labor in this new and rapidly populating portion of Wisconsin, rather than the city of Dubuque?

Society in its formative state needs, above all other agencies, the salutary influences of religion. To provide these and give them efficiency among the people, the presence and labors of the Gospel ministry, and the establishment of churches, are a necessity. To secure these at the outset requires the emigration of ministers from the older States as well as people. Perhaps the motives of neither class in coming will always bear a thorough scrutiny; yet who shall say that their coming is not under the general direction of Providence? Nor is it improbable that the hasty steps that seem to bear the unwilling servant from the presence of the Master are the very ones that most speedily bring him face to face with his duty.

CHAPTER II

In March, A.D. 1845, a letter from Rev. Wm. H. Sampson, then Presiding Elder of Green Bay District, Rock River Conference, found me at Waupun. The intervening nine months, since our arrival in the preceding July, had been spent in making improvements upon the land I had selected, and in the erection of a lumber mill, of which I was in part proprietor.

The bearer of the letter found me in the mill, engaged in rolling logs to the saw and in carrying away the lumber. I opened the letter and glanced at its contents. To my surprise and utter consternation it contained a pressing request that I would take charge of the Brothertown Indian Mission until the next session of the Conference, as the Missionary, Rev. H.W. Frink, had been called away by family afflictions. I instinctively folded the letter and then crumpled it in the palm of my hand, inwardly saying, "Hast thou found me, oh! mine enemy?" No rash answer, however, was given. This question of duty was certainly assuming grave aspects. For four years it had haunted me at every turn. And even in the wilds of Wisconsin it was still my tormenter. Like Banquo's ghost, it would not down at my bidding. I now tried to look the question fairly in the face, and make the decision a final one, but found it exceedingly difficult to do so. To yield after so long a struggle, and especially to surrender all my fondly cherished plans for the future, appealed at first to my pride, and then to what I conceived to be my temporal interests, and the appeal for a moment seemed to gain the ascendency. But how then could I answer to God? was the startling question that burned into my soul at every turn of the argument. In the midst of my embarrassment the thought was suggested, "It is only until Conference, and then you can return and resume your business."

Catching at this straw, thus floating to me, and half believing and half hoping that three months of my incompetency would satisfy the church and send me back to my business again, I consented to go. Leaving my temporal interests in the hands of my father, I hastened to make the necessary preparations for my new responsibilities. The outfit was provokingly limited. The horse and saddlebags, the inevitable Alpha, if not the Omega, of an Itinerant's outfit, were wanting, as such conveniences had hardly, as yet, found their way to the northern portions of the Territory. But in their place were put good walking ability and a small satchel. A few pieces of linen, a few books, but no sermons, were put into the satchel, and I was immediately stepping to the measure of the Itinerancy.

My first point of destination was Fond du Lac, the residence of the Presiding Elder, where I must necessarily report for instructions. The walk of twenty-two miles, with no other companion than a plethoric satchel, passing from hand to hand as the weary miles, one after another, were dismissed, was not the most favorable introduction to my "new departure," but, bad as it was, I found relief in the thought that my Eastern friends, who had so kindly and repeatedly proposed to give me a comfortable seat somewhere in the New York Conference, were in blissful ignorance of the sorry figure I was making. Whether Jonah found his last conveyance more agreeable than the first, I cannot say, but certain it is, I found my first entrance upon the Itinerancy a tugging business.

I reached Fond du Lac before nightfall, and was hospitably entertained. Notwithstanding the cordial reception I received, however, from both the elder and his good wife, I felt embarrassed by the searching look they occasionally gave me. Whether it was occasioned by my youthful, green or delicate appearance, or my light, feminine voice, I could not divine.

The conversation soon turned upon the state of affairs at Brothertown, and I speedily forgot my embarrassment. In the course of the conversation I inquired whether the proceeding would not be considered irregular, to place an exhorter in charge of the Mission. The elder replied, "Necessity knows no law, and, besides, our Quarterly Meeting at this place will soon be held, when we will relieve that embarrassment." I was doubtless indebted to this law of necessity for the privilege of holding one office in the church not provided for in the Discipline, and one that has seldom if ever been accorded to others. Carefully instructed in the best method to manage certain difficulties pending in the Mission, I took early leave for a further walk of sixteen miles.

Across the prairie at the head of Lake Winnebago, I found the walk very agreeable. Passing Taycheedah, I then struck out into the deep woods that skirt the eastern shore of the lake. I was now between my guide and instructor, and the difficult work committed to my charge. Thought was busy. An oppressive sense of my own insufficiency for so momentous a work, came over me, as it had done before, but never in such overwhelming power. I was now face to face with the great work from which I had shrank for several years, and there was no retreat. Imagination lifted the little hills of difficulty before me into mountains that seemed impassable. In the deep shade of the wood I found a moss-covered rock for a seat, and gave myself up to reflection. The troubled currents of the stream ran on this wise. To go forward in my present undertaking may involve a committal to a work that a few short months shall not terminate. In such case, there will follow a life of toil and sacrifice, on stinted allowance, beset with trials and perplexities, and clouded by cold unfeeling criticisms, censures and misjudgings, of both motive and labor, of which I can now entertain no adequate conception. But if this work be not the dictate of duty, then why this unrest of soul which has so long disturbed the even flow of my religious life, or why the uniform urgency of the authorities of the church both east and west in this direction? On the contrary, if my feet are now in the path of duty then why hesitate? A brave soul never falters in the presence of difficulty or peril, but always deals the strongest blows where the conflict rages the sharpest. The struggle was brief and the result satisfactory. Kneeling by the side of the rock, prayer was offered for Divine guidance and help, and there fell on the soul a baptism of serene peace and holy joy, which hallowed each remaining step of the journey.

Arriving at Brothertown the letter of introduction from the Elder was presented to A.D. Dick, Esq., one of the Stewards. The residence of this brother was located in the central portion of the town, and gave evidence of good taste and comfort. Both himself and wife were members of the church, and their house the home of Itinerants. It was now nearly twelve o'clock. I was invited to the parlor where I awaited dinner. These few moments afforded an opportunity to survey my surroundings and master the situation. My early reading had introduced me to the Indian, both in his native wilds and as seen on the borders of civilization, the former as the noblest specimen of the natural man on the planet, and the latter as the most degraded of mortals. But now I was in the very presence of the red man and even a guest in his dwelling. Nor is it too much to say that my curiosity was not a little excited. My reception, however, had been so cordial that I soon found myself at ease in my new associations.

The letter was opened and read. During its reading I noticed that the eye of mine host often wandered from the page to the newly arrived guest. By an occasional glance I tried to read the thoughts of the reader, but found that the dark face was not disposed to be communicative. This much, however, I think I read pretty clearly: "Well, the Elder has sent us a pretty slender specimen as a minister, but we will try him and see what he can do."

The dinner was announced, conversation became lively, and before we were aware of it the distinctions of race and color had faded out of sight, and a life-long friendship was founded. It was now arranged that, during my stay on the Mission, I should make my home under this hospitable roof.

The Brothertown people came from the State of New York, and had now been settled in their western home several years. A log chapel had been erected and school houses provided. The location along the eastern shore of Lake Winnebago was excellent, affording a good soil and water and timber in abundance. Along the principal highways the farms had been cleared of timber and brought under a fair state of cultivation. The buildings were mainly constructed of logs, though in later years, there had been erected a goodly number of frame residences.

Brothertown Mission first appears on the General Minutes in 1839, under the name of Deansburg, as will appear hereafter. In 1840 it was called Fond du Lac, as that point had now been added as a regular appointment. The following year, 1841, the charge remained the same, but the name was changed to Brothertown, this name having taken the place of Deansburg, in honor of the Brothertown Nation. But as this charge will further appear in connection with the labors of its pastors I will defer the balance of the record for the present.

Rev. Jesse Halstead entered the traveling connection in the Troy Conference, was ordained Deacon in September, 1837, and transferred to the Illinois Conference. At the session of the Conference, held the same month, he was appointed second preacher to Aztalan Mission. Here he took his first lessons in pioneer work. He traveled over a tract of country reaching from the line of the Territory on the south to Menomonee on the north, and from the Lake Shore Missions on the east to Madison on the west. In these extended journeys he enjoyed the privilege of preaching the first sermon and forming the first societies in many localities.

In 1838 he was sent to Crete Mission on the Kankakee, in the State of Illinois. The following year, 1839, he was sent to Brothertown, as before stated, the name on the Minutes being Deansburg. While on this Mission, he visited Fond du Lac, and preached the first sermon, as will appear in another chapter. He remained on this charge only three months, and was then sent by his Presiding Elder, Rev. Julius Field, to supply Oneida Indian Mission for the balance of the year, that charge having been left to be supplied. In January he was visited at Oneida by the Presiding Elder. While here the Elder fell sick, and desired Brother Halstead to accompany him on his round of appointments. In the line of travel they visited Madison and intervening charges, and then went to Racine, the home of the Elder.

Brother Halstead now started for his field at Oneida. It was in the depth of winter, and the line of travel was through the dense forests along the Lake Shore to Green Bay. But, nothing daunted, our Itinerant packed his books, which had been left with Brother Stebbins at this place on his first trip to the north, and other baggage, and started on his journey. The first day he reached Milwaukee, and here he laid in provisions and other necessary outfit, such as axe, auger, &c. Striking out into the forest he made twenty miles the first day, but during the afternoon found himself in a severe snow storm. The first night he stopped at a house located at the site of the present village of Grafton. On rising the next morning he found the snow three feet deep. He laid over one day, and on the following morning resumed his journey. He only made nine miles, as he was compelled to beat the track in advance of his horse; and at night he found quarters at Port Washington. The next day he pursued his journey, but at nightfall found himself without shelter in the woods. He built a fire, cooked a piece of salt pork to eat with his bread, and made a supper. But now for the night! He emptied his jumper, and in it he made a bed, and, as nearly as possible, a coil of humanity. The next morning he found his boots frozen. But, with a generous amount of tugging, they yielded to the pressure of his feet, and he was again on his way, breaking the roads himself, thereby aiding his horse in carrying his burden.

On the fifth day he found a house in the woods and remained in it for the night. The sixth day he reached Sheboygan Falls, and the seventh day Manitowoc. The eighth day he tried to reach Green Bay, a distance of forty miles, but was compelled to camp out for another night, and take the ninth day to complete his journey.

In 1840, Brother Halstead was sent to Fond du Lac, his charge including, also, Brothertown, of which a record will be made in a subsequent chapter. During this year he made a visit to Oshkosh. He took an Indian trail on the west side of Lake Winnebago, and after traveling twenty-five miles found himself on the bank of Fox River. He found no way to cross the stream, and, it being now dark, he was compelled to spend the night without shelter. A friendly Indian came along and joined him in his preparations for the night. The weather was quite cold and they were obliged to maintain a brisk fire to keep from freezing. In this duty they served by turns, but neither of them had any provisions. On the following day Brother, Halstead returned to Fond du Lac.

During the year Brother Halstead was abundant in labor, and at Brothertown there was an extensive revival, giving large accessions to the charge. The following year, he was returned to the work, but the name was changed to Brothertown. This year was also fragrant with blessing, and many souls were converted. After leaving Brothertown Brother Halstead was stationed at Monroe, and next at Hazel Green, where he had Rev. I.M.

Leihy as a junior preacher. His subsequent charges were Prairie du Chien, Patch Grove, Mequon, Oak Creek, and Brothertown, when he took, in 1852, a superannuated relation.

Brother Halstead was always at his post of duty. In some of his appointments he had long moves, hard work, and very small compensation, but he and his good wife were always equal to the situation. It has been a pleasure to the writer to make this record, as also that of other veterans of the Itinerancy. But of the labors, the sacrifices and trials of such men, but little can be known here. It is a satisfaction, however, to be assured that their record is on high. It is also a pleasure to know with what views they look back upon the past. A line in hand from Brother Halstead only expresses the common sentiment of all. I will give it to the reader. "Among the most pleasant memories of my life, I reckon the hardships endured as an Itinerant minister of the Gospel of Christ. If I had another life to give I should not hesitate to throw myself into the work again with all the strength and purpose the Master has given me."

Rev. Hiram W. Frink was sent to Brothertown in 1842, and had nearly completed his third year when called away. Brother Frink is also a veteran, having entered the Conference in 1837, the year of Brother Halstead's transfer.

His first appointment was Sheboygan, including the territory between Milwaukee and Green Bay, and extending west as far as Lake Winnebago. Its principal appointments were Sheboygan, Port Washington, Brothertown, Two Rivers and Manitowoc.

Having shipped his trunk to Manitowoc, his future home, Brother Frink left Chicago on horseback, Oct. 28th, 1837, for his field of labor. At Milwaukee, the necessary outfit was procured to penetrate the deep forests which lay beyond, including an axe, steele and punk, a tin cup, blankets and provisions. The only road was an Indian trail, which pushed its devious way through the forest, around the swamps, and across bridgeless streams, without regard to the comfort of the traveler or the speed of his locomotion. As there were no houses along the line of travel, Brother Frink was compelled to spend the first night in the woods. Fortunately, however, he found a small, tenantless cabin by the wayside, in which he was safe from the wild, noisy beasts, that prowled without. The following day he reached Sheboygan.

And this journey was but a sample of the travel and exposures of the year of labor, on which Brother Frink had entered. Amid the drifting snows of winter, and the copious rains of summer, he was compelled to traverse the dreary, and almost unbroken forests of his field, and on more than one occasion he found the night around his camp-fire made hideous by the howling of wolves and the screaming of panthers. But in him the cause found a sturdy pioneer who was equal to the demands of the work.

In 1838, his appointment was Elgin, Ill., and, the following year, Watertown, Wis. In connection with the last named, we shall have occasion to refer to his labors in a subsequent chapter. At the close of his year at Watertown the charge was divided, and in 1840, he was appointed to Summit, the eastern division.

In 1841, he was returned to Illinois and stationed at Sycamore, and the following year was brought back to Wisconsin, and, as before stated, appointed to Brothertown. At the Conference of 1845, he took a location on account of family afflictions, but returned again to the work as soon as relieved of his embarrassments.

His subsequent appointments have been Grafton, Agent for Tracts and Sunday Schools, Palmyra, Rock Prairie, Albion, Dunkirk, Fort Atkinson, Footville, Burnett and Markesan. In 1865, he took a supernumerary relation, but the following year, being made effective, he was appointed to the Bible Agency, which position he has continued to hold up to the present writing. Brother Frink is still vigorous, and is doing effective service. He has kept a cheerful spirit up to the present hour, and is highly esteemed by his brethren.

CHAPTER III

My first Sabbath, April 4, 1845, as "Exhorter in Charge," gave me an opportunity to take the measure of my new field of labor. The chapel, as before stated, was constructed of logs. These were hewn on both sides, thus giving a smooth appearance both within and without. The logs were halved together at the ends, and filled between with small pieces of wood laid in morter, and, on the whole, the chapel made a very respectable appearance. It contained rude seats that would accommodate about one hundred and fifty persons, and furnished standing room in addition for one hundred more.

On the advent of the young "Elder," for it was their custom to call all ministers by that name, the chapel was packed to its utmost capacity. Opening the services with great perturbation of spirit in the presence of so vast a crowd, I proceeded with difficulty until the people arose to sing. Instantly I was at ease. I was not a stranger to good singing, for my surroundings had always been fortunate in this particular, but, I am free to say, that, up to that hour, my ears had never been so thrilled by Christian melody. The tones were not as mellow as those of the African, but they were more deep and thrilling. Inclined rather to a high key, and disposed to be sharp and piercing, yet the voices of the vast congregation swept through every note of the gamut with equal freedom. I was thoroughly entranced. And, on coming to myself, I found my perturbation had left me and my soul was on a plane with the responsibilities of the hour.

At the close of the public services, a class meeting was held under the charge of Father Abner, the leader. This brother was a man of age and experience, well adapted to his position, and universally beloved. The meeting was conducted in the usual manner, and was an occasion of spiritual refreshing. The testimonies were direct and touchingly simple, usually accompanied with weeping, and sometimes with the shout of triumph. The singing, however, was the principal feature, both in quantity and quality, for this highly susceptible people had given this part of the services, in all their meetings, a leading place. Among the most noted leading voices were those of mine host, Alonzo D. Dick, Jeremiah Johnson, Orrin Johnson, and Thomas Cummock. My labors were now fairly opened, and I soon found abundant opportunities for usefulness. The regular meetings at the chapel were supplimented by others, principally prayer meetings, in the more remote parts of the town. These meetings were held on the week-day evenings, and in a short time became occasions of great interest. I attended them usually, and found every evening thus employed when not engaged at the chapel. In these excursions through the settlement, I was almost always accompanied by one, or all of the above named brethren, to lead the singing, as I found myself, though belonging to a singing family for three generations, unable to lead in this branch of the service. And in addition to these, I was also favored with the company of a young man of great worth and precious memory. I refer to Lewis Fowler, an Exhorter of great promise, but who soon after fell under the withering touch of consumption, and passed on to the better land.

As these side meetings, as I chose to call them, were multiplied, and awakened general interest in their several localities, we found the meetings at the chapel also gained in numbers and spiritual power. Soon the people began to talk of a revival, and pray for its speedy coming. Nor was it long delayed. The work began at one of the side meetings, where an old backslider was led back to the cross. The next evening, in another part of the settlement, there were three seekers at the altar. The Sabbath now intervened, and it was deemed advisable to open meetings in the chapel during the ensuing week. Here the meetings were held nightly for four weeks. As a result, seventy-five persons professed conversion.

The working force of the Mission was now put into a more thorough organization. Several new classes were formed and the old ones carefully organized, making six in all. A Sunday School was established, bringing into its promising field the latent talent of the church.

But we had hardly got our home work fully in hand, when there came an invitation from Stockbridge, several miles below, to extend our labors into that settlement. There had been a Congregational Mission among the Stockbridge nation for many years, but its condition was not very promising.

The chapel was located in the central portion of the reservation, and the Mission was now in charge of Dr. Marsh, a gentleman of education and ability. He divided his time, however, between the ministerial and medical professions, and, as a result, the spiritual interests necessarily languished.

During the progress of our revival in Brothertown, Brother David Wiggins, who had recently removed to Stockbridge, had been accompanied to the meeting by several of his neighbors, and they had been converted. This fact will explain the invitation now given. We accepted, and a meeting was opened, using the residence of Brother Wiggins as a temporary chapel.

The meetings, however, had hardly been commenced, when there came a remonstrance from Dr. Marsh. The remonstrance, which was expressed in very emphatic terms, assumed that I had no right to embrace any portion of the Stockbridge reservation in my field of labor. But what was I to do? Some of our own sheep had gone down into Goshen to find pasturage, and now a few of the lambs of a strange flock had come to us seeking care and sustenance. Must these be left to the bleak winds that were evidently sweeping around them, to chill their warm blood in their veins and cause them to perish in the wilderness? My answer was respectful but decided. Having been placed, by what seemed to be a providential intervention, in charge of these souls, I could not withdraw my oversight. The Doctor laid the matter before the Presiding Elder, but he refused to interfere, and thus the matter ended. In due time a class was formed, Brother Wiggins was appointed its leader, and several souls was brought to Christ.

At this place I found Brother R.S. Hayward. Before my arrival at Brothertown, this noble man of God, and his most estimable and talented wife, had purchased a farm on the Stockbridge reservation. They had already erected a log house, cleared a few acres of land, and founded a home both for themselves and passing Itinerants. Such a surprise, and such a cordial welcome as I experienced, fall but seldom to the lot of a stranger.

Brother Hayward was also an Exhorter. Two Exhorters together, what a ministerial force! Why, we began to feel that, by the help of the Master, we could take the whole land for Christ! Plans were immediately formed to extend our field of operations.

Among these, we decided to hold a series of two days' meetings, and, that they might prove a grand success, we selected as the localities the grand centres of population. We appointed the first to be held in Father Chick's barn, a mile west of the Mission Chapel in Stockbridge. The day came, and so did the two Exhorters. The people from the two nations came in throngs. The barn was filled, and the groves around it, until my head grew dizzy in looking at the multitudes and thinking of what was to follow. There was a congregation that might awaken the eloquence of a Bishop, and nobody to conduct the services but two young, inexperienced Exhorters. The reader may well imagine that there was genuine repentance on the part of the striplings, and, may be, hastily made vows never again to challenge a multitude, but these did not solve the problem of the hour. Of course, as I was "Exhorter in Charge," though the youngest man, I had to take the morning service. I was so thoroughly frightened that I have forgotten the text, if I took any; but this point I do remember most distinctly. It was my first thought, on seeing the crowd, that I would take for a text, "There is a Lad here with five barley loaves and two small fishes, but what are they among so many?" But the more I thought of it, the more frightened I became. Fortunately, I dismissed it before the hour of service arrived, for I seriously questioned whether I could furnish the people so generous a feast. How I got through the service I am unable to say, for I never dared to ask any one, and my friends, doubtless out of regard to my youth, forbore to tell me. As to the afternoon service, I need say nothing, for, though respectable, I have no doubt Brother Hayward has preached many better sermons since.

But whatever was wanting in the public services, the social meetings of the day were a great success. Here the brethren came in with their singing and earnest prayers, and the sisters with their Christian testimonies, until every heart was moved. In this part of the service Sister Hayward led off with her accustomed ability and spirit, making a marked feature of the exercises.

The part borne by Father Chicks, as he was called, the head chief of the Stockbridge nation, also added not a little to the interest of the occasion. He had been but recently converted, and his heart was overflowing. To see such a religious demonstration on his own premises filled him with joy, and awoke within him the fiery ardor of those other days when his burning words had swayed his people to the good or evil, as the tempest bends the forest at its will. Tall and erect in form, with a brow to rule an empire, he rose in the midst of the great assembly and came forward to the stand. Every eye was fixed upon him. Turning to the writer, that he might have assistance, if necessary, in the use of the English, by the timely suggestion of the right word, he proceeded to say: "Me been a great sinner, as all my people know." For the moment he could go no farther. His noble form shook with emotion, and his manly face was flooded with tears. The whole audience wept with him, for his tears were sublimely eloquent. Recovering himself, he simply added, "All me want now is to love him, Christ." Then turning to his people, with a face as radient as the sunlight, he began to address them in his own language. I could not understand the import of his words, but the tones of his voice to our ears were entrancingly eloquent. As he advanced in his address, his frame, now bearing the weight of four score years, grew lithe and animated. Soon the whole man was in a storm of utterance. Had there been no living voice, the attitudes and swayings of the body, the carriage and transitions of the head, and the faultless, yet energetic gestures of the hand, were enough to move the human soul to the depths of its being. But to these were added the human voice divine with its matchless cadences, now kindling into a storm of invective, before which the audience shrank, like shriveled leaves in autumn, then sinking to sepulchral tones that seemed to challenge a communion with the dead; now wailing an anguish of sorrow utterly insupportable, and then rising in holy exultation, as one redeemed from sin and inspired with the triumphant shout of victory.

The address occupied only twenty minutes. But for effectiveness I never saw its equal. Bending forms and tears, groans and shouts, strangely commingled in the scene. Eternity alone can reveal the results of the day.

Among the converts at Brothertown were several interesting cases. I will only refer to one. It is that of a very noted character, who "feared not God, nor regarded man." This man, whom I shall not name, was specially bitter against all ministers, and lost no opportunity to treat them rudely. His family had taken the precaution to notify me of his bearing, assuring me that my visits to the house would be agreeable to them, yet they might subject me to abuse on his part, if not expulsion. I at once resolved to make an effort to reach him, and in due time found an opportunity. I discovered that he kept a large number of bee hives in his yard, and I concluded that he was fond of bees. Having had some experience in that line, I resolved to make my assault from that stand-point. The favorable opportunity came sooner than I expected. Early one morning, as I was passing the apiary, I found him in trouble. A young colony had left the parent hive and alighted on one of the topmost branches of a tall tree, and the owner was sending curses after them in a most profane manner. Approaching him with the compliments of the morning, I remarked, "These young people are starting out in life with pretty lofty notions." The reply was a volley of oaths that showed him to be no novice in profanity. To relieve his embarrassment, and tranquilize his temper, I suggested that they were not beyond reach. With a new outbreak of oaths, he replied, "The ladder that old Jacob dreamed of would not be half tall enough." I told him if he would bring me a strong cord and a saw I would bring them down for him. He, half doubtingly, glanced at my slight form, then into my face, as if to assure himself of my sincerity, and hastened to bring the desired articles. I fastened one end of the cord to my arm, and the other to the saw. The ascent was then made, the saw drawn up by the cord, and the severed limb with its burden let gently down until it dropped in front of the prepared hive. By the time I reached the ground the bees had entered the hive, and the raging spirit of their owner had became tranquil.

Conversation now turned upon the culture of the bee and its habits, until the way opened to rise from the temporal to the spiritual. The provident wisdom of the little busy worker, in laying up the needed store for future use, was especially commended, "But more especially," it was added, "is this course the dictate of wisdom in such beings as have an eternity before them." I saw that a small act of kindness had won his ear and touched his heart. On leaving, I was cordially invited to call and see the family. The advantage thus gained was prudently improved until, in process of time, both himself and family were garnered for the Master.

But the time had now come to lay aside the anomalous position of "Exhorter in Charge," and take to myself the appellation of "Preacher in Charge." Under the advice of the Presiding Elder I still retained my membership on the Fond du Lac circuit, of which Waupun was a part. The last Quarterly Meeting of the year was held in Fond du Lac May 31st, 1845, Rev. Wm. H. Sampson presiding. The meeting was well attended. I was granted a Local Preacher's license and recommended to the Rock River Conference for admission on trial.

At the close of the quarterly meeting I returned to Brothertown and made up a company of the good people, to attend a camp-meeting to be held at Clason's Prairie.

It was the pioneer camp-meeting in the region, and, though the attendance was not large, it included nearly all the population of the vicinity. There were ten tents, and as many preachers, with the Presiding Elder in charge. The spirit of the meeting was excellent, and a goodly number of souls were gathered for the Master. The services were greatly enlivened, and clothed with additional interest by the presence of the several brethren whom I had brought from Brothertown. Their ready, incomparable spiritual songs, earnest prayers and touching narratives of Christian experience, awakened intense feeling among all classes, and gave abundant evidence of the power of the Gospel to save, even the red man, as well as his brother of lighter complexion and more favorable surroundings.

Another feature of the meeting fastened itself upon my memory. It was the persistence with which the good Elder pressed me into service on the Sabbath before the great congregation, and such a formidable array of ministers. It was indeed a great trial, but, as on other occasions where there is a "boy preacher" around, there was no escape. And besides, the effort took on the nature of a trial sermon, as it was my first effort after I had been duly licensed to preach. Whether I succeeded fairly or not in the estimation of my critics, I am not able to say, for I kept my ear during the balance of the meeting turned the other way, lest I might "have my feelings hurt."

Returning to Brothertown, I now determined to hold a camp-meeting, under "our own vine and fig tree," in July. The arrangements were accordingly made, and at the appointed time, the Presiding Elder and several other ministers came to our assistance. They were Rev. Messrs. H. R. Colman, Stephen Jones, Joseph T. Lewis, G. N. Hanson, S. B. Whipple and my dear father. The attendance was large, the order perfect, and the results of the meeting specially satisfactory.

Among the converts were several persons from Calumet, a small village of white people adjoining Brothertown on the south. We now established an appointment in the village, formed a class and opened a Sunday School.

But the time had come in the history of the Mission when a new and larger chapel must be erected. To further this object, several boxes of goods had been forwarded to the Mission by Ladies Benevolent Societies in the east. They were accordingly opened out in the rooms of the vacant Parsonage, and, when not otherwise employed, I installed myself as a salesman of merchandise. It was not a little amusing to begin the erection of a church after this fashion, but this was not the only queer thing about the building of the Brothertown Church.

In addition, the Missionary put his own hands to the actual labor of preparing the materials. It was done in this wise. It was ascertained that a man in Stockbridge, who owned a fine grove of timber, proposed to give a certain amount of it for the church, provided the church people would cut it. And it was further found that the owner of a mill in the vicinity would give the sawing. We decided at once to accept both propositions. Word was passed among the people, and on a given day a score or more of men and teams, with the Missionary among them, made an onslaught upon the timber. In a few days the task was accomplished, and the success of the enterprise guaranteed.

The conference year, however, expired at this time, Aug. 20th, and terminated my labors among this people.

Well did the Apostle say, "I have laid the foundation and another buildeth thereon." Nor was this experience new to the world in the time of Paul. It was the work of David to prepare the materials, but it remained to Solomon to build the Temple. Thus it is in every calling of life. But it is more manifestly so, perhaps, in the Itinerancy, than in any other.

CHAPTER IV

The first sermon preached in Fond du Lac was delivered at the residence of Hon. Mason C. Darling, by Rev. Jesse Halstead, Missionary to the Brothertown people, on the 17th day of November, A.D. 1839. The meeting, the first of a religious character, was convened at the request of a few families residing in Fond du Lac and its neighborhood, only seven in number, they having learned that the ubiquitious Itinerant had struck their trail, and was making a visit to their settlement. Having been accustomed to religious services in their eastern homes, these few scattered families had felt deeply their privations in these western wilds. The advent of a minister, therefore, opened an era of no common importance. Few and scattered as were the families, some of them living several miles away, the small log house was filled.

From this lowly, rude dwelling the songs of Zion ascended in grateful praise, floating out over the prairie and lingering in the branches of the old forest trees along the river until they fell upon the ear of the roaming savage, and arrested his careless footsteps. The voice of prayer was heard, breathing to heaven in fervid accents a recognition of the Divine goodness, and an humble consecration of devout worshippers, and the fair land they had adopted as their home, to God. The Gospel Message heralded the dispensation of grace, mercy and peace alike to all, bearing in its wings the gift of healing, and a glorious prophecy of the coming reign of the Messiah over "the wilderness and solitary place." Under the word, the pentacostal blessing came down on the people and filled the humble sanctuary. To many, the memories of other days, and their dear old homes in the east, were overpowering. The fountains of feeling were opened and tears came welling up from their depths, until they brimmed the eyelids of all, and fell in showers, as when the cloud angel shakes his wings. Those only who have mingled in the first religious meetings of the new settlement, can rightly appreciate the intense interest or gauge the overwhelming emotions of such an occasion.

Fond du Lac appears on the General Minutes at the session of the Rock River Conference, held Aug. 26th, 1840. At that time the entire Territory was included in two districts. The first swept across from the southwest to the northeast, making Platteville and Green Bay its extreme points. And the other embraced the southeastern portion, and extended as far west and north as Watertown and Summit. The Presiding Elder on the latter, the Milwaukee, was Rev. Julius Field, and on the former, the Platteville, Rev. H.W. Reed. The year following the northeastern portion was erected into a separate district, called Green Bay, and Rev. James R. Goodrich was made the Presiding Elder. Brother Reed remained another year on the Platteville District, but during that year it retained only two charges that are at the present writing included within the bounds of the Wisconsin Conference. After this date, the labors of Brother Reed fell within other Conferences, where doubtless a record will be made of them. His visits, however, have not been forgotten. He was a man of kindly spirit and great practical wisdom. Wherever he laid the foundations, they showed the labors of a skillful hand. He still remains in the Itinerancy, and is the Patriarch of Iowa Methodism.

Brother Goodrich, who succeeded him on the Green Bay portion of the district, is also remembered with great pleasure by the people. He remained three years on the district, and during the first two, served the Green Bay station also. He was transferred to the Chicago District in 1844, and was succeeded on the Green Bay District by Rev. Wm. H. Sampson. At the close of the year, Brother Goodrich took a superannuated relation.

Rev. Jesse Halstead was appointed to the Fond du Lac charge, as before stated, and the Mission was made to include both Fond du Lac and Brothertown. He was also continued on the same charge the following year, the circuit now being changed from the Platteville to the Green Bay District.

We have spoken at length of the Brothertown portion of the charge in previous chapters, and may now confine the record to that of Fond du Lac. During this year a class was formed at Taycheedah with Francis M. McCarty as leader.

At the session of the Conference, held Aug. 24, 1842, the name of Fond du Lac again fails to appear on the minutes, showing, doubtless, that, up to this date, it had not assumed sufficient importance as a religious centre to retain the name of a circuit. But at this session a charge appears under the name of Lake Winnebago, with Rev. John P. Gallup as Pastor. This new charge contained so much of the old Fond du Lac Mission as had been separated from Brothertown, and, in addition, it swept down along the west side of the Lake as far as Oshkosh.

At the Conference of 1843, the charge was continued, and Rev. Harvey S. Bronson was appointed the Pastor. The meetings during the year were still held in log houses, Dr. Mason C. Darling, Hon. Edward Pier and Mr. Norman Pier furnishing the accommodations. It was in the residence of the second named that the first class was formed during this year by Brother Bronson. The class was composed of Mr. and Mrs. Charles Olmstead, Mrs. Edward Pier, Mr. and Mrs. Daniel C. Brooks, Mr. and Mrs. Norman Pier and Mrs. Parsons. Brother Charles Olmstead was the first leader.

During his pastorate, Brother Bronson also formed a class at Wilkinson's Settlement, of which a record will be made elsewhere.

In 1844, Fond du Lac again appears on the Minutes as a charge, and Taycheedah is joined with it. Rev. Joseph T. Lewis was appointed the Pastor, and Rev. Wm. H. Sampson the Presiding Elder. At the beginning of this year the meetings were transferred to a frame school house that had been erected in the village. The tide of emigration was now setting strongly in the direction of Fond du Lac and vicinity, and new settlements were being rapidly formed. The charge, following the general drift of things, extended its boundaries, adding several appointments, and among them Waupun.

Soon after our settlement at this place, as detailed in a former chapter, we were informed that a Quarterly Meeting would be held in Fond du Lac, at a given date, in the near future. We decided to attend. The day came, and my father and I started on foot for the Quarterly Meeting. On reaching Fond du Lac we enquired for the Presiding Elder, in order to ascertain the time and place of meeting, and found that he had already gone over to the school house where the meeting was to be held. Being directed, we soon found the place and entered. The Elder sat behind the desk, ready to begin the services. The Preacher in charge sat at his right hand, wearing a thoughtful mood. As we took our seats, both glanced at us, as did several of the congregation, doubtless thinking, "Well there are two more pioneers, and they must be Methodists to come thus to church on Saturday."

As soon as I felt assured that the eyes of the congregation were withdrawn from me, I ventured to look up and take the measure, in turn, of those present. There were, perhaps, twenty-five in attendance. They were so like, in their general appearance, congregations usually seen on such occasions in the east that it was difficult to realize we were in the far west.

The service proceeded, and at its close the Quarterly Conference was held. We tarried, and after the opening services, my father arose and addressed the Elder, stating that we had recently settled at Waupun, and supposed we were outside of the boundaries of any charge. Yet such was the flexibility of Methodist institutions, he had no doubt the boundaries of Fond du Lac Circuit could easily be thrown around Waupun. If so, we would like to be recognized as members of the church. We were received on our credentials, my father as an ordained Local Preacher and I as an Exhorter. Before we left the Quarterly Meeting, it was decided that Brother

Lewis should establish an appointment and form a class at Waupun. But of this further mention will be made in a subsequent chapter.

Rev. Wm. H. Sampson, the Presiding Elder of the District, had been a member of the Michigan Conference. On invitation, he was transferred to the Rock River in August, 1842. His first appointment was Milwaukee, of which mention will be made in another place. The next year he was sent to Kenosha, then called Southport, to save the church property which had fallen under financial embarrassment. Having accomplished this task, he was, in July, 1844, appointed to the charge of Green Bay District.

A better selection for the position could not well have been made. He was just in the strength of his early manhood, an able preacher, a sound theologian, a wise administrator, and a man of agreeable presence. The country was new, society in a formative state, and the material limited. Under these embarrassments, it required no little skill to lay the foundations wisely and successfully rear the superstructure.

The District extended from Green Bay on the north to Whitewater on the south, and from Sheboygan on the east to Portage City on the west, and included eight charges. To encompass the labor of a single year required the travel of four thousand miles. The roads were almost impassable, especially in the northern and eastern portions of the District. During certain seasons of the year, the buggy and sleigh could be used, but, in the main, these extended journeys were performed on horseback. A wagon road had been cut through the timber from Fond du Lac to Lake Michigan, but only one family, as yet, had found a home between the former place and Sheboygan Falls.

Between Sheboygan and Manitowoc, a distance of twenty-five miles, there was no house. The road, if such it might be called, was an unbroken line of mud of uncertain depth, and any amount of logs, stumps, roots and stones, to give it variety. The northern portion of the district was a wilderness, and the few points that had been invaded by settlements, were almost wholly inaccessable. In the southern portion the roads were better, but even here, and especially through the Rock River woods, they were not inviting.

The position of Presiding Elder on the Green Bay District at this time was no sinecure. The long journeys, the great exposure and the meager accommodations among the people, were trying in the extreme. But it was found that Brother Sampson was equal to every emergency.

At this time there were only three churches on the District, and these were located at Green Bay, Oneida and Brothertown. Brother Sampson remained a full term on the District, and at its close became connected with the Lawrence University, in connection with which a record of his labors will appear. In this work he was engaged until 1851, when his health failed, and he was stationed at Kenosha. He was recalled the year following, and until the year 1856 performed such services as his broken health would permit. He was now made effective and appointed Professor, but in 1861 he again entered the regular work, being stationed at Whitewater. His subsequent appointments have been, Presiding Elder of Milwaukee District, Pastor of Racine, Janesville, Evansville, Sharon, Milton and Waukau, where he is, at the present writing, doing efficient work. Brother Sampson has given to the cause long service, a noble life; and is an honor to the Conference.

The Fourth Quarterly Conference of the year was held at Fond du Lac. It was at this meeting that I was granted license to preach and recommended to the Conference, as before stated. The meeting was held in the school house and convened on the 31st day of May, 1845. The members of the Quarterly Conference were Rev. Wm. H. Sampson, Presiding Elder, Rev. Joseph T. Lewis, Preacher, Rev. Silas Miller, Local Preacher, Francis M. McCarty, Isaac Crofoot, Joseph Stowe, Charles Olmstead, D.C. Brooks, Cornelius Davis, and myself.

The population of Fond du Lac proper, at the time of our first visit, was very small. It contained seven buildings and numbered only five families, including the family of the Presiding Elder. The school house was the only public building, and for years was used for all public meetings known to civilization. Subsequently this public convenience fell a prey to the devouring element. The papers, in announcing the fire, gravely enumerated the losses incurred by the disastrous conflagration in this wise: "The Court House has been burned, every church in the town has been consumed, and even the school house and all the other public buildings have shared the same fate. There is no insurance, and the loss cannot be less than two hundred dollars."

During the year an appointment was established at the residence of Joseph Stowe, Esq., on the old military road, four miles west of Fond du Lac.

To accommodate the settlement, now rapidly increasing in population, Brother Stowe built a hall for public worship. Two square buildings were erected at a suitable distance from each other, with an open court between. Over this court, and extending from one building to the other, and including the upper part of one of them, the hall was built, thus furnishing an upper chamber. The hall was fitted up with seats and formed a Chapel of no mean pretensions for that early period.

Brother Stowe's Chapel, as the place was sometimes called, soon became a great institution in that region. A class was formed, and, under the leadership of Isaac Crofoot, greatly flourished. A few years after, the leadership passed to the hand of Ethiel Humiston. The members of this class were Joseph Stowe, Priscilla Stowe, Isaac Crofoot, Ethiel Humiston, Almira Humiston, Amos Lewis and Susan Lewis.

The class meetings, as well as the public services at this Chapel, now became objects of general interest. Brother Humiston had been raised under calvinistic teaching, and, until recently, had utterly failed to discover "the way of Faith." But, coming to the light under the special teaching of the Spirit, he had become a most remarkable illustration of this great arm of strength. In short, nothing could stand before his victorious Faith. In this Chapel there were most extraordinary displays of divine power. Nor, under such leadership, need it be deemed strange that revivals sometimes swept the entire circuit of the year. Nor were Brother Humiston's labors confined to his own neighborhood exclusively. He was often invited to other appointments on the charge, and even to other charges, to aid the preachers in their revival meetings, and his labors were always greatly blessed. I have known whole congregations melted to tears under the recitals of his Christian experience. And could a record be made of the wonderful displays of divine grace in the experience and labors of this dear brother, it would be a priceless legacy to the church.

But Brother Stowe was amply compensated for the erection of this temple for the Lord. In one of the remarkable revivals enjoyed in it, and that, too, in the midst of harvest, his son, William Page, now the Presiding Elder of Milwaukee District, was converted. The home of Brother Stowe was always a stopping place for the preachers. The writer, in going up and down the land in his early Itinerant labors, has been often entertained by this dear brother, and his excellent wife and family. Repeatedly, when weary, I have gone to this home of the pilgrims as I would have gone to my own father's house, and in doing so, always found a generous welcome. William, then a lad, was always ready at the gate to take my horse, and the mother, a motherly, godly woman, as ready to spread the table.

Another appointment established this year was that of Byron, where a class was formed by Rev. Joseph T. Lewis on the 18th of July, 1845 The class was at first formed as a branch from Fond du Lac, but has since became the head of an independent charge. The first members were Orrin Morris, Leader, Olive Morris, Abraham Shepherd, Eliza A. Shepherd, Mary C. Shepherd, and Maria Shepherd. The first sermon preached in Byron proper was delivered by Rev. Morgan L. Noble, Pastor of Fond du Lac, January 25th, 1846, and thereafter this place became a regular appointment.

A very comfortable church was built at Byron in 1855, under the labors of Rev. S.V.R. Shepherd, Pastor of the charge. In later years Byron has become distinguished as the place where the Fond du Lac District Camp Meetings are held.

Rev. Joseph T. Lewis was received on trial at the Conference held in Chicago, August 24th, 1842. His first appointment was Elgin, Ill., and his second, Mutchakinoc. He was born in Wales, and, at the time of his appointment to Fond du Lac, had been in America only five years. Such had been his success, however, in acquiring the English language, that he was now able to speak it with remarkable fluency and correctness.

Brother Lewis was a man of robust constitution, above medium height, had a strong face, adorned with a Roman nose, and a piercing eye. He had a vigorous mind, was a thorough student and was already taking rank as a preacher. During his brief year on the charge, he found time not only to master the Conference studies, but, by the aid of the writer, to make considerable progress in the study of Greek. At the end of the year he reported ninety members. His subsequent appointments were: 1845, Sheboygan; 1846 and 1847, Beloit. During his last year at Beloit, he was called from labor to reward. His illness was brief, eight days duration, but he was ready for the Messenger. Just before his departure, he said to his most estimable companion: "Tell my brethren of the Rock River Conference that I die *shouting happy*." Thus fell, on the 22d day of May, 1848, one of the most promising young men of the Conference. Truly it is said: "God buries his workmen, yet carries on his work." The Conference extended to the accomplished and devoted widow their profound sympathy. Nor will it be amiss to say in this connection, that the widow several years after became the wife of Rev. Stephen Adams, of Beloit, and up to this hour is most highly esteemed by all who have the pleasure of an acquaintance.

In 1845, Rev. Morgan L. Noble was appointed to the Fond du Lac charge and remained two years. He was received by the Rock River Conference in 1843, and was appointed to Du Page Circuit with Rev. Elihu Springer as Preacher in Charge. Brother Noble was a man of superior talent, but his health was not equal to the Itinerancy. At the close of his term at Fond du Lac, he took a location and entered secular pursuits.

In 1847 Rev. Henry R. Colman was sent to Fond du Lac, and also remained two years.

Brother Colman entered the New York Conference in May, 1831, and his first appointment was Warren Circuit, with Rev. Joseph McCreery as his colleague. This charge was located forty miles from his residence and included twenty-four hundred square miles. His visits to his family were few, and the year was one of most severe labor. His receipts were only one hundred and forty dollars, showing that pioneer work had not at that period wholly ceased in the older States. Luzerne, his next field, gave him one hundred and twenty dollars. The next year he traveled Bridgeport, a large, four weeks circuit, and had for colleague Rev. J.G. Whitford. On this charge the receipts for the first two quarters were not equal to his moving expenses. He was next stationed at Ticonderoga, Westport and Essex, and Berne, successively, when he was invited by Rev. John Clark, who was east attending the General Conference of 1840, to come west and take charge of the Oneida Indian Mission. He consented, and at the following session of the Troy Conference he was transferred to the Rock River and assigned to that field, where he arrived September 19th, 1840.

He remained on this Mission five years and was then appointed to Brothertown as my successor. At the expiration of two years he was appointed to Fond du Lac, as above stated, where he contracted a severe cold, but thinking to remove it without difficulty, continued his labors. It was a fatal step. Bronchitis set in and he lost his voice. He was granted a superannuated relation at the session of the Wisconsin Conference, held at Beloit, July 27, 1849. From this attack he has never sufficiently recovered to resume his labors.

The loss of Brother Colman from the work in the Conference was severely felt. Of solid endowments, respectable attainments, large practicable knowledge and excellent administrative abilities, his services seemed almost necessary to the success of the work. We can only refer such difficult problems to the Great Head of the church for solution.

During the nine years of Brother Colman's service in Wisconsin, he was abundant in labor. He was emphatically a man of one work. His salary, like that of his co-laborers, was small, making an average of only two hundred and fifty dollars a year. Certainly this was a small provision for himself, wife and five children. By a judicious investment at an early day, however, he is placed beyond the reach of want. He still lives in the affections of his brethren, and, after a superannuation of twenty-five years, his visits to the sessions of the Conference always assure him a hearty greeting from his old friends.

CHAPTER V

The Rock River Conference, for the year 1845, held its session at Peoria on the 20th day of August. At this Conference I was received on trial and appointed to Green Lake Mission. The class admitted this year numbered twenty-three, and among them were Wesley Lattin, Seth W. Ford and Joseph M. Walker.

Green Lake Mission, somewhat undefined in its geographical boundaries, was intended to include the large tract of beautiful prairie and opening country lying west and southwest of Fond du Lac. It took its name from a lake on what was believed to be its northern boundary, five miles west of Ripon. As I did not attend the Conference, I awaited the return of the Presiding Elder at Waupun. Being informed of my appointment, I enquired after its boundaries. The Elder facetiously replied, "Fix a point in the centre of Winnebago Marsh," since called Lake Horicon, "and draw a line to the north pole, and another due west to the Rocky Mountains, and you will have your eastern and southern boundaries. As to the other lines you need not be particular, as you will find no Dr. Marsh in your way to circumscribe your ambition." At the date of which we write, a few small settlements only had been formed within the limits of the Mission, but emigration was moving rapidly in that direction, and it was believed that an ample field would soon be found.

At Waupun a class had been formed during the preceding year, as above stated, consisting of my father's family, six persons in all, as follows: Rev. Silas Miller, Eunice Miller, Henry L. Hilyar, Malvina F. Hilyar, Ezekiel T. Miller and myself. This band consisted of three officers and three privates. My father was the Local Preacher, my brother the Class Leader, and I the Exhorter. My mother, sister and sister's husband were the members.

Rev. Samuel Smith, an aged Local Preacher, and father of Rev. Charles Smith, a worthy member of the Wisconsin Conference, had settled, with his family, in Waupun during the preceding year, and had held religious services in private dwellings, whenever convenient.

Soon after the class was formed, Father Smith, as he was called, and his family identified themselves with the infant society and became efficient laborers in the Lord's vinyard. At the same time the class was strengthened by the addition of Dr. Brooks Bowman and his good lady. Others were added during the year, including S.J. Mattoon, Mr. and Mrs. S.A.L. Davis, Mr. and Mrs. G.W. Sexmith and Mrs. F.F. Davis. The class now numbered twenty-two members.

A building had been erected by the contributions of the people in the village and country adjacent, for the purpose of a chapel and a school house. Regular services had been held in the new edifice for several months, both morning and evening. But during the absence of the Pastor at Conference, two ministers of sister denominations came to the village and established appointments, occupying the house on alternate Sabbaths, thereby displacing the former occupants altogether.

On taking charge of the work, I called on the new comers and expressed a desire to occupy the house for the regular appointment once in two weeks, but found they were not disposed to meet my wishes. I suggested that such had been the previous custom and that our appointments were so arranged, we could not work to any other than a two weeks' plan. But finding them still indisposed to accommodate me, I merely stated to them that the house, having been built mostly by my people, and in part by myself, I could claim as a right what I had begged as a favor, but, since I saw they were indisposed to give me the only hour that would accommodate the balance of my work, I should seek a place elsewhere. At this juncture Dr. Brooks Bowman, the physician of the village, generously offered his residence as a temporary chapel, and it was gratefully accepted. The wisdom of the movement was soon shown by the result. The people came to the private house, and, when they could find no room within, they uncomplainingly stood without. The Lord poured out his spirit upon the people abundantly.

The eldest daughter of our generous host, as the first trophy of grace, was converted. Other conversions followed, and in a short time the number increased to twenty. Among them were William McElroy and wife and several others, who became leading and influential members of the church in Waupun.

The opposition soon came to naught, and the house was left to our peaceable occupancy. The Local Preachers rendered valuable services in the protracted meeting, and also alternated in filling the appointment during my absence in caring for other portions of the charge. Father Smith was not able to visit other neighborhoods, but my father was abundant in labors, extending his visits to every part of the charge and preaching usually twice, and sometimes three times on the Sabbath.

Having spent my first Sabbath at Waupun I next visited Ceresco, where a settlement had been made by the Wisconsin Phalanx, a Fourierite Association.

There was no direct route, as all previous travel had taken a circuit to the west, thereby striking the trail from Watertown. But I deemed it best to open a track at the outset across the country to the point of destination. Obtaining a horse and saddle, and substituting a pocket compass for the saddlebags, as that evidence of civilization had not yet reached the village, I started out on my trip. Unfortunately the day was cloudy, and in the absence of the sun recourse at an early stage of the journey was had to the faithful compass, but unhappily not soon enough to avoid perplexity. After having traveled some distance, as I believed in the right direction, I fell into a questioning, whether I should go to the right or left of a marsh lying directly before me. The compass was brought to aid in deciding the question. It was poised on the knob of the saddle, when, to my surprise, it seemed to point several degrees too far to the left. I boxed the truant thing again and again, but could not bring the needle to point in any other direction. So I concluded, if the mountain would not come to Mahomet, Mahomet must go to the mountain. Out upon the trackless wilds, absolutely without any other guide, it would not do to ignore the compass. But now a new question arose. If the needle tells the truth, I must have been going in the wrong direction for, perhaps, some considerable distance. In such case, it is impossible to conjecture how far I may be out of the direct line of travel or how far I may be astray. The needle may point to the north pole, but I cannot be sure that, if I follow its guidance now, I will find Ceresco in the line of travel. But there was no time to be lost. So, deciding that I must follow the compass, I reined my horse into line and started on, I had not gone far, however, before I found myself confronted by another large marsh. This must be avoided, and hence I made a circuit to the west and passed it, but in doing so, much precious time was lost, and speedily the night drew on. I was now without sun, stars or even compass. The stillness of the prairie was painful. And the scattered trees of the openings in the deepening shades of the evening looked more like muffled ghosts with huge umbrellas, than the beautiful groves they had appeared when seen by the light of day. Pushing on through the darkness, I soon found I was nearer my destination than I supposed. Leaving the groves on the right and passing over the prairie to the left, I had not gone far when a light was visible in the distance. On approaching, I found that I had reached Ceresco, where I was most hospitably entertained by Rev. Uriel Farmin, a Local Preacher and a member of the Association.

The Wisconsin Phalanx came from the southeastern portion of the Territory and settled at this point in May, 1844.

Soon after their settlement, Rev. Wm. H. Sampson, Presiding Elder of Green Bay District, visited the place and held the first religious service of which I can obtain information. Not long after the minister in charge of the

Winnebago Lake Mission at Oshkosh visited Ceresco, and formed a class of seven members. The names, as far as ascertained, were Rev. Uriel Farmin and wife, Mrs. Morris Farmin, Mrs. Beckwith and George Limbert. The first named was appointed Leader.

The Association had erected two long buildings, one for a tenement house and the other for a dining hall. The first was built with a wide hall running from one end to the other. On either side of this hall suits of rooms had been provided for the accommodation of the several families, giving to each family at least a parlor and one or more sleeping apartments, according to its needs. Here families were as exclusive in their relations as good neighborhood could well require. The dining hall was a long, narrow building, giving in its width, barely room enough for the table, a row of persons on each side, and the free movement of the waiters behind them. The tables would accommodate one hundred and fifty at a fitting. In the rear of the dining hall, there was a large kitchen in which the cooking was done for the entire Association. The service of the kitchen, as well as every other department, was performed by persons who either volunteered or were assigned to their positions by lot, and were paid by the hour from the common fund. Divided into squads, each section had a foreman or directress, elected at reasonable intervals. It was expected that all the members would take their meals at the common table, yet exceptions were allowed in certain cases. It was affirmed that with this division of labor and a common table, the cost of board for a single individual per week did not exceed fifty cents.

The Association had under cultivation several hundred acres of land and were now putting flour mills in operation. Goods were purchased at wholesale by the Association and re-sold to individuals at the same rate. A school had been established and was under the care of a very competent teacher. Thus, externally, everything appeared to promise well and the people seemed orderly and happy. But, like all other enterprises of the same character, selfishness and corruption finally crept in, and the institution fell into decay, and ultimately disappeared.

The people of Ceresco were always gratified to receive the attention of the outside world, and their hospitalities were proverbial. And, though not a few of the leading men were professed Infidels, they always received ministers gladly and treated them with consideration. They were specially gratified to have religious services held among them, and the ringing of the bell would generally insure a good audience. The dining hall was used as a Chapel until a more convenient place was provided in the erection of a large school house.

Here in the low, long hall I held forth on the following Sabbath. The position was an awkward one. The table stood in the middle of the hall, reaching from one end to the other. The congregation was seated on each side in long rows. The preacher stood at the head of the table and threw his message along the narrow defile, greatly to his own annoyance, if not the discomfort of the people. To me the task was exceedingly disagreeable. My thin, feminine voice seemed to spend its volume before it had reached the middle of the line. Then, my rapid manner of speaking seemed to send the words in wild confusion into the distant part of the hall. But I soon learned to gauge my voice to the place, and, thereafter, I enjoyed unusual freedom of speech.

At the close of the services, the table was spread for dinner. I was assigned the head of the table, with the President of the Association at my right, and the Vice President at my left. Both of these gentlemen were decidedly Infidel in their views, and have since become somewhat distinguished as champions of Unbelief. They always treated me with courtesy, however, and sought to make my visits agreeable.

It was their custom to bring up some item in the sermon as the subject of discussion at the table. These discussions often became animated. But, having been somewhat schooled in that line of things, I always required a definite statement of position on both sides before any discussion could be had on the point assailed. This precaution kept the coast clear, and made these table conversations profitable. The President repeatedly expressed his gratification with the conversations, and also with the religious services of the day. And on one occasion he took the freedom to say, "Though I am not a believer in Christianity, yet I think there is nothing in the world that can so effectually harmonize the views and blend the sympathies of the community as these religious services." I took the occasion to suggest to him that his admission carried with it a complete vindication of the claims of religion and a proof of its Divine origin.

On another occasion, as I was mounting my horse to leave, the President expressed a wish that I would visit Fox Lake and establish an appointment in that village, assuring me that he had friends there, very intelligent people, who would receive me cordially and appreciate my labors. I enquired whether there were not religious services established already in Fox Lake. "Oh! yes," he replied, "but they are not up to the times. They are conducted by a Local Preacher from Waupun, a gentleman whom I greatly respect, but he is quite antiquated in some of his views." I enquired if he was free to state what these views were. He replied: "Why, sir, he retains the old notion that the world was made in six days." "Well, was it not, Judge?" "Why, certainly not," he answered, "any man at all abreast with the times knows better than that." Willing to put the Judge on the defensive whenever I could, I said; "Well, Judge, if it required more than six days, will you have the goodness to tell me just how long it did take to make it?" The Judge felt the awkward position he was in, and before he could recover I had bidden him good bye and was on my way. Nor was he less embarrassed when he came to learn that the old gentleman to whom he referred was my father.

Having spent the Sabbath at Ceresco, I now started in a southwesterly direction to explore the country along the south side of Green Lake, with the purpose to establish an appointment should a suitable location be found. After traveling about three miles, I came to a large log house, which with its surroundings seemed to say, "We have come to stay." Hitching my horse to the limb of a tree near the gate, I approached the house. I was met at the door by a lady of fine presence and intelligent bearing, who invited me to enter and be seated.

I began the conversation with the usual compliments to the weather and the beautiful country about Green Lake. Receiving frank responses to these common places, I next enquired if there were still good locations untaken in the neighborhood. Her intelligent face radiated a smile as her sharp eyes gave me a searching glance, which seemed to say, "You can't come any land-seeking dodge on me, you are a Minister." Changing the conversation, I soon found that the proprietor of the house was a Mr. Dakin, she, his sister, Mrs. White, and that she was a Methodist. At a subsequent visit to Ceresco I had the pleasure to enter her name upon the list of members.

Passing on I came to the residence of Mr. Satterlee Clark, since widely known in the State, but he being absent I stopped only a few moments and continued my exploration. The next house I visited was located near a beautiful spring in a grove of timber. The building was small, but the surroundings indicated thrift. I rode up to the door and saw a lady at her wash-tub. She threw the suds from her hands and came to the door. In a moment I recognized her as a lady whom I had known in the State of New York. She did not recognize me, however, as I had doubtless changed very much since she had seen me. But she was not mistaken in thinking I was a Minister. She invited me to tarry for dinner, saying her husband would soon be in.

When Shadrach Burdick, for that was the name of the husband, came to dinner he found his house invaded by the irrepressible Itinerancy. He gave me a cordial welcome, expressed his satisfaction that his new location did not lie beyond the limits of Gospel agencies, and urged me to make his house my home whenever I might come that way. I saw that he did not recognize me, and concluded not to make myself known until the surprise could be made more complete. Conversation turned on the character of the settlement, the number of families and the prospect of opening an appointment. It was known that a few families had settled in the vicinity, but mine host was not informed as to their religious proclivities. I decided at once to visit every family in the neighborhood.

Passing down along the shore of Green Lake and thence up through the openings to the margin of the prairie, I found a half dozen families. I found also that, without exception, they were desirous to have religious meetings established in the neighborhood. Receiving unexpected encouragement, I decided to hold a meeting before I left. Fixing on the most central residence as our first chapel, we held service on Wednesday evening. After preaching, I proceeded to form a class, and received eleven names. Brother Burdick was appointed the Leader. He demurred, but I was not disposed to excuse him. I then quietly stated to the class that I had known their Leader on the Crumhorn, in the State of New York, where he held the same position, and I was fully persuaded there had been no mistake in the selection. The Leader was not a little surprised at this turn of things, and concluded that he had nothing further to say, yet doubtless thought, "How strange it is that lads in so short a time will grow to be men?"

At a subsequent visit I crossed the Lake in a small boat to explore the neighborhood where Dartford is now located, but found no settlement. An appointment, however, was opened at this point the following year with Wm. C. Sherwood as the leading spirit. At the present writing, Dartford has become a fine village, has a good Church, an energetic society, and has enjoyed the services of several of the strong men of the Conference.

At Green Lake the congregations and class grew rapidly, and before the expiration of the year the appointment had gained considerable prominence. As soon as a school house was built, the meetings were removed to it and continued there until 1870, when a fine Church was erected.

Leaving Green Lake and resuming my journey of exploration, I came to Little Green Lake. Here I found a four corners with a store on one side and a residence on the other. The residence was occupied by a Mr. Jewell, whose wife was a relative of Rev. D. P. Kidder, then in charge of our Sunday School literature. My acquaintance with him soon made me acquainted with this most excellent family. On their kind invitation I established an appointment in their house, which was continued until their removal from the place. It was then removed to the residence of Mr. Roby, who, with his wife, was a member of the church. A small class was now formed. Before the expiration of the year the appointment was moved a mile south to the school house in

Mackford. And after a time it was taken down to Markesan, a mile west of Mackford.

If was at this place that I assumed the role of Chorister, the occurrence transpiring in this wise. I announced my opening hymn, supposing that some one present would be able to lead the singing, but to my surprise not one was disposed to serve us. I had never attempted such a thing in my life as to "raise a tune" in public, and the only claim I had ever set up as a qualification was that I could put more tunes to each line of a hymn than any one that I had ever known. But something must be done, so I concluded to lead off. Hunting through the garret of my memory, I brought out old Balerma for the occasion. To my surprise, I went through the performance very much to my own satisfaction and comfort. And more, when I got along to the third verse, several persons in the congregation began to follow, with a manifest purpose to learn my tune. I dispensed with further singing, and at the close of the service a good brother came forward and remarked: "There were several ladies in the congregation who are excellent singers, and if you had sung a tune with which they were acquainted, they could have helped you very much." Whereupon I concluded that if I were unable to sing the most familiar tune in the book, so that a bevy of good singers could discern what I was trying to render, I certainly could never succeed as a chorister. I never became the owner of a tuning fork.

In the changes which followed in the boundaries of the charges, Markesan was assigned first to one and then to another, but several years ago it came to the surface as the head of a circuit. And it now has a respectable standing as a charge with a good Church and Parsonage.

Resuming my search for new settlement, I next visited Lake Maria. Here I first called at the house of Mr. Langdon. I was kindly received, and when my errand was made known I was pressingly invited to remain for the night, and hold a meeting before leaving the neighborhood. I consented, and on the following evening we held service in Mr. Langdon's house. Lake Maria was now taken into the list of appointments and was visited regularly during the year. At my third visit, which occurred on the 30th day of November, 1845, I formed a class, consisting of Lyman L. Austin, Amanda M. Austin, Mrs. L. Martin, Mrs. Maria Langdon, David C. Jones and Maryette Jones. A protracted meeting was held soon after and thirty persons were converted. The fruit of this meeting carried the membership during the year up to twenty-five. Among the additions were Lansing Martin, Wm. Hare, Mrs. Susan Woodworth, and others, who have been pillars in the church.

CHAPTER VI

It had been arranged at the Conference that Green Lake and Winnebago Lake Missions should hold their Quarterly Meetings together. The first was now to be held at Oshkosh. In going, I took the trail leading from Ceresco to Oshkosh, and traveled the whole distance without finding a house. But at the intersection of the Fond du Lac and Ceresco trails I met Brother Sampson, the Presiding Elder.

On our arrival at Oshkosh we found it had been arranged to hold the services on Saturday in a private house on the south side of the river. The Elder preached, and at the close of the service, the Quarterly Conference was convened under a tree, thereby giving the house to the needed preparations for dinner.

Rev. G.N. Hanson was the Pastor at Oshkosh. He was a single man, several years my senior, of a kind and gentle spirit, given to books and a fair Preacher. I had known him in the State of New York, where we were both Exhorters, and, also, both engaged in teaching. Brother Hanson entered the Rock River Conference in 1844, and his first charge was Manitowoc. He had been stationed on the Winnebago Lake Mission at the recent Conference and was doing a good work. After leaving this charge he rendered effective service in other fields until 1852, when, having almost lost the use of his voice, he took a superannuated relation. But as soon thereafter as his health would permit, he entered the service of the Bible Cause and for three years proved an efficient Agent. In this work his field of labor lay mostly in the new and sparsely settled regions of the Chippewa Valley, and along the frontiers of Minnesota. But here he evinced the same perseverance and self-denial which had characterized his whole life. Leaving his most estimable companion, he took the Word of God, and though he could no longer give it a living voice, he bore it joyfully to the families of the land, through the forest and marshes of those new counties, often throwing his shadow upon the coming footsteps of the Itinerant himself. But at last he was compelled to yield to the hand of disease which had long rested upon him. He passed over the river in holy triumph in 1857.

On Sabbath the meeting was held in a frame building, the first in the place, that had been erected for a store. It had been roofed and enclosed, but there were no doors or windows. Rude seats had been arranged and the accommodations were ample. The Elder preached in the morning and the writer, as the visiting Pastor, in the afternoon. The meeting was well attended and greatly enjoyed by all. The people, of course, were mostly strangers to each other, and, coming from different parts of the world, were accustomed to various modes of worship. But they seemed to forget their differences, and recognize Christ only as their common Savior.

At this time Oshkosh was but little more than a mere trading post. The few families there were mostly on farms or claims in the vicinity of the river or lake. During my stay I was entertained by Brother William W. Wright, whose house, for many years thereafter, was a home for the Itinerant ministers.

The Quarterly Meeting passed off very pleasantly, and at its close I returned to my work of exploration on the Green Lake Mission.

Flushed with the achievements of the previous few weeks, and still sighing for conquests, I now resolved to make a sally in the direction of Lake Apuckaway, lying to the northwest of Lake Maria. I found, on the southern shore, a few families, and made arrangements for an appointment in connection with my next round. I then started to return, but had not gone far, when I found I had lost my reckoning. I looked for my compass as eagerly as Christian for his roll, but I could not find it. This was a double misfortune, to lose both the way and the guide at the same time. I resorted to the device of the backwoodsman, and tried to determine my course by the moss on the trees, but I found this to be a great perplexity and abandoned it. I traveled in divers directions and devious ways until nearly overcome with fatigue and hunger, when I suddenly came upon a newly erected log cabin. The logs had been rolled up to form the body, a roof of "shakes" had been hastily put on, there was no chinking between the logs, there were no windows, and the only door was a blanket. The floor was made of earth, and the fireplace was merely a pile of stones in one corner, from which the smoke ascended through an opening in the roof, at one corner of the building.

I knocked for admittance, and was kindly received. The good man and his wife had but recently come into the country. He had succeeded in erecting his cabin and putting it in its present condition, but had been taken ill with the ague and compelled to suspend operations. He had now been so long confined at home that provisions had become scarce. It was meal time. A few potatoes were taken from the embers and placed on a chest, as a substitute for a table. I was invited to join them in their repast, using a trunk as a seat. Grace was said, under a special sense of the Divine favor. A little salt was added, and the meal was one of the most relishable I had ever eaten. Several years after, I heard the good brother relate the circumstance in a Love Feast, when he took occasion to say the visit was the most refreshing he had ever experienced. It was certainly such to me. The village of Kingston has since sprang up in the vicinity, and has become the head of a circuit.

Returning again to Waupun, I now decided to look over the territory in the more immediate vicinity. Going to the south of the village five miles, I found Mill Creek, where a small settlement had been made. The most central house of the neighborhood was the residence of Brother David Moul, who kindly offered it for a temporary chapel. An appointment was established, and on the 16th day of November a class was formed. Brother Moul was appointed Leader. The class at the first, consisted of the Leader and wife, David Boynton and wife, and two others, but in the revival that soon followed, the number was increased to twenty-two.

Brother Moul was an earnest worker in the Master's vineyard, generous in his contributions to support the Gospel, and eminently faithful to every trust committed to his keeping. At the end of twenty years, I made a visit to Mill Creek. I found Brother Moul had erected a fine house and was living in manifest comfort; but he retained a vivid recollection of the early days and their sacrifices. Two relics remained, both in a fair state of preservation, which he took great pleasure in showing to me. The first was the old class book that I had given him at the time of the organization of the class. It was a single sheet of foolscap paper, folded together in book form, and stitched. The names upon it were mostly in my own handwriting, and the Leader had carefully made his weekly entries of present and absent, until the pages were filled. The other object of interest was the old house, in which the first meetings were held. Here we had seen remarkable displays of Divine power. And as I now looked upon the old structure, the early scenes seemed to return. I could again see the wide room, filled with rude seats, Brother Moul at the door as usher, the crowds of people that thronged the place, the groups of seekers at the mourners' bench, and the lines of happy faces that were aglow with hallowed expressions of delight. I could again hear the songs of praise as they rang out in the olden time, full and sweet, filling the place with rarest melody. Nay, as I held communion with the past, I seemed to feel the hallowed influences, that pervaded the early worshippers, breathing through all my being, as of old, and even fancy myself young again, and standing before the multitude as an ambassador of the Master.

But the scene, like the visions of the night, soon disappeared, and I turned sadly away, half regretting that I was no longer a pioneer, and permitted to feed the hungry sheep in the wilderness.

Brother David Boynton, at this writing, remains on the old farm, which has been growing with the passing decades, until the paternal acres have become a large estate. Situated on a prominent highway, his house, until the days of railroads, was the stopping place of all the preachers who needed entertainment at either noon or night. Brother Boynton, in the person of his son, Rev. J.T. Boynton, of the Wisconsin Conference, has given to the Itinerant work, an efficient laborer.

Leaving Mill Creek, I next visited Rock River, a settlement on the Fond du Lac road, six miles east of Waupun. My father had visited this place during the preceding year, and had already established an appointment. Brother W.J.C. Robertson, a gentleman whom we had known in the East, had tendered the use of his house, and here the meetings were now being held. My first visit occurred on the 18th day of November, 1845, In the evening, I held a service and formed a class. The members were W.J.C. Robertson, Martha Robertson, Mary Maxson, Mary Keyes, James Patterson, Charles Drake, Abigail Drake, and Elizabeth Winslow. The last named subsequently became the wife of Rev. J.M.S. Maxson. The first Leader was Brother Robertson. Both the congregation and class grew rapidly in this neighborhood, and the appointment soon took a leading position on the charge. During the ensuing winter a revival occurred, and gave an accession of twenty-five. From the first, this Society has been blessed with a devoted and spiritual membership, and its prayer meetings have been a living power in the land. As a result, revivals have been frequent, and the number saved a host. Passing from private houses, the meetings were held in a school house, but in course of time the school house became too small, and a larger one was built, with a special view to a provision for religious meetings.

In later years I have held Quarterly meetings in this building, when it was thronged with people. On such occasions, after filling the building to its utmost capacity, the good brethren would fill the court around it with wagons, carriages and buggies, loaded with people. It was at one of these gatherings that the little girl said, "Why, Ma, only see how full the school house is on the outside." During the past year a fine Church has been erected.

Rock River was the home of the lamented Rev. James M.S. Maxson, before he entered the Itinerant work. It was here that he was led to Christ, licensed to preach, and sent out into the vineyard, and certainly the church has had no occasion to deplore her share of the responsibility. Brother Maxson entered the Conference in 1850, and filled with great credit, Omro, Fall River, Grove street Milwaukee, Oconomowoc, Rosendale and Ripon charges. At the last named place, he closed his labors June 19, 1858. He was a man of great force of character, a good preacher, and was thoroughly devoted to his work. He was greatly beloved in his fields of labor, and his death was deeply regretted.

Having organized the class at Rock River, and arranged the plan of appointments to take it into the circuit, I passed on to visit an appointment at the Wilkinson Settlement, which had recently been attached to my charge from the Fond du Lac Circuit. It was situated on the south side of the marsh, nine miles from Fond du Lac and twelve from Waupun. The school house, in which the meetings were held, was located within the limits of the present village of Oakfield.

The class at this place had been formed during the early part of 1844, by Rev H.S. Bronson, when he was pastor of Lake Winnebago Mission, and consisted of Russell Wilkinson, Leader, and Alma, his wife, Robert Wilkinson, and Almira, his wife, Eliza Botsford and Sarah Bull.

To reach the settlement, it was necessary to follow the military road towards Fond du Lac for some distance, and then cross the marsh. At times, the stream in the middle was swollen, and the traveler was compelled to leave his horse and cross on foot. This was especially true when the ice was not sufficiently strong to bear up the horse, and such was the condition in which I found it on this occasion. So, leaving my horse, I hastened to cross the marsh, but when I had reached the middle of the stream, the treacherous ice gave way, and I plunged into the water up to my armpits. I clambered out, but as the day was intensely cold, I was soon a walking pillar of ice. I was now on the school house side of the stream, and there seemed to be no alternative but to go on. I would gladly have found a shelter and a fire elsewhere, but it was out of the question. So, putting on a bold face, I hastened forward, and found the people in waiting for the minister. As I entered the school house, with the ice rattling at every movement, my appearance was ridiculous in the extreme. But not more so than that of the audience. The faces of that crowd would certainly have been the delight of a painter. Some of them were agape with surprise and amazement; others were agonized with sympathy for the poor minister; and others still were full of mirth, and would have laughed outright if they had not been in a religious meeting. As to myself, the whole matter took a mirthful turn. I had been in church before, when by some queer or grotesque conjunction of affairs, the whole audience lost self control. I had witnessed mistakes, blunders and accidents that would make even solemnity herself laugh, and remained serenely grave. But to see myself in the presence of that polite audience, standing at that stove, and turning from side to side, to thaw the icicles from the skirts of my coat, was too much for me. I confess it was utterly impossible to keep my face in harmony with the character of the pending services.

At Fox Lake, the next point visited, an appointment had been established by my father during the previous year. The services were now held on Sabbath afternoon in the tavern. The log house, thus used for the double purpose of a chapel and a tavern, was built with two parts, and might have been called a double house. The one end was occupied as a sitting-room and the other as a bar-room. The meetings were held, of course, in the former. But it was bringing the two kingdoms into close proximity to dispense the Gospel in one end of the house and whisky in the other. In a short time, a better place was provided, and the meetings were removed to it.

With the better provision for religious services, came also the ministers of other denominations. We all labored together in harmony, except in one instance, where a conflict of appointments caused a momentary ripple. My appointment had long been established, and, to the surprise of the people, another appointment was announced by a young store-keeper of the village for the same hour. The word reached me of this attempt to displace the Methodists, when ten miles distant from the place.

I took my dinner and rode forward, without "wrath" or "gainsaying." I reached the place at the hour, went in and began the services. While the congregation were singing, the young man and his minister came in. Finding me in the desk, the minister quietly took a seat and listened very attentively to the sermon. But not so the discomfited young man. Being placed under the eye of the congregation, his condition was pitiable in the extreme. But finding after awhile that I was master of the ceremonies, and that no one in the congregation seemed vexed enough to fight for him, he subsided into a deferential attitude. And, thereafter, there were no further attempts to override my appointments. The minister, or perhaps I should say clergyman, took no offense, but became in after years a highly valued friend and companion.

At this time Mrs. Green was the only member of the Methodist church in the village. In process of time, however, a strong society was established. Then came the erection of a commodious Church and a very pleasant Parsonage. Fox Lake has been furnished with a line of able ministers, and has at the present writing a large and cultivated congregation.

Passing down the stream the following week, I found several families in the vicinity of Badger Hill. I immediately arranged an appointment for a week-day evening at the residence of a brother by the name of Morgan. At the first service held December 7, 1845, I formed a class of six. Brother Morgan was appointed Leader, and at the Quarterly Meeting following Brother Drinkwater was made steward. Some time after, the class was removed to Fox Lake, it being only three miles distant.

I now returned again to Waupun to spend the Sabbath. The Class Leader at this time was S.A.L. Davis, who came to the place during the preceding year. Brother Davis was an old neighbor from the East, a noble and true man, and, withal, had been my first Leader. He was specially adapted to the position; a man of great faith and ardent impulses. Under his Leadership, the class was in a most flourishing condition. The late revival had, however, so swelled the numbers that a division became necessary. An appointment had already been established at Miller's Mill, and it was now deemed best to so divide the class as to establish the meetings of one of them at this point. The change was accordingly made. The class was formed December 12th, 1845, and George W. Sexmith was appointed Leader.

Brother Sexmith was also an old neighbor, who had come West and taken a farm in the vicinity of Miller's Mill. Under his care, the class grew rapidly, and became an efficient company of laborers. Several years after he removed to Fond du Lac, and greatly prospered in business. In 1852 I had the pleasure to present him with a Local Preacher's license. He was employed one year as Pastor of Liberty Prairie circuit, but his health proved unequal to the Itinerancy, and he was compelled to resume his relation as a Local Preacher, in which position he still holds an honored place among his brethren.

The next place visited was Burnett. The services were held in the residence of Mr. McDonald, and a class was formed December 14th, 1845. The members of the first organization were William Willard, Leader, Huldah Ann Willard, Samuel C. Grant, Ruth M. Grant, and Elizabeth Benedict. The class grew rapidly, and the appointment took a leading rank on the charge. Burnett has since become a charge, has a good Church edifice and a strong congregation. Brother Willard became a member of the Conference, of whom mention will be made in another chapter.

Having organized the work at Burnett, I next visited Grand River. I had passed through this place in the early part of Autumn. At that time I found Brother David Wood and his son engaged in making preparations for a home. Finding they intended to have their cabin completed and the family in it before winter, I engaged to visit them and establish an appointment. On reaching the place to fulfil this agreement, I found that besides this family several others had also settled in the vicinity. At the first meeting, appointed before there was a family in the neighborhood, we had a congregation of fifteen persons. The class was formed December 19th, 1845, with David Wood as Leader. The Alto Church, which gives the name to a charge, has been erected in the vicinity, and there is at the present writing a strong society. Father Wood, as he is now called, still survives, and takes special delight in referring to this visit of the 'boy preacher.'

The watch-night meeting was held at Waupun, and was an occasion of great interest, several persons being converted.

CHAPTER VII

The work of the Mission was now well in hand. But already the field was becoming extended and the labor onerous. Thirteen regular preaching places had been established, and invitations were being received weekly to increase the number. To meet this demand, it was now determined to employ an assistant.

The Quarterly Meeting was held soon after at Waupun, and Rev. Uriel Farmin was employed by the Presiding Elder to assist in filling the appointments. The meeting, the first of the kind ever held in Waupun, was one of rare interest. The revival had just added a goodly number to the membership, besides greatly quickening others. There were present a number of visitors from the newly formed classes in other parts of the Mission, and as a spirit of revival seemed to pervade their respective localties also, they struck the same plane as those at Waupun. The Elder preached the Word, "in the demonstration of the Spirit, and with power." But the meeting reached its climax in the Sabbath morning Love Feast. The house was filled, and many were compelled to sit on the writing desks at the side of the room. The meeting was opened in the usual order, by passing to each a crumb of bread and a sip of water, in token of Christian regard. Christian testimonies followed each other in rapid succession, interspersed by singing spiritual songs, for a full hour. At times the tide of feeling rose, like swelling billows, to a great height, threatening to carry the meeting into disorder, but by giving it a happy change at the right moment, the Elder was able to maintain a complete mastery. There were two periods specially critical. One, when a young lady, one of the converts at Waupun, gave her testimony. Standing on a seat, as there was no other place to stand, she first related her own experience, and then, turning to the young people, she delivered an exhortation that thrilled the audience with overwhelming emotions. The other was when a Brother Mosher, somewhat eccentric in his exercises, gave his experience. As he advanced in its recital, he grew excited and eloquent, and the "Amens" and "Hallelujahs" came from every part of the audience. Now, leaping upon the tide of feeling he had raised, he passed from one to another, shaking hands and congratulating them, until he came in front of the desk where sat my father and Father Smith, the two Patriarchs of the occasion. Throwing his arms around their necks, he fairly lifted them from their seats, but in a moment, he discovered his awkward position and resumed his seat. Instantly the clear voice of my father was heard in one of those outbursts of song, which so effectually kindle the fervors of devotion, or if needed, stay the flow of feeling. In a moment more, the meeting had passed the crisis.

The Mission was now put under a new plan, providing for alternate appointments, each preacher making the round in four weeks. But while this arrangement was the general order, the numerous calls received from various localities required frequent changes. In most cases, however, the new appointments were crowded between the others. To meet them, it required three sermons on the Sabbath, besides many others during the week. As to myself, I sometimes rode forty miles on the Sabbath and preached four sermons.

On one of these excursions, I became very much exercised on the subject of Christian holiness. I had before given the subject special thought, but now it seemed to assume unusual importance. Not only did the teachings of our standards bear an unwonted clearness to my perception, but my heart began to realize its essential value.

At my morning service, I preached on the subject, and as I swept over the prairie ten miles, in the face of a driving storm, I resolved to preach on the same subject again at my noon-day appointment. I did so, and with much better satisfaction than in the morning. Twelve miles more of storm, and I was again before a congregation to preach the unsearchable riches of Christ. I had now become so full of my theme that I concluded to make it the subject of my next discourse. So, changing my text, I preached on Gospel purity, showing that experimental religion presents itself to the conception of the mind under three clearly defined ideas. These are Justification, Regeneration, and Sanctification. The drift of thought ran in this wise: By Justification we mean the pardon of sin. The man, who finds this grace through Christ, stands as fully accepted before the Law, as though he had never sinned. By Regeneration, we mean that radical change of man's moral and spiritual condition which subjects all the faculties and powers of the soul to the control of the Divine Spirit. This work of grace, wrought in the heart by the Spirit, includes not only the entire subjugation of the "Man of Sin," but the introduction of the reign of Christ. These two achievements of grace, wrought in the subject at the same moment, we ordinarily call Conversion. By Sanctification, we mean that higher state of grace which contemplates the removal of all sin from the heart of the believer, and the experience of "Perfect Love."

This last attainment comes to the believer through earnest seeking, and personal consecration to God. In thus "going on to perfection," the believer passes through several phases of experience. He finds that if he shall retain his justified state, it is necessary to seek advanced attainments. And if he shall be faithful in the use of grace already received, he will find the Spirit ever leading him to new fields of experience. As the Astronomer rests his calculations on worlds already discovered when he looks into the regions beyond, so the Christian must maintain his present experience, if he will know the further revelations of the Spirit.

But the moral perceptions, quickened by the Spirit, will furnish painful revelations to the justified soul. He will discover that there linger still within him remains of the carnal mind. Pride, the love of the world, selfishness, self-will, and sometimes even anger or other evil passion, will begin to stir in the heart. Such revelations will awaken a profound spiritual concern, and perhaps, become the subject of temptation. But there need be no alarm. It is but an evidence that the good work, began in Regeneration, has not been fully completed by entire Sanctification. The tree has been cut down, but the shoots around the old stump show that there is vitality still in the roots. The "Mightier" than the "strong man" must now come and pluck up the roots. The work of eradication thus accomplished, the absolute reign of Christ will be established. The heart will now become the Garden of the Lord, without briar, thorn, or thistle. Relieved of these hindrances, the graces will speedily acquire maturity.

At the close of the sermon, a good sister referred in very earnest terms to the discourse, and was grateful for the ministry of a man who so well understood the deep things of God. Instantly the thought came, "Ah, yes! but there must be a great difference between merely understanding the theory, and realizing a happy experience of the power." A hasty supper was eaten, and I was away for another ten miles to my evening appointment. The snow was still falling, and the winds were driving it fiercely across the prairie, rendering the track invisible. Out on the prairie, my noble horse dashed forward with great speed, but I scarcely noted the distance, as my thought was busy. The question that was ringing through my heart was this: "How can you preach to others what you do not know yourself?" At length I resolved; and scarcely stopping to measure the movement, or estimate the consequences, I was on my knees, engaged in prayer. My first conscious thought of my surroundings was awakened by the wrestling of my horse, as my right hand held him firmly by the lines. Then came the suggestion, "This is a very unpropitious time to settle a matter of this importance. With a fractious horse by the rein, a terrible storm sweeping over the prairie, and an already blind snow-path, you had better defer the matter for the present." My reply was, "It is time these questions were settled, and I propose to settle them now" "But the snow-path is nearly filled; you will lose your way and perish." I still replied, "It is time these questions were settled, and I propose to settle them now." "But it is getting dark, and your congregation will be waiting for you. You had better go forward, fill your appointment, and then attend to this matter." The Lord helped me to reply once more, "It is time these questions were settled, and, God helping me, they shall be settled now." Instantly the light broke upon me, and I was able "to reckon myself dead unto sin, but alive unto God, through Jesus Christ my Lord." I was found in due time at my appointment, preaching from the text, "He is able to save unto the uttermost all who come unto God by him."

Learning that a settlement had been made on Portage Prairie, at a point where Mr. Langdon, of Lake Maria, had erected a lumber mill, I resolved to visit the locality. I found Mr. Langdon had erected a small house, and had already moved his family. I was welcomed to his new home and again invited to make his house a chapel until better accommodations could be secured. I accepted the kind offer, and thus Cambria was made a regular appointment. I visited the few scattered families in the vicinity, and found sufficient material to organize a small class. The class was formed on the 10th day of January, 1846, and at the beginning included Mr. and Mrs. Irwin McCall, Mr. and Mrs. Wm. Wilson, Mrs. Maria Langdon, and Mrs. H. W. Patton. Cambria has since been largely settled by emigrants from Wales.

In March, I visited Randolph and opened an appointment at the residence of Father Griffin. At the present writing, the village has become a respectable station, with a good Church and Parsonage.

I also opened an appointment at the residence of Mr. Torbit, at Randolph Centre, which place has since become the head of a circuit.

In May following, I formed a class on the north end of Rolling Prairie, with Bro. Greenleaf, a Local Preacher, as Leader.

Wm. A. Cheney and family settled on Wedge's Prairie in the early part of this year. His house was immediately opened for religious meetings. But before I could arrange my plans to visit the neighborhood, my father, who was always on the alert to carry the Gospel Message to the destitute, established an appointment. On his invitation I held a meeting there, on the third day of June, 1846, and organized a class. The following were the first members: Wm. A. Cheney, Leader, Sophronia Cheney, Abigail Cheney, D. S. Cowles, Ann Cowles, Henry Moore, and wife.

At this time Brandon had not taken form or name, but, on its appearance, the honors and emoluments of this society passed over to its keeping.

Rosendale and Reed's Corners were next visited. At the first I held services in the house of Mr. Sanborn, after whom the prairie at that time was called, and at the latter, the meeting was held in the residence of a Brother Lee, a brother of the celebrated Dr. Luther Lee.

Rosendale has since become a very pleasant station, with its convenient Church and Parsonage, and Reed's Corners is a prominent appointment in the Brandon charge, and has also a fine Church.

Having heard frequent reference made to Strong's Landing, on the Fox River, I resolved to visit the place. On approaching the bank of the stream, I looked sharply in all directions to discover the town, but there were no evidences of human skill within the range of my vision. Concluding that I had struck the river at the wrong place, I first passed down the stream for a mile, but failing to find any settlement I turned back. I now went up the stream for a considerable distance, and found a trail that seemed to lead down to the margin of the river. Following it to the water, I found a small canoe tied to a tree. The light now dawned upon my understanding. This was Strong's Landing. Not having prophetic vision, I was unable to see the city of the future, sitting so gracefully on the banks of the Fox. Again the Itinerancy was ahead of the pioneer. Leaving the site of the future city of Berlin, I hastened to return to Waupun, but a starless night overtaking me on the way, I spent its weary hours where the village of Brandon now stands, under the branches of a friendly tree.

The labors of the year were now drawing to a close. The regular appointments had multiplied until they numbered twenty-four. The membership had gone up from a small figure to two hundred, and the spiritual interests were in a highly satisfactory condition.

My colleague had rendered effective service, proving to be a true yoke-fellow in every particular. Besides taking his full share of the regular appointments, he also gave a large portion of his time to the special labors of the charge. He was not expected, at the outset, to give his whole time, but he soon became so fully identified with the work that he was almost constantly employed. In the severe labors of protracted meetings, and in the wide travel of the circuit of appointments, he was equally self-forgetting and faithful. He was a man of good attainments, kind spirit, studious habits, and an acceptable preacher.

The charge being in a formative state, and the necessities of the preachers small, the financial receipts from the people were very limited. My own were only thirty-six dollars, and those of my colleague could not have been greater.

In tracing the work on Green Lake Mission, I have been thus specific for two reasons. I desired, in the first place, to give the reader an inside view of the relations of the Itinerancy to frontier life, and in the second, note the beginnings of a list of charges that have since constituted a Presiding Elder's District.

The Rock River Conference met this year in Galena, Ill. And as it was necessary for my father to attend the Conference to receive Elder's orders, we decided to make the journey in a buggy. The first day, passing through Beaver Dam, we reached Fountain Prairie, where we were entertained by Rev. E.J. Smith, of whom further mention will be made hereafter.

At noon on the following day we reached Madison, and were entertained by Rev. R.J. Harvey, the Pastor of the charge. Madison at this time was a small village, but, besides the Capitol, contained several buildings of respectable size and appearance.

The first Methodist sermon preached in Madison was delivered by Rev. Salmon Stebbins on the 28th day of November, 1837. Brother Stebbins was then the Presiding Elder of of the District, which extended along the western shore of Lake Michigan, from the State line to Green Bay. On visiting Madison, he was entertained by the contractor, who was erecting the State House, and who also kept a hotel. On learning that Brother Stebbins was a minister, this gentleman invited the entire population to a meeting in his bar-room, and here the first sermon was preached. And I am informed that the people were so pleased with the services that on the following morning Brother Stebbins was presented with a collection of fourteen dollars.

Brother Stebbins again visited the capital July 15th, 1838, and spent the Sabbath, preaching twice to respectable congregations. But as Madison, now in the West Wisconsin Conference, has fallen more directly under the eye of Rev. Dr. Bronson, and will doubtless appear in the Western Pioneer. I need not anticipate its historical incidents.

Passing on our way we were entertained the following night by a gentleman residing on the line of travel, some twenty miles beyond the Capital, by the name of Skinner. The following day we reached Platteville, where we were to spend the Sabbath.

It was now Friday night. Early the next morning, we received an invitation to spend the afternoon, in company with others, at Major Roundtree's, with Bishop Hamline. We went. The company was composed mostly of preachers, on their way to Conference. Among them were the Mitchells and Haneys. Of the first, there were Father Mitchell, a grand old Patriarch, John T. James, and Frank. Of the latter, there were the Father, Richard, William, Freeborn, and M.L.

But the central figure among them all was the good Bishop. Of full form, compact frame, broad forehead, and strong features, he would be selected in any group as a princely man. And yet, withal, his spirit was as gentle as that of a child. Though one of the intellectual giants of the country, and one of her greatest orators, he still seemed so humble in spirit that I felt myself drawn towards him at once. In such a presence the conversation was necessarily restrained. Dismissing, for the time, the freedom of debate, anecdote and repartee, that so often characterize ministerial gatherings, the interchange of thought took on a more serious tone. Only once was there an exception. Referring to the labors of some distinguished man of his acquaintance, one of the leading brethren and prince of story tellers, whose name I need not mention, proceeded to relate an anecdote. Immediately the tides of feeling began to rise, and, as the story advanced to its climax, they broke over all restraint. An immoderate laughter followed, in which no one joined more heartily than the brother himself. The storm of merriment, however, had hardly passed, when the Bishop, in one of those indescribably solemn tones for which he was distinguished, said, "Brethren, I always find it difficult to maintain the proper spiritual equilibrium without a good deal of prayer." Then, turning to the offending brother, he added, "Brother, will you lead us in prayer?" The entire company instantly fell upon their knees. But the poor brother! What could he do? Pray he must, for the entire company were on their knees, waiting for him to begin. So, making a virtue of necessity, he made the venture. But, I am free to say, it took a good deal of coasting before the good brother could get his craft well out to sea, and headed towards the desired haven. During the balance of the visit anecdotes were at a discount.

On Monday we went forward to the Conference, that I might appear before the Committee of Examination. The Committee were Revs. Salmon Stebbins, N.P. Heath, and S. Stover.

CHAPTER VIII

At the Galena Conference, Green Lake Mission was divided into two four weeks' circuits, requiring the labor of four men. In view of my impaired health, I was sent to Watertown, the Cabinet believing that I would here find less labor and exposure.

Watertown, up to the preceding year, had been a part of the old Aztalan circuit, and as this circuit was the mother of charges in this part of the Territory, it is proper that our respects should first be paid to her.

The old Aztalan circuit was organized at the session of the Illinois Conference of 1837, and embraced all the settled portion of the Territory east of Madison and west of the Lake Shore Missions. The first preachers were Rev. Samuel Pillsbury and Rev. Jesse Halstead, and the year was one of extended travels and great exposure. During the year appointments were established at Aztalan, Whitewater, Meacham's Prairie, East Troy, Spring Prairie, Elkhorn, Burlington, Round Prairie, Menomonee, Prairieville, Oconomowoc, and Watertown, and at several of them classes were formed. Brother Halstead's horse became disabled, and during a portion of the year this indomitable pioneer, with saddle-bags on his arm, made on foot, the entire round of appointments. Brother Pillsbury was also a man of sterling qualities, and rendered effective service.

The Quarterly Meetings of this year were held by Rev. Salmon Stebbins, the Presiding Elder, at Aztalan, Meacham's Prairie, Troy, and Burlington.

At the Conference of 1839, Aztalan circuit was divided. The eastern part was called Walworth, and Rev. James McKean was appointed its Pastor. The western part, retaining the Rock River Valley, was now called Watertown, and Rev. H.W. Frink was appointed the Pastor. Both charges were now put in the Milwaukee District, with Rev. Julius Field as Presiding Elder.

Brother Frink was now a young man, and this was his third charge. Leaving the seat of the Conference, he returned to Elgin, his last field of labor, filled his saddle bags with clothes and books, mounted his horse as a true knight of the Itinerancy, and was away for new perils and new conquests. In his journey to what was then deemed the wilds of Wisconsin, he passed through Elk Grove, Wheeling, Indian Creek, Crystal Lake, Pleasant Prairie,

East Troy, Whitewater, Fort Atkinson and Aztalan. The last named was the head of the Mission, as a class, the only one on the charge, had been formed at this place.

Without much regard to boundaries, it was the work of the Pioneer to find the scattered sheep in the Wilderness. To do this, he was obliged to undertake long and wearisome journeys, through exposed and almost trackless regions. Without roads, without bridges, and without shelter, our young Itinerant pushed his way through the forests, swimming the streams, when fords could not be found, and seeking shelter under the overhanging branches of the trees, in the absence of the friendly cabin. As the result of these extended journeys and herculean labors, Brother Frink, during the year, formed classes at Fort Atkinson, Jefferson, Piperville, Oconomowoc, Summit, Baxter's Prairie, Waukesha, Poplar Creek, Brookfield, Wauwatosa, Granville, Menomonee, Lisbon and North Prairie, but was unable to gather sufficient materials to form one at Watertown.

Brother Frink, however, enjoyed the honor of preaching the first sermon in this locality. As there was no school house or other public building that could be had, a small log house, twelve feet square, on the west side of the river, was secured. Here the services were held during the balance of the year. The Missionary was kindly received by all classes of people, and when in the place was usually entertained by Hon. Wm. M. Dennis, since Bank Comptroller of the State, and Patrick Rogan, a gentleman whose religious affiliations were with the Catholic Church.

At Fort Atkinson, Brother Frink preached and formed the class, in the residence of Jesse Roberts, during the winter of 1839 and 1840. The members of the first class were Jesse Roberts, Betsey Roberts, Franklin Roberts, Sarah Roberts, Martha Fellows, Anson Stone, and Mr. and Mrs. Harrison. The first Church was built in 1850, and Fort Atkinson became a separate charge in 1854. It now ranks among the first charges in the Janesville District.

The class at Jefferson was formed in the summer of 1840, and the members were Jacob Fellows, Martha Fellows, Mary Fellows, and John Masters.

The name of the circuit was again changed in 1841, Watertown being dropped and Aztalan restored. A change was also made in the name of the Summit charge, which was now called Prairieville.

Another dismemberment again befel the old Aztalan circuit this year. The southern portion, lying down the Rock River, was cut off and joined to territory that had been developed in Rock County, from the east and south, and out of the united parts Janesville charge was constructed. On the old Aztalan charge Rev. John Hodges became the Preacher, and on the

Janesville Rev. Alpha Warren. By these changes Aztalan was again reduced to the condition of a Mission.

In 1842, Rev. C.G. Lathrop was appointed to Aztalan, of whom a further record will be made in a subsequent chapter. Both Aztalan and Janesville were now transferred from the Platteville District to the Rock River, a new District that had just been formed, with Rev. S.H. Stocking as Presiding Elder.

Brother Stocking entered the traveling connection in Oneida Conference, and after filling a respectable class of appointments for a term of years, came to Illinois at an early day. He was stationed at Chicago in 1839, at Rockford in 1840, and was Presiding Elder of Mt. Morris District in 1841, Rock River 1842, Ottawa 1843 and 1844, and Milwaukee in 1845. Brother Stocking was highly esteemed by his brethren, and was an excellent laborer, but, his health failing, he was compelled to take a superannuated relation soon after the writer entered the work. He is spending the evening of life at Beloit.

In 1843 Rev. Stephen Jones was sent to Aztalan. In 1844 the charge was again divided and Watertown charge was formed, Brother Jones being transferred to the new charge. Rev. Asa Wood was now sent to Aztalan, and remained one year, when he was succeeded by Revs. C.N. Wager and S. B. Whipple. At the Conference of 1854 the honors and emoluments of Aztalan circuit passed over to the keeping of Lake Mills, which charge at this writing holds a respectable rank in the Conference.

Watertown, at the time of my appointment, had been a separate charge one year. A Church edifice had been commenced, and a class formed. The members were Mr. and Mrs. Walter Andrews, Mr., and Mrs. Heber Smith, Mr. and Mrs. Calvin Bunton, Mr. and Mrs. Wm. A. Dutcher, Mr. and Mrs. Elihu Higgins, Mr. and Mrs. Albert Cook, Mrs. Simeon Ford, Mr. and Mrs. Cheney Adams, Mr. Sands Cook, and others.

The financial ability of the charge was moderate, and hence the erection of the Church required a great effort. Our meetings were held in the school house until the Church edifice was enclosed, plastered, and furnished with temporary seats.

The fall of 1846 was a season of unusual sickness, fevers in various forms being the principal ailment. Along the valley of the Rock River, the affliction became so flagrant that scarcely a family escaped. And in some families, so universal were its ravages, that not one member was left in condition to care for the balance. In this state of things hundreds suffered, and not a few even died for want of kindly attention.

Repeatedly, when riding through the country to visit the sick and bury the dead, I found flags of distress hung out over the dwellings of sick families, where not one was able to bring a pail of water, or provide a morsel of food. In such cases I installed myself master of ceremonies, kindled fires, brought water, administered medicines, and then went forward to render the same class of services to others.

In attending funerals in the surrounding neighborhoods, I sometimes found there were not well people enough to bury their dead. After performing the sacred functions of my office as a minister, I was obliged to aid, with my own hands, to let the coffin down to its final resting place.

Though still frail from my illness during the previous year, I stood this strain for two months, when I was prostrated by an attack of bilious fever. During the first week of my illness a physician made two visits to my boarding place, and this was more than he could give to the greater portion of his patients. The family with whom I boarded were all sick, and I was dependent for care mostly upon such snatches of service as others could spare from pressing demands at home. At the end of a week, believing my chances of recovery, under such circumstances, precarious, I ordered my horse and buggy, and started for Waupun, thirty miles distant. My friends remonstrated, and thought me insane; but, fortunately, they were too ill to prevent the movement. The attempt was perilous, indeed, but by the aid of stimulants, which I had provided with special care, and a will-power that nerved itself for the occasion, I made the passage safely. At the end of four hours I was comfortably housed at the residence of Dr. Bowman, who bestowed upon me skillful medical treatment, while his family gave me careful and faithful nursing.

At the end of four weeks I was able to return to my post of duty. The sickness had now mostly passed, and I was able to enter more fully upon the regular labors of the charge. I now adopted a plan of systematic labor, giving the forenoons to my study and the afternoons to pastoral visiting. And I soon found that earnest and devoted labor brought its reward. A revival speedily followed, which added a goodly number of probationers.

But the holidays were approaching, and it was expected that I would spend a portion of them at Waupun, where, it was hinted, an event would transpire in which I might have a personal interest. Anticipating the time several days, I went as far as Clason's Prairie, and turned aside to assist Brother Holmes, the Pastor of the charge, for a few evenings in a protracted meeting. Returning, I proceeded on my way to Burnett. By arrangement, I met Brother Sampson here, and spent the Sabbath with him, it being his Quarterly Meeting on the Waupun charge.

The preachers on the circuit were Revs. A.P. Allen and Henry Requa, the latter being employed by the Elder as an assistant. Brother Allen was a man of mature years, though he had been in the work only a short time. He was a man of decided talent, but so full of queer ways and witty sayings that these seemed to give him his status in the general estimation of the people. He filled several leading charges in the Conference, and served a full term as Presiding Elder on the Racine District. But wherever he might be, the same tendency to create laughter was ever present. If an exception ever came to my knowledge, it must have been the one that is said to have occurred on a former charge at one of his outlying appointments. It is related that at this point the people had not shown much regard for the visits of the preacher or the sanctity of the Sabbath, spending the day either in rioting or in the pursuit of their secular business. Becoming disgusted with this state of things, Brother Allen announced at the close of his services, that on the occasion of his next visit, he would preach his farewell sermon. The day came, and the people, shocked at the idea of being left without meetings, came out in large numbers, leaving for once their business and sports. The services were opened in due form. On arising to announce the text, the Preacher told the people that he had come prepared to preach his farewell sermon, and he was glad that so many had come out to hear it. He presumed they knew the reason of his purpose to leave them, and hence he need not consume time over that matter, but would proceed at once to announce as his text, the following passage of Holy Writ: 'Oh, full of all subtlety and mischief, thou child of the devil, how long wilt thou not cease to pervert the right ways of the Lord.' Having repeated the text with emphasis, he looked over the congregation very gravely, and said, "Ladies and gentlemen, you will perceive that I have chosen a pretty hard text. Now it is not polite for people to go out of meeting during the preaching, and if any of you think that this text is too severe for you, you had better go out before we begin the sermon." As might have been expected, none were disposed to go. "Well, then," said the Preacher, "if you are not disposed to go, I will begin. I intend to show, in the first place, that you are all full of subtlety and mischief. In the second place, I intend to show that you are all the children of the devil, and in the third place, I intend to put to you the straight question, whether you intend to cease from thus perverting the right ways of the Lord." The preacher, at this point, again, paused and looked over the congregation. "Now you will say," he added, "this is going to be a hard sermon." "So it is, but if any of you think you can't sit to hear the truth told you, or in other words, to have your portraits taken, you had better leave now, for it is not polite to go out during the sermon." It was now too late to go, if any one felt inclined. So the sermon proceeded, and commanded respectful attention to its close. Before leaving, the Preacher was invited to continue the appointment, and consented to do so.

But to return to the Quarterly Meeting. The people came in great numbers, and the services throughout were deeply impressive. On Saturday evening, several souls were converted, and on the Sabbath others were added to the number. But the crowning meeting was held on Sabbath evening. Before the hour of service had arrived, the school house was full, the seats even having been removed to furnish standing room. And yet crowds of people were coming from all directions. I finally proposed to the Elder, that if he would put a man in my place in the school house, I would go over to the nearest neighbor's house and hold another service. The private house was soon filled, and in each congregation there were several conversions.

On Monday, January 4th, 1847, Brother Sampson accompanied me to Dr. Bowman's at Waupun, where he officiated in introducing the Doctor's eldest daughter to the Itinerancy.

Returning to Watertown, I held protracted meetings at all the outlying appointments, and had the happiness to witness many conversions. But the year was one of hard labor and small financial receipts. At its close I found my receipts from the charge were forty-four dollars and my board. The forty-four dollars were put into the Church enterprise, and I drew on my private funds for my incidental expenses.

The Conference met in Clark Street Church, Chicago, Aug. 11th, 1847. I passed my Conference Examination, was ordained Deacon by Bishop Waugh, and reappointed to Watertown.

Watertown was now placed in Milwaukee District, with Rev. Elihu Springer, as Presiding Elder. At the beginning of the new year we opened house-keeping in the upper rooms of a house on the corner of Fourth and Main Streets. The first floor was occupied as a residence by Judge Enos.

The year opened encouragingly. The Church in the village required two sermons on the Sabbath, and I had established other appointments in the country which required three a week, besides funeral sermons. The appointments were Higgins and Bennetts on the south of the village, and Piperville, Concord and Newhouse on the east. At several of them, during the winter, protracted meetings were held, in addition to the one held in the village. At each several conversions occurred, making a fair aggregate in all. These extensive labors taxed me severely, and finally brought on an attack of fever. I was taken during Sunday night, after preaching in Watertown both morning and evening. The attack was so violent that before morning I had become deranged, and my life was despaired of. But through my wife's faithful watching and the good Providence of God, I was able to resume my labors in three weeks.

It now became apparent that a severe financial pressure was upon us. I had spent what I could immediately command of my own funds, and the good brethren had contributed so generously out of their scanty means, to place the Church in condition for use, that they could not meet the Pastor's salary. I saw clearly that some other provision must be made.

While casting about to find my direction, a Providential opening occurred. Rev. Mr. Hoyt, the Episcopal clergyman, who had been keeping a Latin school for some time in the village, was compelled through illness to desist from teaching. Fortunately, I had gone down several times at his request, and relieved him in hearing his classes in Greek and Latin. This little kindness, added to the fact I was one of the School Commissioners of the county, naturally directed attention to me, as the person to open a select school in the village. I embraced the opportunity. The Trustees kindly consented to the use of the Church for the purpose. As the seats were only temporary, they were easily adjusted to the new order of things, and a school of sixty students was soon organized. This new demand upon me greatly abridged the pastoral work, but there seemed to be no other way to live. Before I could realize anything, however, from the school, we found ourselves in very considerable embarrassment. In this emergency, my wife opened her doors for a few boarders, which met the immediate demands of the table.

But at this juncture of our affairs, an incident occurred that afforded relief in another direction. My coat had become, through long wear and exposure, not a little seedy. On entering the pulpit one Sabbath morning I found a note lying on the Bible. I opened it and read as follows: "Will Mr. Miller have the goodness to preach this morning from the Text, 'I have put off my coat, and how shall I put it on?'" The note was written in a delicate hand and gave evidence of no ordinary cultivation. At the conclusion of the reading, I gave a searching glance over the congregation, but could make no face present plead guilty to the accusation of impertinence.

The opening exercises of the service were not concluded before my course of action was decided upon. I read the note to the congregation, and stated that I had just found it on the desk. I further stated that I was at a loss to determine whether it was intended as a sneer at my old coat, or whether the writer really desired an exposition of the text named. But, believing that no one could so far forget a due sense of propriety as to deride honest poverty, or scoff at so faithful a servant as my old coat had been, even though it now began to show signs of age, I chose to take the latter view of the case. With this conviction, I should proceed to make the text the subject of the discourse. After giving the connection and context, I proceeded to define the subject of coats, arrange them into classes and set forth their uses. The spiritual application was not difficult, but it needed a little skill to cut the several styles so that each one could recognize his own pattern and appropriate the right garment. "Of course," I remarked, "every one has heard of the garment of self-righteousness, though it may be that none in this congregation are aware of ever having seen it. Yet, should you chance to look upon it, with its straight seams and buckram collar, I am quite sure you would not prefer it to my old coat, unseemly as it may appear." Thus the sermon went on, to "cut to order" and "fit to measure," until all the most flagrant styles of coats had been disposed of, being careful, meantime, to institute the comparison in each case with the old coat before the audience. The discourse was perfectly ludicrous, but, like all of its kind, it took amazingly. Its financial success was, doubtless, all that the writer of the note had intended. On the next Sabbath morning the minister walked into church with a new outfit of wearing apparel, from the crown of the hat to the soles of the boots.

Watertown, from the first, was an unpromising field for ministerial labor. The leading influences at the beginning, if not directly opposed, were almost wholly indifferent to the claims of religion.

CHAPTER IX

The General Conference of 1848 divided the Rock River Conference and formed the Wisconsin. The first session of the new Conference was held at Kenosha July 12th, and I was stationed at Waukesha.

It will be remembered that Prairieville was included in the Watertown charge in 1839, and formed one of the appointments established at that early day by Brother Frink. In the following year, when the Summit charge was formed, Prairieville fell into the new circuit. In 1841 Prairieville took the name of the charge, and henceforth became the mother of circuits in this portion of the Territory. Rev. John G. Whitcomb was appointed to the charge in 1842, and Rev. L.F. Moulthrop in 1843.

Brother Moulthrop entered the Conference in 1840, and was first appointed to the Racine Mission. In 1841 he was stationed at Troy, where he performed a vast amount of labor and gathered many souls for the Master. He remained a second year and had for a colleague Rev. Henry Whitehead, so well known in connection with the Chicago Depository. On coming to Waukesha he had Rev. S. Stover as a colleague.

At the close of his term Brother Moulthrop retired from the work, but was re-admitted to the Conference in 1859, it being conceded that so valiant a veteran should be permitted to spend the balance of his life in connection with the Conference.

Prairieville Circuit at this time extended from the lake towns to Watertown, and into Washington county as far as settlements had penetrated. As stated in a former chapter, Brother Frink had passed over this region in 1839, and had formed classes during the Conference year at several places, but it now remained for his successors to extend the field. In doing this Brother Moulthrop opened an appointment at Wauwatosa and in several other neighborhoods.

At Prairieville, the class formed by Brother Frink consisted of Mr. Owen, Leader, Mrs. Owen, Richard Smart, Truman Wheeler, Mrs. Truman Wheeler, Hiram Wheeler, Mrs. Hiram Wheeler, Theophilus Haylett and Horace Edsell, and to these were soon after added, Mr. and Mrs. Winters, Mr. and Mrs. Joseph Hadfield, Mr. and Mrs. Alexander Henry, Mr. and Mrs.

Daniel Clark, Sarah Packham, Mr. Blodgett, Mr. and Mrs. John Bromell, John White, and Rev. Jonas Clark. Brother Henry was soon after made the Leader.

The members of the class at Summit were John Merical, Leader, Levi Merical, John Merical, Jr., Philip Scheuler, Mary Scheuler, Maria L. Frink, Sarah Taft, and Sarah Hardell.

Prairieville charge was now in the Chicago District, and Rev. Hooper Crews was the Presiding Elder. During this year he assisted Brother Moulthrop in holding a protracted meeting at Prairieville, and large numbers were converted.

Brother Crews was one of the choicest men in the Conference. He began his ministerial work when what is now the great Northwest was yet in its infancy, and has mingled in the discussion and settlement of all the great questions which have arisen. His appointments have placed him in the front rank of his compeers, and among them all, none have made a better record, or will go from labor to reward leaving a profounder regret among the people.

At the Milwaukee Conference in 1844, Prairieville charge was divided. The northern portion was set off and erected into the Washington Mission, with Rev. J.M. Snow as Pastor, of whom a record will be made in another chapter. Brother Moulthrop remained on the old charge, and was able to take care of what remained without an assistant.

The following year, 1845, the charge again required two men, and Revs. G.W. Cotrell and Miles L. Reed were appointed, and had a year of great prosperity. This year Pewaukee was detached from the Prairieville charge and added to Washington Mission, and as this change drew the latter to the southward, the name of Washington was dropped, and that of Menomonee substituted. Brother Snow remained on the charge.

Brother Reed was a young man of great promise, but his career was of short duration. At the close of his year at Prairieville, his failing health compelled him to leave the work. Remaining, however, in the village, he was greatly useful and highly esteemed as a Local Preacher.

In 1846, the Pastors of Prairieville circuit were Rev. Washington Wilcox and Rev. J.M. Walker. Both of these devoted and earnest men were abundant in labor. Protracted meetings were held at nearly all of the principal appointments, and large numbers were converted. It is affirmed that the junior preacher was engaged seventy five successive days in these meetings. It is not a matter of surprise that a severe illness followed.

Brother Walker entered the Conference, as before stated, in the class or 1845, with the writer. His first circuit was Elkhorn. During the year he had extensive revivals at both Delavan and North Geneva. After leaving Prairieville he was sent to Geneva, where he again had a prosperous year, and also found an excellent wife. His next field was Rock Prairie, to which he was sent in 1848. Here he had over two hundred conversions. The following year he was sent to Union Circuit, with Rev. James Lawson as colleague, and was returned to the same the next year. But in the early part of the year he was removed to Beloit, to supply a vacancy. His next appointment was Whitewater, where he succeeded in completing a Church, and his next field was Beaver Dam. In 1855 he was appointed Presiding Elder of Beaver Dam District, which post he filled with great acceptability. His subsequent appointments have been Spring Street Station, Milwaukee, Chaplain of the Thirty-Eighth Regiment, Beaver Dam, Oshkosh and Green Bay. At the last named, he is at the present writing doing effective service.

In 1847 Prairieville Circuit was changed to a station, under the name of Waukesha. Brother Wilcox was returned, and during the year built up a strong congregation, giving the station a front rank among the first charges of the Conference.

Brother Wilcox entered the traveling connection in the East and came to the Illinois Conference at an early day. He was stationed in Galena in 1839, and before coming to Waukesha he had served Dubuque, Mineral Point, Dixon, Elgin and Sylvania. At the close of his term at Waukesha he was appointed Presiding Elder of Fond du Lac District At the end of three years he was sent to the Madison District, where he remained a full term. His subsequent appointments fell within the bounds of the West Wisconsin Conference, in all of which he acquitted himself creditably. His last field was Baraboo Station, where he passed from labor to reward, leaving to his brethren the record of a spotless life and unswerving devotion to the Master's work.

Brother Wilcox was an able minister of the Lord Jesus Christ. He was a man of large intellect and strong convictions. His sermons embodied cardinal truth, and with him mere word painting was a sham. Sometimes he was thought to be severe, but it was the severity of what he conceived to be truth. In debate, on the Conference floor, or in discussion before an audience, he was a giant. At times he would seem to push his antagonist relentlessly, but it was only following his inexorable logic to its findings. The same thoroughness entered into all he did. On a committee it was his habit to go to the bottom of things. Especially was this true in the Conference examinations.

I remember distinctly the examination that was had the year I graduated to Elder's orders. With him as chairman, and another strong man, whom I need not name, as second, we were under the fiery ordeal seven sessions. I have never ceased to wonder that anything was left of us, after having been thus ground between the upper and nether millstones. And yet there was no unkindness, for in his feelings he was as tender as a child. The fact is, this noble man could never do anything by halves. If the faithful discharge of duty, the persistent adherence to the right, and unsparing self-denial, constitute the standard of nobility, then Washington Wilcox. had a right to claim his patent.

At Waukesha, a respectable Church edifice had been erected in 1841 and 1842. At a later period a small Parsonage had been built, and on our arrival it was in readiness to receive us. The public services of the Sabbath were held at half-past ten in the morning and at one in the afternoon. The latter had been so arranged to accommodate families in the country, who desired a second service before returning home. The plan, however, did not fully satisfy the people in the village, as it failed to provide for an evening service. It was suggested that in a village, a certain class of people could be induced to attend an evening service that would not go to any other. To test the matter, I opened an evening service. The arrangement proved satisfactory, and was continued, though it involved the necessity of having three services a day.

The good seed of the kingdom, scattered among the crowds who gathered at the evening service, in due time began to bear fruit, and an extensive revival followed. As the good work in the village increased, and the number of converts was multiplied, the people of the surrounding neighborhoods became also interested, and attended the meeting. Many of these were induced to accept the obligations of a holy life, and as a result, invitations began to multiply, requesting me to open appointments in their respective localities. I now selected five of the most central neighborhoods and established in them week-day evening services. But as the summer drew on, they were discontinued except two, and these, as the most promising, were assigned to the Sabbath, and were filled on alternate days at four o'clock in the afternoon. To meet these appointments, in addition to the regular services in the village, required four sermons each Sabbath. As to the propriety of undertaking this amount of labor, I need say nothing. Some may deem it an evidence of zeal, but others that of folly.

During this year the Milwaukee District established a system of platform missionary meetings on the several charges. To further the object, it was decided to appoint two or three ministers to attend each meeting, and by dividing the labor throughout the district, bring thereby all the preachers upon the platform. On several of these occasions, I found myself associated with a brother who was beginning to attract considerable attention as a speaker. We usually put him on the programme for the closing speech, that he might furnish the "rousements," as Bishop Morris would say, for the collection. And in this particular we were seldom disappointed. The good brother was always ready for what might be called a flaming speech. And though he always ran in much the same channel, his craft, to use a figure, was always full-rigged and under full sail. But, to change the figure, and bring it more fully into harmony with the department of nature, from which the brother had evidently derived his name, I might say his pinions were always full fledged and in full tension for a lofty flight. Unfortunately, however, he could never fold his wings in time to make a graceful descent when he desired to come down to the plane of ordinary mortals. In the descent he would sometimes "swap ends" so many times, that it was a marvel that a broken neck was not the result. But to his own mind these airy flights were always sublime, and especially so when he struck the quotation, which usually closed each missionary speech, that placed the herald of the Gospel on the highest pinnacle of time, and made him "look back over the vista of receding ages" and "forward over the hill-tops of coming time," and "lift up his voice until it should echo from mountain top to mountain top, from valley to valley, from river to river, from ocean to ocean, from isle to isle, and from continent to continent, the whole earth around." Of course the collection always followed this speech, and if it proved to be pretty good, a few additional feathers went into the pinions for the next flight.

On one of these occasions our orator became greatly elated with his success, and rallied me upon the difference between the broad, velvety wing of the miller and the long, sharp pointed wing of his species. The opportunity was too good to be lost. I replied, "Well, my brother, I had a thought last night, when I saw you towering to such dizzy heights in your speech." "What was it?" he enquired, eagerly. "Oh!" I replied, "I would hardly dare to tell you." "Yes, yes," said he, "let us have it." I still hesitated, until the several brethren present joined him in his persistent request. "Well," I answered, "if you insist upon it I will state it. When I saw you making your lofty flights, I thought if you could only have a few feathers plucked from the wings of your imagination and placed in the tail of your judgment, you would make a grand flyer." The next flight was made with greater caution.

The balance of the year at Waukesha was given to the ordinary demands of the work. To the Church there had been large accessions and to the Parsonage a welcome guest, in the person of our eldest daughter.

The Wisconsin Conference for 1849 was held at Platteville. I crossed the State in a buggy and was assigned to Father Mitchell's for entertainment. To enjoy the hospitality of this truly Christian gentleman and veteran patriarch for a week was a privilege that would mark an era at any time in a man's life. At this Conference I was ordained an Elder by Bishop Janes, and received my appointment for a second year at Waukesha. Rev. Elihu Springer was returned to Milwaukee District for the third year.

At my first Quarterly Meeting the Elder insisted on a reconstruction of my work, in which he was joined by the Local Preachers and several other brethren of the charge. The noon-day sermon was dispensed with and the Sabbath afternoon appointments were given mainly to the care of the Local Preachers. These were William Carpenter, Hiram Crane, and Miles L. Reed, a trio of noble and devoted men.

Assisted by these faithful men and a united and earnest church, the work grew upon our hands, and this second year was also blessed with a precious revival. It was in connection with this revival and the garnering of the converts that the controversy arose between us and the Baptist friends on the subject of baptism. As many of our converts had not enjoyed favorable opportunities to become informed on this subject, the Pastor was desired by formal request to preach a sermon on the mode of baptism. This was done, and soon after the official board requested a copy for publication. The writer, supposing it was merely intended to secure a few copies through the columns of the village newspaper for convenient reference, hastily furnished the discourse. Instead, however, of procuring a few slips only, it was published in pamphlet and given a more extensive circulation. In due time it was taken up by the Pastor of the Baptist Church and reviewed at length in his pulpit. On the following Sabbath the reviewer was himself reviewed, and here ended the controversy. It is a question whether such controversies are really beneficial. They usually engender strife and party feeling, and not unfrequently alienate the servants of our common Master. But that such was not the case in this instance is pretty evident from the fact that at the session of our Conference in Waukesha the following year, the writer was requested to fill on the Sabbath the pulpit of his former antagonist.

On this charge also the writer took his first serious lesson in Church trials. The matter in question arose out of a misunderstanding between a man and his wife, growing out of a want of interest, perhaps, on the part of the one, and jealousy on the part of the other. Like other inexperienced administrators whom I have known, in trying to make crooked things straight, I invoked an agency that became a fire and a sword in my hand. Neither the Church nor the individuals concerned derived any advantage in the result, and though the wisdom of the administration was never called in question as far as I knew, yet I could not suppress the conviction that Church trials can only be commended as a last resort. It is much easier to awaken than allay the spirit of strife. Abating this discordant note, which did not long disturb the harmony of the Church, the two years we spent on this charge are freighted with most precious memories. Full of incident, and fragrant with blessing, they form a bright link in the chain of our itinerant life. Happy in our work, with only occasional calls for special services abroad, the years passed swiftly and joyously.

Referring to services abroad reminds me of the Quarterly Meeting I held for the Presiding Elder, on what was then called Howard's Prairie, some twenty miles distant. Seated in my buggy with my wife and child, I started on Friday afternoon for the place. We reached the neighborhood at nightfall. We were directed by the Elder to call on a given family for entertainment, the gentleman being the most wealthy Methodist in the settlement. We halted the buggy at his gate, and I went in to crave his hospitality. As I approached the door and addressed myself to the master of the premises, he put on a frigid expression of countenance, and answered me coldly. I decided at once that I would not make myself known, but try the spirit of the man. I inquired whether there was to be a Quarterly Meeting in his neighborhood. He replied in the affirmative. I then inquired where the Methodist preachers put up when they came into the settlement.

He said, "They usually put up at the second house further on." I concluded the old gentleman was not expecting company until the Presiding Elder should come, and so concluded we had better go on. As I retired the old gentleman looked sharply after me, but doubtless thinking so small and young a man as I then was could not be the Elder, he permitted me to go on my way. We went on to the house indicated, and inquired of the gentleman at the gate whether the Methodist preachers who visited the settlement usually found entertainment with him. He replied, "I am not a Methodist myself, but my old woman is one, I believe, and she sometimes takes in the preachers on her own hook, but she is not at home to-night. Why didn't you stop up at the white house on the hill? He is the loudest Methodist in this neighborhood." I inquired, "Who lives up here in this small house that we have just passed?"

"Oh," said he, "that is my son, the Class-Leader." It was now quite dark. I returned to the buggy and asked my wife how she liked the Presiding Eldership. She laughed heartily, and said, "The fact is, they are all waiting for the Presiding Elder, for no one would ever take you for one."

I concluded she was right, and on returning to the Class-Leader's house I made bold to announce myself in due form. We were most hospitably entertained, and were so pleased with our kind host and hostess that we felt constrained to decline, the next day, urgent invitations from both of the large houses. My wife has often queried since as to what became of the pies and cakes that were intended for the Presiding Elder on that occasion.

The services of the Sabbath were held in a school house. At the close of the morning sermon the Pastor, Rev. Jesse Halstead, volunteered to carry the hat through the congregation, to receive the collection for the Presiding Elder. After performing this service, he requested the good people to sing while he should count the funds. On completing the count, he found a deficiency, and concluded to carry the hat again. He started and moved leisurely along, taking special pains to afford all an opportunity to contribute, until he came to the dear man, whose acquaintance I had made the night before. He now paused, placed the hat on the desk, under the face of the reputed miser, put his hands in his pockets, and looked unconcernedly over the congregation, remarking, "Well, brethren, there is no great hurry about this matter. If you have not got the money with you, we will give you plenty of time to borrow it from your neighbor." This new feature in the programme directed all eyes to the brother in whose custody the hat had been placed. For a moment he was frigid, but under such a concentration of piercing rays as were now turned upon him, he soon began to melt. Turning to his neighbor, he borrowed a contribution, whereupon the hat moved on.

CHAPTER X

The Conference of 1850 was held June 26th at Beloit, Bishop Hamline presiding. Brother Springer was returned to the Milwaukee District, and I was appointed to Spring Street Station, Milwaukee. The charge included the entire city except Walker's Point, where a Mission had been established, but before speaking of the Station in connection with my labors, I should, in harmony with my general plan, first refer to its earlier history. In doing this, I can only give in these pages the briefest outline, and refer the reader, who may desire further information, to a pamphlet entitled "Milwaukee Methodism," published by the writer in 1873.

The name of Milwaukee has, doubtless, come down to us from some extinct tribe of the aboriginal inhabitants of the country, as there seems to be nothing that will fully answer to it in any of the tongues now in use. In 1680 Zenobius Membre mentions the river of Melleoke, flowing into Lake Dauphan, in latitude forty, with an Indian village at its mouth. Three generations later Lieut. Gorrell visited Milwacky River, and found a village on its bank, with an Indian trader.

Another interval of a generation occurred, and Solomon Juneau appeared and took up his residence in Milwaukee in 1818. Other fur traders came soon after, but the real settlement of the country did not begin until 1835, when nine families came, forming the nucleus of the future city.

The first Protestant sermon preached in Milwaukee was delivered by a Methodist clergyman in June, 1835. The meeting was held in a log house, erected by Dr. Enoch Chase for a residence, near the mouth of the river.

Milwaukee Mission was organized by the Illinois Conference in the summer of 1835, and Rev. Mark Robinson, who had been admitted that year, was appointed to the charge. The Presiding Elder of the District, which extended from Chicago to Green Bay, was the veteran pioneer, Rev. John Clark. The Presiding Elder visited Milwaukee during this year and preached a sermon in the residence of Dr. Chase, this being at that time the principal place in which meetings were held. Both the Pastor and Presiding Elder were entertained by the Doctor.

The population of the village was very small, but before the expiration of the Conference year Brother Robinson was able to form a class of four members. These first members were David Worthington, Mrs. Samuel Brown, Mrs. J.K. Lowry, and Mrs. Farmin.

In the autumn of 1836 Rev. William S. Crissey was sent to Milwaukee. The congregations were now growing, and it was found expedient to provide some place, other than a private residence, for the meetings. The Society was not able to build, and to rent a suitable place seemed impossible. In this embarrassment a carpenter's shop belonging to two members of the church, W.A. and L.S. Kellogg, was deemed the most feasible arrangement. This building, located on the corner of East Water and Huron Streets, was a frame structure, and stood on posts. Beneath and all around it was a pond of water, and to gain an entrance a narrow bridge was constructed from the street to the door. The first Quarterly Meeting was held in this place by Rev. John Clark, on the 8th and 9th of January, 1837. At this meeting the Pastor reported the conversion of Mr. J.K. Lowry, doubtless the first in the village.

The legal organization of the Church, according to the laws of the Territory, was effected July 22d, 1837, with Elah Dibble as Chairman and W.A. Kellogg as Secretary. The first Trustees were Elah Dibble, David Worthington, W.A. Kellogg, L.S. Kellogg, J.K. Lowry, Jared Thompson and Joseph E. Howe. The fourth Quarterly Meeting was held July 29th, and the Pastor reported a membership of forty-five.

In September, 1837, Rev. James R. Goodrich was appointed to the Station and Rev. Salmon Stebbins to the District. Among the members enrolled at this time I find the names of Thomas McElhenny, Jared Thompson, Local Preacher, Mr. and Mrs. L.S. Kellogg, Wm. A. Kellogg, Theresa Kellogg, Ophelia Kellogg, Amelia Kellogg, Mr. and Mrs. Alexander, David Worthington, A.T. Wilson, Mrs. Samuel Brown, Mrs. Henry Miller, Mrs. J.K. Lowry, James Ash, Mr. and Mrs. Elah Dibble, and Sisters Adams, Church, James and Vail.

During this year Leader's Meetings were established, and at the one held March 12th, 1838, James Ash, David Worthington, Francis Metcalf and Hiram Johnson received Exhorter's license. The first named became subsequently a member of the Conference, traveled several years acceptably, was greatly beloved by all his brethren, and finally died within the bounds of New Berlin Circuit. Brother Worthington was a clerk in Solomon Juneau's store. In 1840 he entered the Conference, was stationed at Burlington and was returned the following year. In 1842 he was stationed at Davenport, Iowa, and thereafter his fields of labor fell within that State. He held an honored place among his brethren, represented them in the General Conference, and a few years since closed a useful life and passed to his home on high.

The other brethren became Local Preachers, and the former departed this life in Christian triumph at Appleton, Nov. 3, 1863, while the latter has become a successful business man, and is awaiting his summons. Thus the infant society of Milwaukee need not blush for her first contribution to the Ministerial staff of the church.

In 1838 Rev. Wellington Weigly was appointed, but as the great financial disaster had prostrated the business of the country, leaving the people in poverty, he only remained a short time, and the pulpit was largely left to the care of Brother Thompson, the Local Preacher. In 1839 Rev. Julius Field was appointed to the District, and the charge was left to be supplied.

Brother Field entered the New York Conference in 1821, and before coming west had filled leading appointments, including New York city. He was transferred this year to the Illinois Conference, and assigned to the District. He remained two years, and was then appointed General Agent of the Bible Society for Northern Illinois, Wisconsin and Iowa. He served in this field four years, was then stationed, in 1845, at Racine, but at the close of the year was re-transferred to his old Conference, where he continued to render effective service, with but brief intervals, up to 1871. Having now completed a half century of labor, he was invited by his Conference to deliver a semi-centennial sermon. Having taken a superannuated relation, Brother Field, happy in spirit, is spending the evening of life among his friends, and awaiting the call of the Master.

The pastorate of Milwaukee was soon filled by Rev. Daniel Brayton, a superannuated member of the Troy Conference. It was now determined to build a Church. Hon. Morgan L. Martin came forward and generously donated a lot, situated on the east side of Broadway, and between Biddle and Oneida Streets, but the financial derangement still continuing, it was not deemed advisable to undertake the erection of the building.

At the General Conference of 1840, the Illinois Conference was divided and the Rock River took its northern territory. Rev. John Crummer was this year appointed to Milwaukee. As the carpenter's shop could no longer be had as a chapel, the meetings passed from one private house to another for a time. But this state of things could not long continue. The erection of a Church was decided upon, and before the close of the year the edifice was completed. It was dedicated by Rev. Julius Field in May, 1841. The building remains at this writing, on the same lot, but placed with the side to the street, it has been fitted up for residences.

At the session of the Rock River Conference in 1841, the Milwaukee District was discontinued, and the city was placed on the Chicago District.

Rev. John T. Mitchell was appointed to the District, and Rev. Sias Bolles to the station.

Brother Mitchell was one of Nature's noblemen. Tall and erect in form, high and broad forehead, symmetrical and shapely cut features, dark and lustrous eyes, his bearing was princely. Such was Brother Mitchell in the years of his strength. He was second to no man in his Conference or State as a pulpit orator. In 1844 he was elected Assistant Book Agent, Cincinnati, where he served the church with distinguished ability. After leaving this position he re-entered the regular work in the Cincinnati Conference, from the ranks of which he passed on, several years ago, to the companionship of the white-robed in Heaven.

Brother Bolles, on coming to the city, first proceeded to liquidate the indebtedness of two hundred dollars on the Church, and then entered upon a protracted meeting, which resulted in an extensive revival. Among those converted was a German Catholic boy, of whom the following incident is related: The first night he attended the meeting, Brother Bolles preached on the duty of Christians to let their light shine. Taking the instruction of the Preacher in its most literal sense, the young man greatly surprised the good people on the following evening by stalking into church bearing a well-lighted lantern. On enquiring of the young man the reason for so strange a procedure, he answered: "Why, the Priest said I must let my light shine, and so I have brought it with me." The Preacher carefully explained his sermon, bringing it down to the capacity of his auditor, and had the pleasure to see him thoroughly converted. Many years after, Brother Bolles was happily surprised to meet his convert, who had grown into a Christian gentleman of exalted position in society.

In 1842, Rev. Wm. H. Sampson was sent to Milwaukee, of whom a record is made elsewhere. The following year Rev. James Mitchell was appointed, and it was decided to enter upon a new Church enterprise. A lot was purchased July 3d, 1844, of John Clifford, on the northwest corner of West Water and Spring Streets.

At the time of the purchase the location was considered by not a few to be unfortunate, as the population at that period on the west side was quite limited, and it was even hinted that a leading member of the Board of Trustees had unduly influenced the selection in order to enhance the value of certain property in the vicinity. But whatever may have been the complications of the case at the beginning, certain it is that it was found in due time to be a very excellent location. The building, forty-five by ninety feet in size, was commenced soon after, and carried forward as rapidly as possible to completion.

It was a brick structure, trimmed with stone. Standing with its front to West Water, the side was turned to Spring Street. On the first floor there were four stores fronting Spring Street, and having cellars in the basement beneath them. The auditorium was on the second floor above the pavement and was reached by a broad flight of steps in the front of the edifice. Between the outside entrance and the auditorium there was a vestibule with a class room on either side, and above it a commodious gallery. The auditorium was finished in a neat yet plain manner, and furnished sittings for about six hundred people. The whole structure cost upwards of ten thousand dollars. To defray the current expenses and erect such an edifice taxed the good people to the utmost limit of their resources, besides imposing on them a heavy indebtedness. But there was no lack of courage, and the good work went forward.

In 1844 the Milwaukee District was again revived and Rev. James Mitchell was assigned to it, and Rev. F.A. Savage was sent to the station. In 1845 the station was left to be supplied, and Rev. Abram Hanson was called to fill the pastorate. Finding it difficult to rent a house, Brother Hanson procured a boarding place for himself and good lady with Mr. Lindsay Ward, where he spent the year and founded an abiding friendship. He was a man of superior pulpit ability and engaging manners. The congregation filled the new Church edifice, and many valuable accessions were made to the membership.

Brother Hanson after leaving Milwaukee filled several important charges, and then retired from the work. For several years he served as the representative of our national government at Liberia, where he fell under the fatal malaria of the African coast, and passed on to the better country.

The next session of the Conference was held Aug. 12, 1846. At this Conference Rev. S.H. Stocking was continued on the District, and Rev. W.M.D. Ryan was appointed to the station. Mr. Ryan entered the Ohio Conference in 1839, and came by transfer to the Rock River Conference in 1844. After spending two years in Chicago, where he had wrought a good work for the Master, he was sent to this charge.

The fame of the Preacher had preceded him, and he was greeted by immense congregations. His ministry formed an epoch in the history of the church. He brought the same earnest manner, the same fiery eloquence, and the same shrewd business tact that had characterized his labors in Chicago and elsewhere, and which have since placed him in the front rank of successful laborers in Baltimore, Philadelphia, and the Metropolis of the nation. The stores in the Church edifice were rented or sold for a term of years to liquidate the indebtedness of the society, and the church was placed on a substantial financial basis. But Mr. Ryan could hardly feel at home among his new associates, and in this new field of labor. His earlier associations were formed in a more southern latitude. The Puritan type of society that, traveling westward on a line from New England, had struck Milwaukee, was not congenial to his tastes and not wholly in harmony with his methods of ministerial labor. At the end of nine months he was invited to a pastorate in the city of Baltimore, and he deemed it advisable to accept the invitation. His place in Milwaukee was filled by Rev. Francis M. Mills, who came, by exchange with Mr. Ryan, from the charge in Baltimore to which the latter had been invited. Mr. Mills filled out the balance of the year.

Among the accessions to the charge this year was Hon. John H. Van Dyke. Soon after his arrival, though a young man, he became an official member, and has continued to hold positions of trust to the present writing. A man of thorough mental training, sound judgment, and unswerving integrity, he cannot fail to command the respect and esteem of all. His legal abilities have specially fitted him for the Presidency of the Board of Trustees, the position he has long held, while his superior business sagacity has been of great service to the church in guiding her through the extraordinary trials she has been called to endure. Nor has he proved less valuable financially. Being possessed of large means, he is generous towards the Church and the benevolent enterprises of the city.

In 1847 Rev. Elihu Springer was appointed to the District, and Rev. Francis M. Mills was returned to the station. Brother Mills was an able preacher, but in his style of delivery was almost the reverse of his predecessor. He was a noble representative of Baltimore Methodism, but his health suffered from the bleak winds of the Lake, and at the close of his term he was compelled to seek a milder atmosphere.

The following two years Rev. James E. Wilson was stationed at Milwaukee.

Brother Wilson came to the Conference from the Protestant Methodist Church, in which he had held a prominent position both as a Preacher and Secretary of the Conference. He was a man of genial spirit, affable manners, and commanding eloquence. His sermons were well prepared, and especially in given passages, were delivered with an unction and pathos that could not fail to produce an abiding impression. The great concourse of people who waited upon his ministry attested how highly he was appreciated by those who were permitted to listen to his weekly ministrations. A revival occurred during the winter, and at the close of the year he was able to report one hundred and sixty-four members and thirty-nine probationers.

During the pastorate of Brother Wilson an unhappy controversy arose between the managers of the Sunday School and the leaders of the social means of grace with reference to the hours of meeting. The Official Board decided in favor of the School, and an alienation of feeling was the result. A few of the disaffected withdrew, organized a Wesleyan Church, and called Rev. Mr. McKee as their Pastor. Though an unpleasant affair, the old church moved on as usual.

But as another charge was now growing up in the southern part of the city, it is proper that I should refer to it before closing this chapter.

In the fall of 1847 Osmond Bailey and a few others became specially interested in establishing regular religious services at Walker's Point. Soon after a class was formed consisting of Mr. and Mrs. Osmond Bailey, Mrs. Capt. Stewart, Mrs. Warren. Mrs. Almena Waite, Mrs. Worden, Mr. and Mrs. Daniel Waite and M.S. Velie.

At the Conference of 1848, the small society was erected into a Mission with Rev. Warner Oliver as Pastor. The Meetings were held in a school house, located on lots eleven and twelve, in block one hundred and one.

Brother Oliver was a man of fine talent, but was compelled to give a portion of his time to business, through the financial feebleness of the charge.

In 1849 Rev. William Willard was appointed to the charge. It will be remembered that this good brother was a member of the class formed at Burnett in 1845. He entered the Conference in 1847, and had been stationed two years at Aztalan. He was an earnest laborer, and under his administration the work was encouragingly prosperous. The congregations were growing and the people were beginning to agitate the measure of building a Church.

After leaving Walker's Point, Brother Willard remained in the regular work, with a few brief intervals, for many years, doing efficient service for the Master. At this writing he is in Nebraska, using such openings as may offer to help forward the good work.

Hiving thus briefly sketched the beginnings and progress of the good work in the city up to the time of my appointment, I will defer the balance of the record for the next chapter.

CHAPTER XI

The Spring Street Station had now attained the reputation of being the first charge in the Conference. The Church edifice, as we have seen, was decidedly respectable, both in size and character. The membership was enterprising, and full of the spirit of labor. In its official Board were found L.S. Kellogg, G.F. Austin, John H. Van Dyke, Geo. E.H. Day, James Seville, J.C. Henderson, W.W. Lake, Wm. Rowbotham, George Southwell, Wm. R. Jones, Wm. L. Boughton, John Kneene, Wm. Cossentine, C.F. Larigo and Charles Randall. And during the year John Kemp, Cornelius Morse, Mitchell Steever, C.C. Chamberlin and Henry Seiler were added.

My salary was fixed on the basis of the old Disciplinary allowance: Quarterage, $216; Table Expenses, $200; House Rent, $125; Traveling Expenses, $5; making a total of $546. This amount would be considered a small allowance at the present time, but at that early day it was believed to be a generous provision for a family of three persons.

My first Sabbath, always a trial day to the Preachers as well as the people, passed without any special disaster. Perhaps it was owing in part to the presence of the Presiding Elder, who sat at my back. Whatever he or the people may have thought, I certainly felt that I was a mere stripling going out with nothing in my hand but a sling and a pebble. Nor did it relieve my embarrassment when I saw the great congregation, and remembered that they had enjoyed for two years the ministry of the most eloquent man in the Conference.

It is said that a minister ought always to be ready to preach or to die. I think, on that occasion, if I had been permitted to choose between them, I would have accepted the latter. As it was, I very nearly did both. And that I really did neither, I have always considered a special intervention of Providence. On the part of the people there was evidently a suspension of judgment. They were doubtless puzzled by my contradictory appearances. In form I was slight and fragile, not weighing more than one hundred and thirty pounds, but in my face, though only twenty-eight years of age, I bore the appearance of being ten years older.

At the close of the service a large number of people remained and gave the new Minister a hearty greeting. It was timely, giving me to realize I was not quite gone to the land of shadows.

I was informed afterwards that one good brother went home from the service and told his wife, who had not been present, that he had shaken hands with the new Minister and his daughter. "No, father," said the daughter, "that lady was not the Minister's daughter, but his wife." "Well," replied the father, "she must be his second wife, for she looks young enough to be his daughter." Whether this opinion should be interpreted as complimentary to the Minister or his wife, I was never fully able to decide.

Having passed the crisis, the first Sabbath, and survived the following week, I now began to adjust myself to my work. I was happy to find that the good people were strongly attached to Prayer and Class-Meetings. This gave an assurance that there were at least some efficient laborers in the Church, who could be relied on if we should find ourselves in a revival. I also found that the people could endure a large amount of pastoral visiting. These discoveries were enough for a start, and I entered upon the work without delay.

About this time I was called to attend a funeral in one of the families that had gone out from the church the previous year, and were now members of the Wesleyan organization. The next Sabbath morning this family and several others were in my congregation. In the opening prayer I made the poor slave a special subject, as I often did. At the close of the service, the head of one of the families came forward and stated that Mr. McKee, the Pastor of the Wesleyan Church, had gone to the Conference, and hence they were without services for a few Sabbaths. But as for his part, he did not care if he never came back, for I was abolitionist enough for him.

In a few weeks Rev. T. Orbison was sent to the city, in the place of Mr. McKee. After the first Sabbath, he called on me and said that he found his people quite disposed to return to the old Church, and that in consequence, he had dispensed with his services the previous evening, and attended our Church with them. He was now inclined to advise them to return, as he saw no occasion for two organizations. The leading members having previously decided to return, the balance now joined them in the movement, while those who had been gathered from other organizations, returned to their respective homes.

Brother Orbison, in coming to this country from Ireland, fell among the Wesleyans on his arrival, and became identified with them, supposing they were the same body he had left at home. On learning his mistake, he now came over to us, and for many years was a worthy member of the Wisconsin Conference. After doing faithful service for many years, and winning the esteem of all, he laid aside the armor and took up the everlasting crown of rejoicing.

The work of the year was now well begun. The house was filled with people, the finances were in excellent condition, and everything indicated a year of special success, But how strangely light and shadow, hopes and fears, rejoicing and mourning commingle in this life! While we were thus full of hope, and even exultant over the indications of a prosperous year, little did we imagine that we were then on the threshold of a deep affliction, arising from the sudden death of our Presiding Elder.

Brother Springer left the city to hold his Quarterly Meetings at Watertown and Oconomowoc, the writer accompanying him to the city limits. On the 21st of August he closed his Quarterly Meeting services at Watertown, took dinner at the Parsonage with the Pastor, Rev. David Brooks, and then rode on to Oconomowoc. He stopped for the night with Brother Worthington, ate sparingly, and retired at the usual time. At three o'clock in the morning he was seized by the cholera. The attack, severe at first, soon became alarming. Medical aid was called, but without avail. He lingered until six o'clock P.M., and passed away in great peace. His family were sent for, but failed to reach him before his departure. The Funeral Sermon was preached in the Spring Street Church by the writer, from Second Timothy, 4. 6-8.

Brother Springer was received on trial by the Illinois Annual Conference in September, 1833. His appointments before coming to Milwaukee District had been, Carlinville, Iroquois, Oplaine, Saminoc, Bristol, Lockport, Joliet, St. Charles, Mineral Point and Hazel Green.

Brother Springer was a man of commanding presence. In form erect, full and athletic, with a broad, high forehead, and an intellectual face. The whole cast of the man indicated strength. He was a sound theologian, an able Preacher and a wise and vigilant administrator. He was emphatically a true man, and, as a Presiding Elder, very popular. The loss of such a man, at forty years of age, was a great disaster to the Conference.

Soon after the death of Brother Springer, Rev. I.M. Leihy was appointed as his successor on the District. Brother Leihy entered the Conference in 1843, and before coming to the District, had been stationed at Hazel Green, Elizabeth, Mineral Point, Platteville, Southport, and Beloit He was a man of marked ability both as a Preacher and administrator. His leading endowment was strength, and on some chosen subject, a subject to which he had given special attention, his preaching was overwhelming. He was a man of immense will force, and not a whit behind the chief of his brethren in his devotion to the Master's cause. Neither storms nor other impediments deterred him from his work. With a face set as a flint against every obstacle in his path of duty, he drove straight on to fulfil the convictions of his dauntless spirit. By some he was thought to be severe, and not a little exacting, but those who knew him best were tolerant of his idiosyncrasies, and were prepared to assign him a chief place among his brethren. After completing his term on the District, he filled several important appointments, but finally located and removed to California, where at the present writing, as for several years past, he is again engaged in the regular work.

During the fall and early winter there was manifest a growing spiritual interest among the people, which culminated ultimately in an extensive revival of religion. The protracted meeting continued five weeks, and resulted in the conversion of seventy-five souls.

The plan of holding Platform Missionary Meetings was continued during this year, and largely increased the contributions of the people. While on my way in company with Brother Leihy, to attend such a meeting at Port Washington, I formed the acquaintance of Brother Jesse Hubbard and his good lady at Mequon, where we halted for dinner. For many years this residence was the home of Itinerant Preachers and the nucleus of Christian society in that region.

The dedication of the German Methodist Church at Sheboygan occurred in April of this year. I went down to perform the service in a steamer, but when ready to return, the waves were running too high for the boat to make the pier. The mishap left my Pulpit without a supply for the Sabbath, an event which seldom transpired, but gave me an opportunity to make the acquaintance of our people in that part of the Conference, and the pleasure of preaching twice at Sheboygan and once at Sheboygan Falls.

During the summer of 1851 the cholera raged in Milwaukee in a most appalling manner. The whole city was a hospital. For several days together it was claimed there were fifty deaths per day. Though earnestly entreated to leave the city, as many others had done, I declined, feeling that my life was no more precious than the lives of others. Besides, it seemed to me, if there is ever a time when a people need the aid of their Pastor, it is when they are in peril and affliction. When at the height of its ravages, I repeatedly attended six funerals a day, and visited a dozen sick persons. The very men whom I met at a funeral one day, I would bury the next. Mingling thus daily with the sick and dying, I could not well escape myself. I suffered two attacks during the season, but through great mercy, the lives both of myself and family were spared.

During this terrible visitation I had frequent opportunities to test the value of the Christian religion. So marked was the difference between the death-bed scenes of Christians and the unconverted that even Infidels themselves could not refrain from referring to it. As if to teach the people this great lesson, there were a few instances of triumphant deaths, and a few of the opposite class. One good sister, as she was gliding across the stream, enquired, "Is this Jordan?" She was told it was. "How calm and placid are its waters," she added. "I expected to find the billows running high, but, glory to Jesus! there is not a ripple upon all the stream."

Unlike this scene was the death of a young man who had sent for me in great haste. On entering the room, I recognized him as a young man whom I had repeatedly urged, during our meeting of the previous winter, to give himself to the Saviour. He was now in the throes of dissolution and I could hardly hope to reach him. Wild with frenzy, he seemed to pray and curse with the same breath. As a momentary interval occurred between the paroxysms, I sought to arrest his attention and divert his thought to Christ. He turned his piercing eyes on me and said, "Oh! it is too late. Last winter, if I had yielded to your kind admonitions, all would now be well, but it is too late, too late." Another paroxysm seized him, and he was lost to all consciousness, and soon ceased to breathe.

Another event occurred this year of which mention should be made in this connection. It is the notorious riot. I quote from "Milwaukee Methodism." "Rev. Mr. Leahy, a minister in the Protestant Methodist Church, after visiting several of the principal cities of the Union, came to Milwaukee. Having spent many years in a monastery, and having become convinced of his error, he now sought to enlighten the people on the subject of the confessional. He proposed, in coming to the city, to give a course of lectures in a public hall during the ensuing week. On the intervening Sabbath he was invited to occupy several of the Pulpits of the city. He had already filled one in the morning, another in the afternoon, and then came to the Spring Street Church in the evening. The house was filled as usual. He opened the services in the regular order, took his text and began the delivery of his sermon. Immediately a crowd of strange men began to press in at the door and push along up the center aisle. At a given signal, a rush was made towards the Pulpit. Comprehending the situation in an instant, the Pastor, from his position in the Pulpit, ordered them back, and at the same time directed the men nearest the aisle and altar to intercept their advance. A stone was hurled at the Pastor's head, but it missed its mark and crashed against the wall in the rear of the Pulpit. But L.S. Kellogg, L.L. Lee and others stood firmly in the aisle and dealt some vigorous blows in response to the clubs and other missiles with which they were being severely bruised. At this moment Dr. Waldo W. Lake, who was sitting in the altar, drew a revolver which he on leaving home had put in his pocket, expecting after service to visit a patient in an exposed part of the city, and instantly the rioters fell back and retreated through the entrance to the street. During the conflict the audience room was a wild scene of confusion. The ladies became greatly alarmed, and required the attention of a large number of gentlemen in making their escape from the building. The door being thronged with the rioters, the principal egress was found to be the windows next to the street, and these were elevated a full story above the pavement. Ladders, wagons, and other impromptu scaffolding were provided, and large numbers of ladies were rescued in this way, while others were crowded against the sides of the room until the rioters had withdrawn. After quiet had been restored measures were taken to convey the speaker safely to his lodgings at the hotel. But a good number of revolvers, carried by a posse of earnest men, were a sufficient protection against all evil-minded persons that thronged the streets on the way."

The city was rocked with excitement. Early next morning a meeting was held in the Church edifice that had thus been made the scene of a riotous assault. The populace interpreted the affair rightly. It was not so much an attack upon a Protestant Church as an assault against the freedom of speech, one of the most sacred rights of the people. After expressing suitable indignation against the actors and abettors of the riot, and resolving to protect the freedom of speech so long as it should not offend against public morals, the meeting appointed a committee to wait on Mr. Leahy, and, on behalf of the community, guarantee him protection in his rights. Under this protection a lecture was given in the Free Congregational Church, and another on the public square, when, all danger of assault having disappeared, he was permitted to go on his way.

The only persons seriously hurt were L.L. Lee and L.S. Kellogg. The first was compelled to carry a hand in a sling for a long time, and the latter was considerably injured by a blow from a club on the head. The blood ran freely, but he was able to attend the Law and Order Meeting the following morning. His speech on the occasion became a watchword among the people. He said in a very resolute manner, "Our Fathers fought for freedom, both civil and religious, and if we have got to fight the battle over again I am ready, and I am willing that my blood should be the first to flow." The city appropriated one hundred and fifty dollars to repair the damages done to the Church edifice.

Bishop Waugh made us a visit near the close of the year. He was on his way to the Conference to be held at Waukesha, and went with us to the Camp-Meeting at Brookfield. Spring Street Station made no inconsiderable part of the Meeting. She pitched a tent that would accommodate one hundred and fifty persons, and it was well filled from the beginning to the end of the Meeting. It was a Meeting of great power. None who heard the exhortations of the good Bishop at the close of his Sunday morning sermon can ever forget it. After holding the vast congregation spell-bound for more than an hour in the delivery of the sermon, the old man, with locks as white as the driven snow, came down from the stand, and, standing on a seat in the Altar, began to invite mourners. The motives of the Gospel were presented one after another, the tide of feeling rising, until the Bishop was master of the occasion, and seemed to sway the people at his pleasure. The Bishop's voice grew grandly eloquent as his great soul rose to the level of the effort, and before it and its burden of truth, the people began to bend, then brake, and finally flew to the Altar. Nor did the exhortation cease until the Altar was literally crowded with seeking penitents.

The Scandinavian work was this year opened in Wisconsin. To further this object the Missionary Management at New York sent forward Rev. C. Willerup, placing him at the beginning under my care. On reaching the city he found the population using the Scandinavian language too small to organize the work, and we deemed it advisable to explore the interior. To do this he must have an Itinerant's outfit, consisting at least of horse and saddle-bags. While he was employed in settling his family in a rented house, I visited the market and purchased a horse for him and the other necessary articles, using my own funds until drafts should be received from the Missionary Treasury. The desired location for the first Mission was found at Cambridge, where Brother Willerup organized a Society and subsequently erected a Church edifice. From this small beginning has since grown a family of charges and a line of able Ministers, constituting a Presiding Elder's District.

The Conference year had now come to a close. Many changes had occurred in Spring Street Station. In consequence of the cholera, and the consequent stagnation of business, large numbers of the people went into the country. But notwithstanding this depletion, such had been the number of accessions, one hundred and seven in all, that I was able to report one hundred and fifty-seven members and sixty-three probationers, making a total of two hundred and twenty.

The financial plan, adopted at the beginning of the year, that of collecting the funds in the classes, had proved a success. At the close of the year, the Pastor was fully paid, and the Society was out of debt.

CHAPTER XII

The Conference for 1851 was held June 25th, at Waukesha. The Sessions were deeply spiritual, and were characterized by general harmony among the preachers. At this Conference the Committee on Periodicals, of which I was a member, reported in favor of the establishment of a North Western Christian Advocate, and the report was unanimously adopted.

In the arrangement of appointments I was assigned to the Fond du Lac District. The appointment was a great surprise to myself, and doubtless to others. Besides, it was not in harmony with my judgment or wishes. It seemed to me to be an unwise measure to take so young a man, only twenty-nine, from the companionship of books and the details of the Pastoral office, and place him on a District where both of the Departments of labor, so essential to success in the Ministry, must necessarily be abridged. And in the next place, it appeared to me that, since there were so many other men in the Conference, who were better qualified than I for the position, my appointment was but doing violence to the work. But I soon came to the conclusion that when an appointment has been made there is no further need to debate the question. In such a case, the sooner both the Ministers and people adjust their views to the new order of things, the better for all concerned. Accepting this view, I hastened to conform to the situation with as good grace as possible. And to aid me perhaps a little, several of the preachers surprised me by the presentation of a cane.

I had heard it remarked that when a man used a cane, it was an evidence that he had a weak place somewhere between the crown of the head and the sole of the foot. I was now puzzled to know what the cane meant. There was doubtless a weak spot somewhere, in the opinion of the brethren. It must of course be either in the District or the incumbent. But my query as to which was soon answered. Dr. Bowman, my father-in-law, was traveling soon after in company with a good brother, when the conversation turned upon the appointments of the recent Conference. It had not proceeded far when the brother remarked, in referring to my appointment, "The Conference must have been hard up for material when it appointed that young stripling Presiding Elder." The mystery of the cane was now explained. The good brethren of the Conference doubtless thought the matter could be helped out by the use of a cane.

But a sharper joke than that was passed upon the people of Fond du Lac. Only six years before they had given me license to preach, and sent me to the Conference, and now, in sending me back so soon, the Conference seemed to say, "Brethren, we return you as good as you gave." I have heard it said that sometimes Quarterly Conferences grant licenses with the implied understanding that the recipients are not expected to serve the home Church, but are good enough to preach to less highly favored people abroad. If this course had been adopted by these Fond du Lac brethren as their policy, certainly it was a cruel joke to return the labor of their hands on such short notice.

But fortunately I was not supposed to know anything about this matter, and hence, on the principle that "where ignorance is bliss, 'tis folly to be wise," I had nothing to do but to gather up my family and hasten to my new field of labor.

Fond du Lac District at this time embraced that portion of the State lying North and East of the city of Fond du Lac, and included thirteen charges. A few of the charges could be reached by steamers on the Fox and Wolf Rivers and Lake Winnebago, but the balance could only be visited by the stage or private conveyance. I chose to adopt the latter. Having provided board for my wife and child with Rev. M.L. Noble, and secured a horse and buggy, I was ready to enter upon my work.

The First Quarterly Meeting was held at Fond du Lac. The Church edifice was unfinished, and the celebrated school house having been burned, as stated in a former chapter, the Meeting was held in the Court House. At that time the building, though now so dingy, was new, and aspired to be the most respectable edifice in the village. To prepare the Court House especially for the Quarterly Meeting, the floors were newly carpeted with sawdust, even then a famous product of the village, and the seats well broomed. The place was crowded with people, and the occasion one of rare interest. The Gospel was dispensed from the "Seat of Justice," the Sacrament was administered within the "Bar," now vacated by the lawyers, and the people knelt outside to receive the sacred emblems. Several of the Members present had attended the Quarterly Meeting in the school house six years before, and among them were a few who had known me from my boyhood. It afforded me great pleasure to meet them and receive their friendly greetings.

Rev. J.S. Prescott, the Pastor at Fond du Lac, had been bred to the legal profession in the State of Ohio. He came to Wisconsin as a Local Preacher, and joined the Conference in 1846. He had been stationed at Sheboygan, Waupun, and Green Bay. He was a man of sharp, decisive movements, sometimes angular in his opinions and measures, but full of energy and not afraid of hard work. He kept no horse, even when on the largest circuits, as he could not afford to wait for so laggard a conveyance. In this particular he became notorious, and marvelous stories are related of his pedestrian abilities. It is affirmed that, on one occasion, in going to the Conference, he walked from Waupun to Platteville, and reached his destination in advance of the long line of ministerial buggies that were headed in that direction. Carrying the same energy into every Department of his work, he always left his "footprint" behind him. But his most devoted friends would sometimes question the wisdom of his measures. Even in the small village of Fond du Lac, he had now two churches in process of erection. But such was his skill in raising funds at home and abroad that one of them was dedicated by Bishop Ames at the close of the year and the other by the writer in the year following.

Subsequently he served for several years as Agent of Lawrence University, and then entered upon the project of founding an Institution of learning at Point Bluff. The selection of a location, however, was unfortunate, and his expectations were only partially realized. After this disaster he addressed himself to business pursuits.

The Fond du Lac charge had now gained an influential position in the Conference. Among her membership she had several leading business men. And in addition, this place had now become the home of Rev. H.R. Colman and Rev. M.L. Noble, the last two Pastors of the charge.

My next Meeting was held on Greenbush Circuit. This charge was midway between Fond du Lac and Sheboygan, and had been established only two years. Its Eastern portion had been opened from Sheboygan, and its Western from Fond du Lac. It had neither Church nor Parsonage, and the Minister lived in a shanty.

The Quarterly Meeting was held in Mr. Tunis Burhite's barn, about nine miles east of Fond du Lac. I found the Pastor, Rev. David Lewis, at his post. As was his wont, he had made every needed preparation, and had brought out nearly the entire strength of his charge. The barn was filled with people, and the neighborhood taxed to its utmost to entertain the visitors. Nor was it surprising that, with such a preparation, the Meeting was an occasion of rare interest. For months and even years after, it was referred to with great satisfaction. At the time the opinions of people were found to differ. One good sister said in my hearing, "I think it is better to have old men like Elder Wilcox for Presiding Elders, rather than such young men, because they can keep a meeting steady and not let the people get so excited." But at the close of the services a veteran Local Preacher said, "The old Elder gave us a straight talk this morning." Both remarks were suggestive, and I resolved to bear myself with becoming dignity.

Brother Lewis entered the Rock River Conference August 24th, 1842, and was sent as Junior Preacher to Indian Creek, Ill., a four weeks' circuit, the labor of which greatly taxed his strength. His next appointment was Manitowoc, the charge extending from Port Washington to Two Rivers, and requiring one hundred and fifty miles of travel to each round of appointments. Through these dense forests, as I have had occasion to remark in a former chapter, the roads were almost impassable, with long distances intervening between residences, and involving great fatigue and exposure. Like the good Brother Frink, who preceded him in this field, he was compelled to swim rivers, suffer hunger and endure fatigue, that would appall a man of less nerve. During the winter his horse became disabled and he made the entire round on foot, carrying his provisions in a knapsack. Such were the trials and exposures of the pioneers who planted the standard of the Cross in the "Sheboygan Woods," as this region was called. They were indeed heroic men.

There were a few scattered sheep in the wilderness, and these were gathered into the fold. At Manitowoc, Brother Lewis formed a class.

In 1844 Brother Lewis was sent to Pewaukee, where he had eleven appointments. Though at the beginning of the year there was no class on the charge, at its close Brother Lewis, was able to report sixty-five members. It was during this year that our sturdy pioneer took to himself a worthy helpmeet, in the person of Miss Adelia Morley, who, as an inmate of the Presiding Elder's family, spread the table for the writer's first meal as an Itinerant. Brother Lewis was next appointed successively to Root River, Kankakee, and Brothertown, in which charges he enjoyed his usual share of hard work and spiritual prosperity.

In 1849 he was appointed to Sheboygan Falls. The circuit was very large, taking the entire tract of country between the Lake and Fond du Lac, but the year was one of marked success. Finding the Parsonage under a mortgage that imperiled the safety of the property, Brother Lewis stepped forward and offered his horse, saddle, and a dollar and a half, all the money he had, in liquidation of the indebtedness. They were accepted, and as a result, the dear brother traveled his circuits on foot for two years before he was able to procure another horse. Such is the sterling material out of which the early Itinerants were made. With such men in the field, it is not a matter of surprise that, under the Divine blessing, the "Wilderness and solitary place" were made to rejoice.

At the close of his labors on this circuit, Brother Lewis was again sent to Manitowoc for one year, when, the Greenbush charge having been created, principally out of the west part of his former work, he was appointed to it, as before stated. After leaving Greenbush he was stationed at West Bend, Columbus and Fall River, Oneida Indian Mission, New London, Markesan, Caldwell's Prairie, and New Berlin. At the Janesville Conference in 1870, Brother Lewis, having served the church nearly thirty years with great devotion, took a superannuated relation. At this writing he is residing in Fond du Lac, maintains a happy frame of mind, and is still doing what he can for the cause. He certainly deserves well of his Conference.

Sheboygan Mission, the next point visited, appears on the Minutes, as stated in a former chapter, in 1837, with Rev. H.W. Frink as Pastor. During this year Brother Frink formed a class at Sheboygan, consisting of the following members: Mr. and Mrs. Morris Farmin, Uriel Farmin, Benjamin Farmin, Mr. and Mrs. Elder Farmin, and Mr. and Mrs. McCreedy.

At the close of this year Sheboygan disappears from the list of appointments, but in 1843 the Manitowoc mission appears with Rev. D. Lewis as Pastor, and Sheboygan, it will be recollected, is named as one of the appointments. In 1845, however, the name re-appears, and Rev. Joseph T. Lewis was sent to the charge. From this time until 1849 the strength of the circuit consisted largely in the outlying appointments. But at this date Sheboygan Falls was erected into a separate charge, taking from Sheboygan its several interior appointments.

Rev. Daniel Stansbury, the Pastor, had commenced his labors in 1849, and was now on his second year. The Membership numbered only thirty-three, but Brother Stansbury had achieved a great work in the erection of a large and convenient Church edifice. I had visited the village the preceding year, as before stated, to dedicate the German Church, and had formed a very agreeable acquaintance with this truly noble man and his most estimable family.

Brother Stansbury was from Baltimore, and brought with him to Wisconsin a goodly portion of the warm and cheerful type of Baltimore Methodism. He was received on trial by the Wisconsin Conference in 1849, and hence Sheboygan was his first appointment. His subsequent appointments were Janesville, Union, Portage City, Beaver Dam, Berlin and Janesville District. In July of his second year on the District, and while preaching at his Quarterly Meeting on Cambridge circuit, he was stricken down by paralysis. He was taken to his home in Janesville, where he lingered in extreme feebleness until Oct. 28, when he died in great peace.

Brother Stansbury was a man of warm impulses, practical mind, and abundant labors. In the protracted meeting, his rare gifts of prayer and exhortation, made his labors a grand success, and, in the bright world beyond, it will be found that his comparatively short ministry gathered a large harvest of souls.

I next visited Sheboygan Falls. The charge first appears on the Minutes in 1849, it having been created out of the interior portions of the Sheboygan circuit. Its first Pastor, as we have seen, was Rev. David Lewis. In 1850, the following year, Rev. Matthias Himebaugh was appointed to the work. At this time the field embraced fifteen appointments, and required the travel of two hundred miles each month. Like his predecessors, Revs. J.S. Prescott and D. Lewis, Brother Himebaugh traveled this circuit on foot. The Society in the village consisted of thirteen members, and included the names of Mr. and Mrs. L. Cheeseman, Mr. and Mrs. Parrish, Mr. and Mrs. Goodell, Mr. and Mrs. Sully, Mr. and Mrs. Jackson, Mr. and Mrs. Waite, and others.

The public meetings were held in a school house outside of the village, and the prayer meetings in private houses. A lot had been purchased for a Church and Parsonage, and the latter had been partly built. On the arrival of Brother Himebaugh a hall was obtained in the village for the meetings, and soon after he commenced a subscription for a Church.

A revival occurred during the winter, and there were a goodly number of accessions, but they did not bring very much financial strength. The Society, though small and in moderate circumstances, were very enterprising and generous in their effort to erect a Church, subscribing towards the building one-fifth of their entire property. Having secured pledges, amounting to twelve hundred dollars, the Pastor now led a strong force of volunteer laborers in the manual labor of the undertaking. Felling the first tree for the timber in the woods with his own hands, Brother Himebaugh gave the keynote to the movement. Nor did he stay his hand until he had expended sixty days of labor.

After accomplishing what he could at home, he visited Milwaukee, Chicago, and several towns and cities in the Erie, Pittsburgh and Genesee Conferences, to obtain aid to complete the enterprise. The edifice, forty by sixty, with a basement, was so far completed that the lecture-room was ready for dedication in December, 1851. With this good work accomplished, our Quarterly Meeting at Sheboygan Falls was an occasion of great rejoicing.

Brother Himebaugh entered the Erie Conference in 1839, then twenty years of age. His first circuit was Red Bank, on the Alleghany Mountains.

At the end of eleven years he was transferred to the Wisconsin Conference, and Sheboygan Falls was his first charge. After leaving this work, he was stationed in the North Ward charge in Fond du Lac. Here he also did a good work towards completing the Church edifice, which had been begun by Brother Prescott. He also had a good revival during the year.

In 1853, Brother Himebaugh was stationed at Oshkosh, where he performed prodigies of labor, preaching during a portion of the first year, on every other Sabbath, four sermons, and walking fourteen miles. He also gathered large accessions, which rendered the charge self-sustaining thereafter.

His subsequent appointments have been: Madison, Madison District, Appleton, Appleton District, Agent of Lawrence University, and Assistant Superintendent of the Western Seaman's Friend Society. At the present writing, he still holds the last named position, and represents the Bethel interests in this city. He is yet strong physically and intellectually, and bids fair to give to the good cause many additional years.

Oshkosh was the next place visited. Instead of finding, as in 1845, a few small cabins, I now found a respectable village and a flourishing Church.

The first Methodist sermon delivered in Oshkosh was preached by the veteran pioneer, Rev. Jesse Halstead, at the residence of Mr. Webster Stanley, in 1841. The place was now taken into the list of his appointments, and was supplied by Brother Halstead with considerable regularity.

At a subsequent visit he was accompanied by his Presiding Elder, Rev. James R. Goodrich. The services were again held in the residence of Mr. Stanley, and at this meeting, which was held in the fall of 1841, the first class was formed. The members were: Ira Aikin, Mrs. Aikin, his mother, Rachel Aikin, his sister, Mrs. Chester Ford, Miss Ann Brooks, and Mrs. Electa Wright. Brother Aikin was the first Leader, but soon after Brother William W. Wright and his wife becoming members, the Leadership passed over to Brother Wright. Before other provision was made, the meetings were held at the residences of Mr. Stanley, Mrs. Electa Wright and William W. Wright, but subsequently they passed to the school house and ultimately to the Court House.

In 1842, Rev. John P. Gallup was appointed to the Winnebago Lake Mission. His plan of labor gave to Oshkosh every fourth Sabbath, and the intervening time was filled by Rev. Clark Dickinson, a highly esteemed Local Preacher, and others. A revival occurred this year that brought into the Church the larger portion of the people living in Oshkosh and vicinity.

Rev. Harvey S. Bronson was the Pastor in 1843, and was succeeded the following year by Rev. Joseph H. Hurlbut. The first Church edifice was erected under the Pastorate of Rev. Robert Everdell in 1851. Being the Presiding Elder of the District at that time, the writer performed the dedicatory service. The building was enlarged in 1856 and again in 1861. Under the Pastorate of Rev. Wm. P. Stowe there were large accessions, and he found it necessary to enlarge again, when in 1870 the writer was called to preach the re-opening sermon.

The mother charge at this writing ranks among the leading stations of the Conference, and rejoices in the companionship of two promising daughters. The first is located on the South Side, where a lot was purchased and the contract for a building let, under the Pastorate of Rev. J.M. Walker, in 1868. The charge was organized the following year, and under the successive Pastorates of Revs. C.W. Brewer and Joseph Anderson, the Church was completed and the station assigned an honorable place in the Conference. The other, located in the Western part of the city, was erected into a separate charge at the last Conference session, a Chapel having been previously built.

CHAPTER XIII

Green Bay, the next point visited, is the oldest town within the bounds of the Wisconsin Conference. Its site was explored by Jean Nicollet in 1639, but its settlement did not begin for more than a century thereafter. In 1785 it contained seven families, and in 1816 there were one hundred and fifty inhabitants located in the village and its vicinity. The population now began to increase more rapidly, and in 1819 there were sixty dwellings and five hundred inhabitants.

Green Bay was made a United States trading port in 1815, with Col. John Bowyer as Indian Agent. And on the 16th of July of the following year, Col. John Miller commenced the erection of Fort Howard. The first frame house built, and perhaps the first in the State, was erected in 1825, by Col. E. Childs.

Col. Samuel Ryan came to Green Bay in 1826 and was the first Methodist, as far as I have been able to ascertain, who settled within the bounds of the Wisconsin Conference, and was probably the first in the State. From the time of his arrival until 1833, the religious Meetings were held in the Garrison school house and in an old Commissary store. Thereafter, and until a Church was erected, the services were held in a new yellow school house, or in the Garrison building at Fort Howard.

At the General Conference, which was held in Philadelphia in 1832, action was taken looking to the extension of the Missionary work of the Church in the Northwest. In furtherance of this object, Rev. John Clark, then of the New York Conference, was sent out as Superintendent of the work. This eminent Minister and able administrator, whose special record I need not enter in these pages, as his Life has been published, arrived at Green Bay July 21st, 1832. Immediately after his arrival he began his labors, preaching the first Methodist sermon within the limits of the present boundaries of the Wisconsin Conference. The sermon was delivered in the Fort, to both soldiers and citizens.

The first class was formed by Brother Clark immediately after, the services being held also in the Fort. This class consisted of four members, as follows: Col. Samuel Ryan, Sen., Mrs. Sherman, Mrs. Gen. Brooke, and a young man whose name cannot be given. Mrs. Brooke was the wife of the Commandant of the Fort, and Col. Ryan was the Leader.

Col. Ryan was born in Ireland, May 22d, 1789, and in early youth entered upon the military profession. He was in the engagement between the Shannon and Chesapeake off Boston Harbor, fought June 1st, 1813, and during the conflict was severely wounded. He was converted at Sackett's Harbor, N.Y., under the ministry of Rev. Mr. Irwin, in 1821. In 1822 and '23, he resided at Sault St. Marie, and while there was Leader of a class. During the year there was no Minister at the Sault, but Brother Ryan held religious services regularly among the soldiers, and as the fruit of his labors, seventy souls were converted. On coming to Green Bay, as above stated, in 1826, he resumed his labors, and continued to devote himself to the good work in that locality for twenty-six years. The Land Office, in which he held the first place, being now, 1852, removed to Menasha, he also took up his residence in that village.

Brother Ryan was a man of ardent temperament, full of vivacity, and not a little eccentric, but a true soldier of the Lord Jesus Christ. As in his youth his dauntless spirit never cowered in the presence of an earthly foe, so, in maturer years, he was a fearless champion for the spiritual reign of the Master. Honored by all, the Patriarch is now, "leaning upon the top of his staff," with his dimned eye looking across the river, ready to move on at any moment.

One of the early laborers at Green Bay was Rev. George White, who came from Oneida Conference, N.Y. He was stationed at Green Bay in 1835, Brother Clark having been assigned to the Presiding Eldership. Under the labors of the new Pastor, the work continued to prosper. On the 2d day of February, 1835, Brother Clark reported to the Christian Advocate and Journal as follows: "Brother White is in the spirit of his work, and the Lord is blessing his labors in the conversion of souls, both in the Fort and among the citizens."

The first Church enterprise was entered upon in 1836, when a lot was donated to the Society for the purpose of erecting a Church edifice. The Deed was given on the 6th day of September, 1836, by John Jacob Astor, Ramsey Crooks, Emily Crooks, Robert Stewart and Eliza Stewart, and was executed by James Duane Doty, their attorney. The Trustees of the Society, to whom the Deed was made, were Philip W. Nicholas, Francis McCarty, George White, Thomas P. Green, William White, Edwin Hart, and John P. Gallup. The edifice was completed during the year, but in the effort the Society became seriously involved, and were compelled to mortgage the property. The indebtedness hung as an incubus on the Society for ten years, and finally, through some strange mismanagement, the property was sold at a great sacrifice to the Roman Catholics.

At the session of the Illinois Conference, held Sept. 27, 1837, Rev. Philip W. Nicholas was sent to Green Bay, and Rev. Salmon Stebbins was assigned to the District. The congregations had now become highly respectable both in numbers and position. Hon. M.L. Martin had settled at Green Bay, and his good lady, who was a Methodist, had become a member of the Society. Sister Martin had been raised in affluent circumstances, and was a lady of fine culture and rare judgment. Her husband, a member of the legal profession, and subsequently a Delegate to Congress and Member of the Constitutional Convention of the State, was a man of good attainments and superior abilities. His family not only formed the nucleus of cultivated society, but also furnished a pleasant home for the Itinerant.

Besides this excellent and cultured family, the congregation embraced Col. Ryan and family, as before stated, Mrs. Gen. Brooke, and Mrs. Capt. Kirby Smith, whose husband was killed in the Mexican War, she being now the wife of Gen. Eaton, Quartermaster General of the U.S.A. In addition, Gov. and Mrs. Doty were constant attendants upon the Chapel, as were also Gen. and Mrs. Marcy, whose daughter, Mrs. George B. McClellan, was born here, and the most excellent of all the officers, Capt. Merrill and his young wife.

Referring to the class of society that constituted at first the class and congregation at Green Bay, reminds me of a case of Church discipline which occurred there about the days of which I am now writing. It happened on this wise:

One of the young members of the class, and perhaps the youngest, for she had but recently come West as the bride of a distinguished citizen whose name has already been mentioned, had become the owner of a new bonnet. The lady herself had never, though fashionably raised, shown a fondness for gaudy apparel, but, being obliged to send to Detroit for all millinery accommodations, she sometimes felt constrained to wear articles that were not selected in harmony with her tastes. The new bonnet fell somewhat into this category. If I were gifted in that line, I would attempt a description of the new comer, but, as I am not, I will simply say it was made in the height of the then fashion, with a small crown and a very high, flaring front, with ornaments atop. On the Sabbath following its arrival, the good sister put on her bonnet as innocently as in childhood she had ever said "Our Father" at her mother's knee, and went to Church. She walked modestly to her seat, bowed her head as usual, and the services proceeded. She certainly felt devout, and she had not the remotest idea that there was anything in the

Church that could disturb the devotion of others. But alas! for poor human nature. A horrible nightmare was that moment lurking under the wings of the beautiful dream of our innocent sister. In that highly respectable congregation, there were evil eyes that could not look at the Minister or close in prayer. They were fixed upon the gaudy bonnet.

At the close of the services comment was rife. Some of the good plain people christened the newly arrived, "The Methodist Flower-Pot," while others looked exceedingly unhappy. But there was one resolute brother who could not permit matters to go on in this way, and hence the case was brought before the Church. The zealous brother stated the case and declared that if Mr. Wesley's rule in regard to "high heads and enormous bonnets" meant anything, this was "the time to put it to the test and prove its efficacy." He further stated that it was "better to begin at the top round of the ladder and work down, rather than take up some offending sister from a lower round as an example." Of course all things were now ready for a decapitation, but judge of the surprise of the brother, when the good sister showed herself not to be very "high-headed," though big-bonneted, by offering the offensive article to her accuser, to manipulate into orthodox form, if he were pleased to do so, otherwise it would have to remain, like Mordecai at the King's gate, steadfast and immovable.

The bonnet was not manipulated, and the good sister continued to wear what neither her accuser nor any other person in Green Bay could put into another form.

Before the expiration of his second year, Brother Nicholas gave up the Pastorate of the charge, and his place was supplied by Rev. Stephen P. Keyes. In 1839, Rev. F.A. Chenoweth was appointed to the charge, and Rev. Julius Field was assigned to the District. In 1840 Green Bay was left to be supplied, and Rev. Boyd Phelps was employed as the supply, and the charge was assigned to Platteville District, with Rev. H.W. Reed as Presiding Elder. The following year, 1841, the Green Bay District was formed, with Rev. James R. Goodrich as the Presiding Elder, and his name appears also as Pastor of the charge, but it is probable that Brother Phelps also assisted him in the Pastorate as a supply. In 1842 the appointments remained the same, but in 1843 Rev. G.L.S. Stuff was appointed to the station. Brother Stuff and Brother Keyes are remembered with great pleasure at Green Bay, as men of sterling qualities and marked ability, but as their labors have mostly fallen within the Rock River Conference, their record will doubtless be made in connection with that field. In 1844, Rev. Wm. H. Sampson was appointed to the District, as stated elsewhere, and Rev. C.N. Wager to the station. He was followed in 1845 by Rev. T.P. Bingham, and the year following by Rev. R.P. Lawton.

Brother Lawton entered the Rock River Conference this year, and in this, his first appointment, acquitted himself creditably. As this good brother, who may be set down as one of the pioneers of the Conference, began his labors, so he has continued to the present hour. His appointments after leaving Green Bay, have been Dixon, Ill., Delavan, Mineral Point, Waukesha, Reed Street, Milwaukee, Palmyra, Grafton, Root River, Elkhorn, Delavan, East Troy, Evansville, Rosendale, Wautoma, Plover, New London, Hart Prairie, Utter's Corners, Footville, and Jefferson, where he is located at this writing. Brother Lawton is a good preacher, has a genial spirit, and is devoted to his work. He has passed over the greater portion of the Conference, and has a host of friends wherever he has been stationed.

Rev. A.B. Randall was sent to Green Bay in 1847, and it was during this year that the Church edifice was sold. This Church was dedicated, doubtless, by Rev. John Clark, and had been used for ten years for religious purposes, yet it is surprising to find how much of time and labor it required to purify it after it fell into the hands of the Catholics. I am told that they spent days of labor and nights of vigil, exhausted miniature rivulets of holy water, and pounds of precious "gems, frankincense, and myrrh," exorcising the devils and scattering the Methodist imps of darkness from the holy place.

The balance of the money, after paying the indebtedness, was applied to the purchase of the Second Church, which was still in use at the time of my visit.

On coming to Green Bay I found Rev. Seth W. Ford as Pastor, who was commencing his second year on the charge. He was in the midst of a revival, and the charge appeared to be in a prosperous condition. The Quarterly Meeting passed off very pleasantly, and gave me the opportunity to share the hospitality of Hon. M.L. Martin and his excellent family. I also visited the Fort, and had the pleasure to enjoy the companionship of Col. Ryan and his family.

Brother Ford entered the Conference in 1845, as a classmate of the writer, and passed with him through the course of graduation. I have referred in a former chapter to the seven sessions through which we passed between the upper and nether millstones. Whether the result was flour or bran in the estimation of the Committee would have been forever hidden from us, doubtless, had not the good brethren, after our election to Elder's orders, moved that Brother Ford and myself be a Committee to examine those of the class who had not been before the Committee. With our own experience fresh in our minds, I have no doubt the balance of the class had an easy passage.

Brother Ford's fields of labor had been Hamilton Grove, Macomb, and Oneida Indian Mission. In each he had made a good record, and was now rapidly rising in his Conference. Since he left Green Bay he has continued to hold good appointments, and has served his Conference six times as its Secretary. Though slender in form, and apparently not vigorous in health, he has nevertheless taken his full share of work and is highly respected by his brethren.

The Oneida Indian Mission, lying twelve miles to the northwest of Green Bay, next claimed my attention. Seated in my buggy, I was soon at the Parsonage, where I found Rev. Henry Requa, the Missionary, and his kind family.

The Oneidas came from the State of New York. A few of them came as early as 1821, but through some hitch in the negotiations with the Menomonees for the lands constituting the Reservation, the removal did not become general until 1832. Meantime, a Mission had sprung up among the western branch of the nation. In 1829 a young Mohawk, who had been converted in Canada, began the good work and established meetings. Among the early Missionaries the names of Rev. Mr. Poe and Rev. John Clark are especially fragrant, but I have been unable to find satisfactory data until 1840, when Rev. Henry R. Colman was appointed to the Mission.

Brother Colman remained until 1845, when he was succeeded by Rev. C.G. Lathrop. Brother Ford followed next, and remained until 1850, when he was succeeded by Brother Requa. Meantime, the old log church had given place to a respectable frame edifice. There was also a good frame Parsonage, occupied by the Missionary, and a school house, in which a school was kept either by the Missionary or some one employed by him. The membership at this time numbered one hundred and twenty-five.

The Quarterly Meeting was held on Saturday and Sabbath, as on the other charges. On Saturday the Quarterly Conference was held, composed of the official members, but it was somewhat unique in its method of transacting its business. The Conference was opened with singing and prayer. The next thing in order was an address from the Elder, or "Big Missionary," as he is called. The address simply expressed the gratification of the Elder with his visit, and the encouraging things he has heard of the good work of God among them, and then suggested such items of business as would require their attention. This done, I took my seat, for what more could I do. The business must now be done in a strange language, and in the method of the red man. After sitting in absolute silence for some minutes, the head Chief of the Nation, "Big Jake," as he is called, being one of the Stewards, turned to a brother on his right and spoke a few words, and received a reply.

Then turning to another, he did the same, and thus continued to address each personally, until all had been consulted. At intervals there were long pauses, indicative, as I judged, of the gravity of the matter to be considered. At the end of an hour the Council had completed its work. The Chief then arose in a very dignified manner, but without ostentation, and, calling to his aid an interpreter, proceeded to reply to the opening address. He began his speech by expressing thanks, on behalf of himself and people, that the "Big Missionary" had come once more to see them. He next referred to the good work that had been performed by the Missionary, and the special blessing of God upon his people. And in conclusion, he reported the items of business they had considered, and the action taken in each case. If anything further was desired at any time, it was always presented in a most respectful manner. In this case it was represented that they needed some repairs on the Church, and a bell, and they desired that the Missionary might be permitted to go abroad and raise the necessary funds. Permission was granted, and the Missionary, taking several fine singers of the Nation with him, went to New York, Boston, and other places, and secured the needed help.

At the close of the public services came the hand shaking. The Missionary understood the matter and detained me in the Altar for a moment, Commencing with the ladies and ending with the children, every person in the Church came forward and shook hands with the Elder.

I was greatly pleased with "Chief Jake." He was a man of stalwart frame, standing with head and shoulders above the people around him. That giant frame supported a large head, adorned by an expressive face. His movement was dignified simply because he was a born nobleman, and did not know how to appear other than like a prince. He was benevolent and tender to all who were trying to do right, but he was a terror to evil-doers. Standing for his people or the rights of the oppressed, he was absolutely invincible.

Brother Requa entered the Conference in 1847, after having been employed one year as second preacher at Waupun. He was appointed to Brothertown in 1847, to Lowell in 1848, and Fond du Lac in 1849, Here his health partially failed, and, in consequence, he was sent to Oneida. From the first, Brother Requa attracted attention as a Preacher. The first time I heard him was at the Camp-Meeting at Sun Prairie, in the summer of 1846. He had only recently been converted, and was now called out to exhort at the close of a sermon. He had been known in the community as an Infidel, which greatly increased the interest felt by all when he arose to speak. But the first utterance of his eloquent tongue, so full of feeling and so decided in its tone, disarmed all criticism. As he advanced, he threw off restraint, until he was master of himself and the congregation. Once free, he seemed to lose sight of all but the condition of a perishing world. With lost men he reasoned, expostulated, entreated, until it seemed that the whole audience was moving towards the Altar.

While at Oneida, as before stated, he went East to raise funds for the Mission. Wherever he went, he was recognized as a man of rare eloquence. Throngs followed him from Church to Church, and, as might be expected, his mission was a great success. On his return with the bell, the people were overjoyed. For the first week after it was hung in the steeple, it was kept going, almost night and day. The friends came from every part of the reservation, and no one was satisfied until his own hand pulled the rope. And so high did the enthusiasm run that one man said, "As soon as we get able, we will put one on every house in Oneida." After Brother Requa left Oneida, he served one year as Agent of Lawrence University, and was specially engaged in raising an Indian Scholarship Fund. His appointments subsequently were: Janesville, Fond du Lac District, Oshkosh, Sheboygan Falls, Sheboygan, Brandon and Ripon. In March, 1865, his second year at Ripon, he went as a Delegate of the Christian Commission to the army. His field of labor was Little Rock, Ark. While here he was taken ill with the chronic diarrhoea, and on the 19th of May departed to his home above. During his illness, he was attended by his old friend, Brother A. B. Randall. Just before he died, he requested his attendant to bear this message to his brethren of the Wisconsin Conference: "Tell them that Henry Requa died at his post." He then added, "Take my ashes back to be interred among my brethren. I have labored with them for twenty years past, trying to preach Jesus. My present acceptance with God is a great comfort to me now. I am very unworthy, but I believe there are some in glory who call me father. In looking over my whole life I cannot see an act upon which I would risk the salvation of my soul; the best of them need washing in the blood of Jesus. I know I have a home in glory. How precious Jesus is. Jesus, I love thee for what thou hast done for me. I will praise thee forever."

Brother Requa was a man of ardent temperament, and at times impulsive, but he was a true man and a faithful minister. His attachments were strong and abiding. He loved the work in which he was engaged, and was very generally popular among the people. A born Radical, he was liable to push matters beyond what more conservative minds deemed wise, and it is possible that in some instances his extreme methods defeated his purpose, but even then, no one questioned the rectitude of his heart. In the death of Brother Requa the Conference sustained a severe loss. His remains were interred in College Hill Cemetery, at Ripon.

CHAPTER XIV

Leaving Oneida, I next visited Appleton, where I was kindly received by Rev. C.G. Lathrop, the Pastor, and his good wife. Though three years had scarcely passed since the echoes of the woodman's axe first rang through the forests of this locality, yet I found Appleton to be a village of considerable pretensions. The location of Lawrence University at this point, and the great promise of business, given by its almost unparalleled water-power, had already drawn together an enterprising community. Good buildings had been erected, and the village was putting on an air of thrift.

The first sermon preached in Appleton, and probably in Outagamie County, was delivered by Rev. Wm. H. Sampson, Oct. 8, 1848, in a shanty occupied by Brother John F. Johnson and family. The first class was formed by Rev. A. B. Randall, the Pastor of Oshkosh circuit, whose charge included Appleton, in February, 1849. The first members were Robert R. Bateman, Leader, Robert S. Bateman, Mary Bateman, Amelia Bateman, Electa Norton, Theresa Randall, L. L. Randall, J.F. Johnson and D.W. Briggs. Brother Randall organized the first Sunday School in March, 1849, with Robert R. Bateman as Superintendent.

The meetings were held in private houses until the Chapel of the Institute was ready for use. They were held in the Chapel thereafter until the first Church was erected. In June, 1854, the corner-stone of the Church was laid by Edwin Atkinson, Dr. Edward Cooke officiating. The lecture-room was occupied during the following winter, and the Church was dedicated by Dr. N.E. Cobleigh in June, 1855.

The Quarterly Meeting, the first held in Appleton, was convened in the Institute Chapel, Sept 27, 1851. The members of the Quarterly Conference present were C.G. Lathrop, R.O. Kellogg, Jabez Brooks, D.L. Atwell, George E. Havens, Charles Levings, John Day, H.L. Blood, A.C. Darling, L.L. Randall, D.C. Weston, William Rork, and J.F. Johnson. The meeting was well attended, and the services indicated a healthy spiritual condition.

Rev. Curtis G. Lathrop entered the Rock River Conference in 1842, and his first appointment was Aztalan. Before coming to Appleton he had been stationed at Lancaster, Oneida Indian Mission, Green Lake and Fall River. After leaving Appleton his fields of labor have been Green Bay,

Oneida, Indian Mission, Presiding Elder of Watertown District, Menasha, Neenah, Waupaca, Dartford, Fox Lake, Vinland and Randolph. He took a superannuated relation in 1868, but during 1870 and 1871 he was able to serve as Chaplain of the Western Seaman's Friend Society, at Washington Island. Having removed to Nebraska, he was made effective in 1874 and transferred to the Nebraska Conference.

Brother Lathrop is a man of vigorous mental endowments. He is an able Preacher, has a reliable judgment, and possesses a kind spirit. He hates shams and thoroughly detests the superficial. He never hangs out a flag to catch the popular breeze, and does not turn the prow of his craft down the stream. His convictions are strong, but Curtis G. Lathrop is the soul of integrity, and is most highly appreciated where best known.

The Lawrence University, located at Appleton, deserves special notice, it being the first, and, at the present writing, the only school of the Church within the bounds of the Conference.

In the Spring of 1846, Rev. Wm. H. Sampson received a letter from H. Eugene Eastman, Esq., of Green Bay, informing him that a gentleman in Boston, Mass., proposed to donate ten thousand dollars to found a school in the West. And as the gentleman entertained an exalted opinion of the adaptations of the Methodist Church to the work contemplated, he was authorized to give the proposition that direction. The conditions on which the trust must be accepted were, that the School should be located on the Fox River between Neenah and Green Bay, and that an additional ten thousand dollars should be contributed by other parties.

Brother Sampson submitted the proposition to the Conference, which met in August, and was instructed by that body to continue the correspondence, and, if possible, reduce the negotiations to a definite form.

In December following, Rev. Reeder Smith, who had been employed as Agent of the School at Albion, Mich., came to Fond du Lac, bearing the proposition directly from Hon. Amos A. Lawrence, the gentleman referred to. Not finding Brother Sampson at home, he went down to Brothertown and secured the co-operation of Rev. H.R. Colman in making an exploration of the Fox River. They went to Green Bay, thence to Kaukauna, and, accompanied by George W. Law, Esq., thence to Grand Chute, the present site of Appleton. After looking over the grounds now constituting the campus of the University, they passed on to Oshkosh, and thence to Fond du Lac.

Brother Sampson had now returned, and it was decided to hold a meeting in Milwaukee for consultation. The meeting was convened December 2 8th, 1846, and was composed of the following members of the

Conference: Wm. H. Sampson, Henry R. Colman, Washington Wilcox, and Wm. M.D. Ryan. To these were added Reeder Smith, Geo. E.H. Day, and doubtless several others whose names I have not been able to learn. At this meeting a Charter was drafted for the Lawrence Institute, and Rev. Reeder Smith was sent to Madison to lay it before the Legislature. The Charter received the signature of Gov. Dodge, Jan. 17, 1847, and the following gentlemen were constituted the first Board of Trustees: Henry Dodge, Loyal H. Jones, Jacob L. Bean, Wm. H. Sampson, N.P. Talmadge, Henry R. Colman, H.S. Baird, Wm. Dutcher, M. C. Darling, M.L. Martin, Geo. E.H. Day, D.C. Vosburg, and Reeder Smith.

The first meeting of the Board was to have been held in Fond du Lac, June 30, 1847, but as there was not a quorum present, the meeting was adjourned to Sept. 3d. At this meeting the Board was duly organized by the election of the following officers: Hon. M.C. Darling, President; Hon. N.P. Talmadge, First Vice President; H.S. Baird, Esq., Second Vice President; Rev. Wm. H. Sampson, Secretary, and Hon. Morgan L. Martin, Treasurer. Rev. Reeder Smith was appointed Agent.

Geo. W. Law, Esq., and Hon. John F. Mead now offered a donation of thirty-one acres of land each, on condition that the Institute should be located at Grand Chute. The offer was accepted, and the location was made, the name of the place being soon after changed to Appleton. In due time the Law Tract was conveyed to the Trustees, but, by some strange mismanagement, to say the least, on the part of the Agent, the Mead land was conveyed to another party, and it was lost to the Institute.

At the Conference of 1848, Brother Sampson was appointed Principal, and was expected to serve as Agent until the building to be erected was ready for occupancy. In pursuance of this arrangement he left Fond du Lac, Sept. 7th, to enter upon his new field of operations. He took the steamer to Neenah, and then obtained an Indian "Dug-out" for the balance of the journey. As the craft carried no sail, he was compelled to put her before the "white ash breeze" across Lake Butte des Morts, and down the river to the point of destination, his craft being nearly swamped by a gale on the Lake.

On the 8th of September he began to cut a road to the grounds and clear the brush from the campus, thereby making the beginning of both the Institute and the city of Appleton. The lumber for the building of the Preparatory Department was purchased of Hon. M.L. Martin, and was delivered at Duck Creek. The timber was furnished by Col. H.L. Blood. Through the indomitable energy of Col. Blood and the co-operation of the agents, the building, seventy by thirty feet in size, and three stories high, was ready to receive students on the 12th day of November, 1849.

The Faculty with which the school opened were Rev. Wm. H. Sampson, Principal, Rev. R.O. Kellogg, Professor of Ancient Languages, Mr. James M. Phinney, Professor of Mathematics, and Miss Emeline M. Crooker, Preceptress. The first catalogue, published in the fall of 1850, showed a list of one hundred and five students, which was certainly a very creditable beginning. The name of the Institute was now changed to Lawrence University.

A record of the early years of struggle and sacrifice necessary to found the University would fill a volume, and cannot be given at length in these pages. Having been a member of the Board for nearly a quarter of a century, I could say much of the noble men who performed double service on half pay, but such a recital cannot here be given.

Rev. Dr. Edward Cooke was installed President of the University June 29, 1853. At the same time the corner stone of the College building was laid by Hon. M.C. Darling, Rev. Alfred Bronson, D.D., delivering the address. The edifice, a substantial stone structure, one hundred and twenty by sixty feet, and five stories high, was pushed forward to an early completion by the untiring energy of the agents, Rev. J.S. Prescott and Col. H.L. Blood. For college purposes the building ranked among the first in the West.

In both Students and Faculty Lawrence University has been fortunate from the beginning. As to the former, she has sent out not a few representative men to the several occupations of life, several of whom will find mention in these pages. As to the latter, she has enjoyed the labors of a class of instructors whose names have found an honorable place in both the clerical and literary circles of the Commonwealth.

Of Rev. Wm. H. Sampson, the first head of the Faculty, a record has been made in a former chapter, and it would afford me pleasure to refer at length to the several members of the first Faculty, as also to all the Professors who have followed, but I find it will be impossible to do so in these brief pages.

Rev. Edward Cooke, D.D., the first President, entered the New Jersey Conference in 1843. He was a graduate of the Wesleyan University, Middletown, Conn. His first appointment was Principal of the Pennington Male Seminary, N.J. In 1847 he was transferred to the New England Conference, and stationed at Saugus. His subsequent appointments were Union Church Charlestown, D. Street, Centenary, and Hanover, of Boston, Mass. He was transferred to the Wisconsin Conference in 1853, having been elected President of the University. As a President he was very popular, and during his administration of six years had the satisfaction to see the Institution rise from a feeble preparatory school to a full-fledged University. In addition to the ordinary duties of his position, he was largely concerned with the financial matters of the enterprise, but in every portion of the work Dr. Cooke showed great wisdom, tact and devotion. And during his term he laid the friends of education in the State under lasting obligations.

After leaving the University, he was stationed at Summerfield Church, Milwaukee, but, returning to Boston at the close of his term, he was elected Principal of the Wesleyan Academy, Wilbraham, Mass., where he has enjoyed great success in his administration. Dr. Cooke is a man of fine presence, and a good Preacher. Genial in spirit, full of anecdote and well read, he is very companionable. He has a multitude of friends in Wisconsin.

Rev. Nelson E. Cobleigh, D.D., was elected Professor in 1854. He was also a graduate of the Wesleyan University. On coming West, he was first elected Professor in the McKendree College, Ill., from which position he came to Appleton. His first visit to these "northern wilds," as Appleton was then called, was a memorable one. It was a Commencement occasion, and in connection with the other exercises, the annual Missionary Meeting was held. Under the leadership of Dr. Cooke, Brother Cobleigh was appointed to deliver one of the addresses. There were three speakers appointed as usual, and the second place was assigned to Dr. Cobleigh and the last to Dr. Cooke. The first speech, brief and to the point, was made, and as Chairman I introduced Dr. Cobleigh. The speech opened in a quiet, clear, and common-sense way, none expecting more than a good, average effort. But before the speaker had proceeded far, his sentences began to grow intense, and the blood began to shoot upward in deep, livid lines along the neck and face, and wreathe his forehead. All eyes were turned upon him, and each hearer began to feel the kindlings of a strange inspiration. But the speaker was lost to everything except his theme. He dashed on from one burning thought to another, carrying his audience with him, in such storms of eloquence as had never before enchanted the walls of the University Chapel.

At the expiration of a full hour, the great orator came to himself and resumed his seat, amid the shouts of the people. As soon as quiet intervened, I introduced Dr. Cooke. The Doctor came forward and stated that as the speakers had been limited to thirty minutes each, and as his good friend, Dr. Cobleigh, had used an hour, without any fault of his own, however, as he could not help it, he would not attempt to make a speech himself, but would adopt the last half of the last speech, which was infinitely better than he could do if he were to speak. The fine turn of the Doctor was taken with a good zest.

After serving the University several years, Dr. Cobleigh went back to McKendree College as President. He next served as Editor of Zion's Herald, in Boston, then was President of our College in Tennessee, and at the last

General Conference he was elected editor of the Advocate at Atlanta, Ga. But his work was soon finished, and he passed on to join the great and good who have entered the Heavenly gates.

Dr. R.Z. Mason came to the University as a Professor in 1855, and continued to hold this position until the resignation of Dr. Cooke, when he succeeded to the Presidency. He remained at this post until the election of Dr. Steele, when he entered upon business pursuits in Appleton. The Presidency of Dr. Mason was distinguished by great anxiety and severe labor. Like the Presidents who went before, and those who have followed, he was greatly burdened with the financial management. The several schemes which had been adopted to secure an Endowment Fund for the University, had not fully met expectations, and in consequence, an indebtedness had been incurred. To lift this incumbrance became the special concern of President Mason. He traveled over the State, visiting the charges in person, and taking subscriptions wherever they could be obtained. And I am happy to say that through his great ability in this direction, and his unbounded persistence, the work was carried forward to a grand success.

Rev. Loren L. Knox, D.D., was another member of the Faculty. Brother Knox had also given the greater portion of his life to educational work. His successful administration of the interests of leading institutions of learning in the East had fully prepared the Board to expect in him a valuable accession to the Faculty, and they were not disappointed. He was found to be a thorough scholar, a wise and careful instructor, and a Christian gentleman of the highest and purest style. After leaving the University, Dr. Knox did good service in the pulpit for several years, but, finally, his health so far failed that he was compelled to take a superannuated relation. At the present writing he is residing at Evanston, where he is giving such attention to literary work as he finds himself able to perform.

Rev. Geo. M. Steele, D.D., the President of the University at this present time, is a man of fine literary attainments, an able administrator, a superior preacher, and a writer of pronounced reputation. He is also a graduate of Middletown, and has had considerable experience as an instructor. He was elected President of the University in 1865, and has more than met the highest expectations of the Board. In addition to his duties at the head of the Faculty, he has given his personal attention largely to the financial interests of the Institution. In this particular he has achieved a grand work, both in managing the current expenditures, and in increasing the Endowment Fund. The Doctor is a great acquisition to the University, and is highly esteemed by his brethren. The Conference have delighted to honor him in all appropriate ways, and especially in sending him to both General Conferences which have occurred since he became a member of the body.

Having thus paid our respects to Appleton and the University, we are prepared to pass on to other fields. To complete the round there were two charges yet to visit, but as these will claim our attention hereafter I need not refer to them now, except to give an incident that transpired at the Quarterly Meeting held on one of them.

The meeting was held in a school house. The new schoolteacher, a nice youngster, concluded to lead the singing. Gathering a few young people around him, and displaying a tuning-fork, he was ready for the services to begin. I gave the hymn commencing,

"Come, Holy Spirit, Heavenly Dove."

When I had finished the reading, the chorister arose with superlative dignity, and gave the key. Unfortunately, the choir dropped a tone or two too low, and the first verse was sung at that disadvantage. Discovering the blunder, the key was again given, but the singers were now getting nervous, and instead of rising, they went still lower, as they sang,

"Look how we grovel here below."

Certainly the chariot wheels of Pharaoh did not roll more heavily than the numbers from that orchestra. I remembered old Balerma, and felt deeply for them. But our young knight of the tuning-fork was not to be vanquished. With a dash he brought the fork down upon the desk, and gave the key again. But alas! for all human expectations! The choir dropped down to a dead monotone, as they went on with the next verse:

"In vain we tune our formal songs,
In vain we strive to rise;
Hosannas languish on our tongues,
And our devotion dies."

Both the choir and congregation felt a relief when the Minister said, "Let us pray."

Having completed the first round of the District, I returned to Fond du Lac to begin the second. But it is not my purpose to give the details of each round or year, as the labors of a Presiding Elder are too monotonous to furnish a record that would be entertaining to the general reader.

CHAPTER XV

The Conference of 1852 was held at Fond du Lac, Sept. 1st, and was presided over by Bishop Ames. This was the first Conference held by the good Bishop after his election to his high office. The visit was also the first the good people of Northern Wisconsin had enjoyed from a Bishop of the Church. Both parties appeared delighted with the acquaintance.

On the Sabbath preceding the session of the Conference, the new Church in the upper town was dedicated by the Bishop, the preachers of the Conference generally being in attendance.

At this Conference I performed my first labor in the Cabinet. I felt the responsibility to be one of great gravity, but sought to bear it in the fear of God. In fact, the adjustment of the appointments had been the subject of careful thought and earnest prayer during the last three months of the year. From the first I felt that the adjustment of the Ministers and their work required the nicest discrimination and the most absolute self-abnegation. Resolving to discharge my duty fearlessly, and yet fully in the spirit of the Golden Rule, I entered upon the responsibility. Whether I succeeded or not, is a matter I have referred to the day when "The Books" shall be opened.

There were but few changes made in the appointments in the District, as I then cherished, as I have since, the conviction that changes, other than by limitation, should only be made for grave reasons.

Fond du Lac was divided into two charges, Rev. M. Himebaugh, of whom a record has been made, being sent to the North Ward, and Rev. Ezra Tucker to the South Ward. The year in both charges was generally prosperous.

Brother Tucker was a new man in the work, and entered upon his labors with great zeal. Having the new Church, and the inspiration usually experienced in such cases, he was encouraged with an extraordinary promise of success, but before the expiration of the year he fell sick, and was compelled to suspend his labors. After resting two years he was again able to resume work. He filled several appointments thereafter in the Wisconsin

Conference, and then removed to Minnesota, where, on both stations and Districts, he has rendered effective service.

Rev. Jabez Brooks was appointed to Oshkosh, but as he was still needed in the Professorship he had formerly held in the Lawrence University, I changed his appointment. Brother Brooks subsequently filled out the balance of Brother Tucker's year at Fond du Lac, and was then stationed at Jackson Street, Milwaukee. He was subsequently made President of the Hamline University, and at the present writing is Professor in the State University of Minnesota. Dr. Brooks, for such is his present title, is a prime man in every respect. Scholarly, logical, clear-headed, kind-hearted and diligent, he is a general favorite, wherever known.

During this year a Camp-Meeting was held on the District. The ground selected was Father Bower's Grove, on the east shore of Lake Butte des Morts, six miles above Oshkosh. The meeting was held June 8th, 1853. The attendance was good, there being ten tents on the ground, and there were fifty conversions.

The year closed pleasantly, and on my way to the Conference, to be held at Baraboo, Aug. 31st, I attended a Camp-Meeting at Lodi. The meeting had been appointed with a view to intercept the Bishop and the Preachers on their way to the Conference. The attendance was large and the meeting spirited. Bishop Scott came early in the week, and before Friday night there were not less than sixty-five Preachers in attendance. After preaching twice, the Bishop left on Saturday, as he was to dedicate the new Church in Baraboo on the Sabbath. As it was desirable also for the Presiding Elder to go forward with the Bishop, I was requested to remain and take charge of the Camp-Meeting until Monday. I consented on condition that the Bishop would take the clergy with him to the dedication. I selected a few men from the Fond du Lac District, and a few others from the vicinity of the meeting to remain with me, and the balance mostly went with the Bishop.

The change in the state of affairs, as I anticipated, was felt immediately. The Laity, who must always form the basis of a successful meeting, now came forward and took hold of the work. On Saturday night the Spirit fell on the people in great power. Before the conclusion of the sermon it was manifest that there would be, to change the reference, an abundance of rain. In the Prayer Meeting which followed, not less than thirty souls were converted. On Sabbath the meeting went forward with great spirit. But the climax was not reached until Sabbath evening, when, at the close of a sermon by Brother Himebaugh, the whole audience seemed to respond to the invitations of the Gospel. The Altar was thronged and the adjacent seats were filled far back into the congregation. It was impossible to tell how many were forward as seekers, or how many were converted, but those immediately engaged in the work, expressed the belief that not less than one hundred persons passed into the Kingdom of Grace.

The meeting had now received such momentum that it was impossible to close it on Monday. It was put in charge of brethren who were not immediately needed at the Conference, and was continued nearly the entire week.

On this trip to the Conference, I was permitted to enjoy the companionship of Rev. N.J. Aplin, who rendered signal service in the meeting on the Sabbath.

The Conference at Baraboo was one of unusual interest. The greetings of the Preachers were cordial, as they always are where persons make sacrifices and put forth labor in a common cause. It was the first visit of Bishop Scott to the Conference, and his urbanity and self-sacrificing labors endeared him to all. The business of the Conference was done in the spirit of the Master, but an unhappy trial made the session a very protracted one. This being the second year of my Presiding Eldership, the Disciplinary limit required several removals, but I need not give them in detail, as they can be ascertained, if desirable, by consulting the Minutes.

On our return from the Conference we reached Fall River on Saturday evening, and remained there over the Sabbath. On arriving at the forks of the roads on the crown of the prairie, the several Preachers who were in company halted for a proper distribution among the good people. Rev. A.P. Allen, the inimitable joker, who had served as Pastor on the charge, installed himself master of ceremonies, and proceeded to divide up the company. After assigning the balance to their respective quarters, he said, "Now, I guess the young Presiding Elder and the old Pastor had better go to Aunt Martha's, as that is the place where they do up the chicken-fixings scientifically." We were delightfully entertained by Rev. E.J. Smith and family, with whom, it will be remembered, I became acquainted in 1845. On Sabbath morning, accompanied by Brother and Sister Smith and their daughters, now Mrs. Pedrick and Mrs. Coe, of Ripon, we attended religious services at the school house in Fall River, where the serving fell to the lot of the writer.

At the beginning of the new year, special attention was given to the finances in the several charges. And during the first round the work was planned for the winter campaign. Fixing on the localities where I could render special assistance to the Pastors, it was arranged to commence the services with the Quarterly Meetings, and if the work should require more than the following week, I could return after the succeeding Quarterly Meeting had been held.

The first meeting was held at Appleton, Rev. Elmore Yocum being the Pastor. This noble man, one of the excellent of the earth, came to the Conference in 1849 by transfer from the North Ohio Conference, and was appointed Presiding Elder of the Platteville District. At the close of his term, he was stationed at Appleton, where his family could enjoy special educational advantages. At the end of two years he was made Presiding Elder of the Appleton District, and at the close of his term went to the West Wisconsin Conference, as he had become identified with the Educational Institution at Point Bluff. Both as Pastor and Presiding Elder Brother Yocum was deservedly popular.

The meeting at Appleton awakened intense interest. The good work grew upon our hands from day to day, until the business of the village was largely suspended during the hours of religious service. All classes fell under the good influence, and both students and citizens shared in the result. One hundred and thirty souls were converted.

The next meeting was held at Sheboygan Falls. As I drove into the village, the severest storm of the winter was raging, and by Sabbath morning the snow was two feet in depth. During the following night the winds piled it into drifts that made the roads nearly impassable. What was to be done? The prospect certainly looked dubious. But it occurred to me that a little preparation for the meeting would be of service, and this could now be done before the crowd should rush in upon us. We decided to go on. Illustrating the saying, "Where there's a will there's a way," the good people opened the streets in the village, and a small congregation was brought together. The Spirit of God came down in sweet, melting influences, and, under the Divine inspiration, the faith of the Church grew strong. Before the end of the week the place was filled, and souls were being converted.

The Pastor was Rev. R.W. Barnes. And as soon as the meeting was well established, the Pastors of the other Churches, Rev. Mr. Marsh, of the Congregational, and Rev. Mr. Lull, of the Baptist, came in with their people. They were received cordially, and set at work as opportunity offered. Besides these, several of our own Laymen gave themselves almost wholly to the work. Among these, Rev. L. Cheeseman, a Local Preacher, and E.T. Bond, Esq., a merchant, deserve special mention. Too much cannot be said in praise of these lay workers and the Church generally. With their Pastor, they were instant in season and out of season. After the regular labor of the evening was concluded, it was no uncommon thing for them to organize a second meeting for such of the seekers as had not obtained a satisfactory evidence of conversion. Here, in prayer and Christian Conference, they would labor until midnight, and in some instances until the dawn of day. The shout of victory usually signalled the close of the meeting. A more thorough work than this I never witnessed. I left the meeting twice before its close to attend to my work elsewhere, and was brought back by a messenger. During the meeting one hundred and fifty souls professed conversion, and among them were both men and women, who have since shown themselves to be valiant soldiers for Prince Immanuel.

The next meeting was held in the South Ward charge, Fond du Lac. The Pastor, Rev. E.S. Grumley, who had been appointed to the charge at the recent Conference, entered the North Ohio Conference in 1842. He had been stationed at Lower Sandusky, Bucyrus, Ashland, Shanesville, Ohio City, Tiffin, Sandusky City and Norwalk. Since his transfer to the Conference in 1851, he had been two years at Council Hill. After filling his term in Fond du Lac he was, for a full term, Presiding Elder on Racine District. After leaving the District he continued to hold respectable appointments until 1871, when his health failed and he was compelled to take a superannuated relation.

Brother Grumley was a man of small frame and apparently of feeble health, yet he was able to do effective work to the last. He had a sound head, and a heart equally sound. He was a good Preacher, and a superior Pastor. Revivals usually attended his labors, and he was always highly esteemed by the people.

The meeting at Fond du Lac immediately followed the one at Sheboygan Falls. With my family I left the latter place in time to reach Fond du Lac at noon on Saturday. But through detention I was just driving into the city as the bell was ringing for the service. Hastily caring for my horse, I went immediately to the Church. Before the services were concluded, I saw evident assurances that the Pastor had been making careful preparation for the work before us. The opening sermon was addressed to the Church, and found a ready and hearty response. Before the Quarterly Meeting had passed, it was manifest that a glorious revival was impending. Seekers of religion came to the Altar and found a prepared Church to lead them to Christ. The meeting went on from night to night, and before the end of the week, each night brought scores of seekers. The good Pastor was now at home. In prayer, in exhortation, and in labor at the side of the seeker, he was a tower of strength. Among the laity there were also several excellent laborers, who rendered valuable services in the meeting. The revival reached all classes, from youth to old age, and gave to the Church many reliable accessions. At the beginning, sister Churches joined largely in the meeting, but as the work extended among their people, they opened meetings at their own places of worship. The change, however, did not check the revival. It swept on through the community, and all the Churches shared in the harvest of souls.

During this year Sheboygan was also favored with a revival. Rev. N.J. Aplin, the Pastor, came to Wisconsin during the previous year. He came from Western New York, where he had been engaged in business, bringing a note of introduction from Rev. Moses Miller, my uncle, who had been for several years his neighbor. I employed him at once, for the balance of the year, at Charlestown, a new charge that I had just formed. He was admitted on trial at the ensuing Conference, and appointed to Sheboygan.

After leaving Sheboygan, Brother Aplin's appointments have been: Manitowoc, Waukesha, Brookfield, Watertown, Beaver Dam, Oconomowoc, Berlin, Geneva, Sun Prairie, Sharon, and Clemensville. At the last named place, he is still rendering the cause effective service. Brother Aplin has been a successful man, and has seen, at various times, extensive revivals under his labors. He is a man who "seeks not his own but the things of Christ."

At Sheboygan he was assisted in his meeting by Fay H. Purdy, Esq., of Palmyra, N.Y., with whom he had enjoyed an acquaintance in the East. Brother Purdy had already become distinguished as the "Lawyer Evangelist." Under the united labors of these devoted and earnest men, there was a great quickening in the Church, and though the population of the town was largely German, there was an accession to the Church of forty members.

It was during this Conference year the celebrated Greenbush Camp Meeting was held. The meeting was held in June, 1854. The people came in great numbers, and many of them were fresh from their revivals at home. On invitation, Brother Purdy came to the meeting and brought with him, from Western New York, Rev. Amos Hard, Seth H. Woodruff, Esq., and several others. The meeting was one of great power. Large numbers of professing Christians entered into a new consecration to God, and many souls professed conversion. Throughout the week, the meetings continued to increase in spiritual interest, but culminated in the services of Sunday night. After the close of the sermon, seekers were invited to the Altar. Then followed prayers, singing, and Christian testimony without intermission, until the morning light broke upon the encampment. The prayers of the penitent and the shouts of the saved greeted every hour of the night. The voices of prayer and song did not cease until the meeting was closed on Monday.

Nor did the formal closing of the services in the grove close the meeting. It was now adjourned to the school house in the village, where the services were continued with unflagging interest. But there now came an interchange of labor. Whenever it was necessary to look after domestic affairs, the meeting was left in the hands of others, and on returning its duties were again resumed. Thus by these changes there was no cessation of the meeting throughout Monday, Monday night, and a portion of the following day. This meeting is still referred to with great interest by those who were permitted to participate in its thrilling exercises.

The Pastor of Greenbush at this time was Rev. A.M. Hulce. He was a young man in the work, having been received into the Conference at its last session. Both himself and good lady were fully engaged in the work, and greatly assisted in perfecting the arrangements for the meeting. Brother Hulce was a well-read man, a good thinker, and earnestly devoted to his work, but his health was not equal to the toil and exposures of the Itinerancy. After laboring a few years he was compelled to retire to the local ranks, in which position he still holds an honorable place.

Other charges than those mentioned also shared in the revivals of the year, giving a net result for the District of nearly one thousand conversions. My labors throughout the year were severe, making an average of nearly seven sermons per week.

The Conference for 1854 was held at Janesville, and I was returned to the District for a fourth year. Several changes of Ministers were made, several new fields were opened, and six new men were brought into the District.

Omro was one of the charges to claim my attention at the beginning of this year. It had now assumed considerable importance, it being the home of the Brother Cowhams. James M., the elder, was the Recording Steward, ranking among the most efficient I have ever known, and John M., the younger, was a leading spirit in all Church work, becoming subsequently a Local Preacher of most excellent standing.

The Pastor of the charge was Rev. T.C. Golden, who entered the Conference in 1850, and had been stationed at Cascade and Sheboygan Falls. He was a man of mark. Of a vigorous mental development and logical cast, he early became an able Preacher and commanded a leading place in the Conference. After leaving Omro, he was stationed in Fond du Lac. He was then transferred to the West Wisconsin Conference, and stationed at La Crosse, after which he served several years as Presiding Elder with great acceptability. At the present writing he is a Presiding Elder in the Upper Iowa Conference. Dr. Golden, for such is his present title, has made a most gratifying record.

A Quarterly Meeting held at Brother John M. Cowham's during this year, is remembered with great pleasure. This dear Brother had built both a house and a barn of large dimensions, and the meeting, to be held in the latter, awakened general interest throughout the circuit, bringing together a multitude of people. Every house in the neighborhood was filled with guests, and the balance, not less than fifty in number, were entertained at what was called the Cowham Mansion. But great as was the outpouring of the people, the manifestations of the Spirit were still more extraordinary. Under the preaching of the Word, the Holy Ghost fell on the people. The shout of redeemed souls and the cry of penitents, "What shall I do to be saved?" commingled strangely together. And yet, out of the apparent discord, there came the sweetest harmony. The minor strains were lost in the rapturous paeans of the major movement, as each seeking soul received "the new song." The days of the Fathers seemed to have returned to the Church, when, under the Pentecostal baptism, believers fell to the floor, and multitudes were saved in a day.

It was during this year that I was called to experience a severe trial in the death of my dear father, which occurred on the 30th day of May, 1855. After remaining at Waupun six years, he removed, in 1850, to Waupaca, where he purchased the lands comprising the site of the present village, laid out the town and erected a lumber mill. Soon after his arrival he opened religious services, preaching the first sermon and organizing the first class. In due time, others came to his assistance, and a small Church was built. Waupaca having been taken into the regular work, my father now visited the adjacent neighborhoods and established religious meetings, preaching usually two or three times on the Sabbath. Not a few of these early appointments ultimately became the nucleus of independent charges.

My father's illness was brief. In the latter part of the winter he met me at my Quarterly Meeting at Oshkosh, but, to the regret of the people, he was unable to preach. He felt that his work was nearly done, and in referring to the matter, said: "I have no occasion to feel anxious about it, since, through Divine help, I have been permitted to preach, on an average, about two sermons a week for thirty years." I visited him two weeks before his death, and found his mind tranquil and his Faith unwavering. When I enquired as to his state of mind, he said, "It is like a sunbeam of glory." He continued in the same satisfactory frame, until he passed over the river to join the white-robed throng in the Heavenly realm. The multitudes who gathered with tearful eyes around his grave, gave but a fitting expression of their high appreciation of a noble life.

The labors of my first term as Presiding Elder were now drawing to a close. Though my labors had been arduous, yet such had been the kindness and co-operation of both Preachers and people, I felt an interest in them. During the four years the District had nearly doubled its strength, and was now ready for a division.

Feeling that it was due to myself, being so young a man, and due to the Church also, that I should now go back to station work, I favored at the Conference a resolution asking the Bishop to appoint no man to a District for a second term until there had been an intervening service of two years on circuits or stations. The action of the Conference doubtless, sent me to a station instead of a District.

CHAPTER XVI

The Conference for 1855 was held at Racine on the 29th day of August, and was presided over by Bishop Janes. During the session I was quartered with Rev. Moses Adams, a superannuated member of the Black River Conference.

The business of the Conference was transacted with the usual dispatch, and there were only two items which engrossed unusual attention. These were the distribution of the missionary appropriations and the election of delegates to the General Conference.

As to the first, a new departure was made in the organization of the Committee on Missions. The Presiding Elders of the Conference had been hitherto appointed on this Committee. But now a few restless spirits, who fancied that, as seen from their limited opportunities to judge correctly, the appropriations had not been judiciously made during the past few years, determined to appoint this Committee from among the Pastors. The Elders, well knowing that the farcical proceeding would in time come to naught, concluded to offer no opposition to the movement. The Committee was accordingly appointed and proceeded to the discharge of its duties. At the first meeting, however, it was found that the Committee was unable to proceed for want of information. At the next meeting, to remedy this difficulty, the brethren who had occupied Mission fields the previous year were invited to be present. This measure was found to afford only a partial relief, as these brethren knew nothing of the border territory that ought now to be organized into new fields. The next move was to ask all the Pastors to meet the Committee at the next session. To afford room to accommodate the Committee and its invited guests, the audience room of the Church was appropriated for an entire afternoon. Here the great work of the Committee was entered upon in right good earnest, with the special champions of the movement as managers of the exhibition.

But now, alas! for the success of the meeting, there was too much light. At once a large number of fields that had been supposed to be self-supporting was brought forward, and their respective representatives were so successful in setting forth their feeble and helpless condition, that many of them were entered upon the list by the Committee as Missions. The question as to the number of Missions having been settled, the next thing in order was the amount of money that should be given to each.

From the information already received, the amounts were jotted down briskly until the entire list had been gone over. The footings were now made, and to the Committee the result was appalling. They had appropriated three times the amount of money at their disposal. Then came the rub, which had been so often experienced by the Presiding Elders. The Missions must be cut down in two ways. First, all that could possibly manage to get through the year without aid must be struck off the list, and then such as remain will need to be cut down to the lowest possible figure. But still brave, our Committee would not see their impending defeat, and proceeded at once to the labor of cutting down.

One of the champions had been a surgeon in his time, and had cut human flesh with becoming recklessness, but now he, as well as the entire Committee, struck a new experience. To strike Missions off the list, and cut down the appropriations to others, is comparatively an easy task in the quiet and secluded confines of a committee room, but to do either in the presence of the very men who expected to occupy those fields the coming year, and who knew the poverty of the people, was quite another thing. The flood-gates of speech-making had been opened by the Committee, and it was now impossible to close them. The balance of the afternoon was given to stormy debate, and into what disorder the meeting might have drifted, if the coming evening had not made its appearance, it is impossible to conjecture.

The next day the Committee took another new departure, and invited the Presiding Elders, who had studied these matters and looked the ground carefully over for a whole year, before them. The Committee were now able to complete their labors and make such a report as had usually been presented to the Conference. But the Conference became fully satisfied that this experiment needed no duplicate, and, for years after, the mention of the "Committee of the Whole on Missions," did not fail to excite mirth.

Early in the session, the election of delegates to the General Conference occurred. As I was too young to be thought of in that connection, I was permitted to sit quietly and take notes. The only issue of any great importance in the election was the slavery question. And as this institution had already been put in issue in the general elections of the country, it could not well be left out on this occasion. So it was made the chief subject of discussion. To be a thorough-going anti-slavery man was the stubborn test of qualifications for a delegate. And that there might be no mistake on this point, it was deemed advisable to have an able committee present to the body as a platform a report that should make the absolute prohibition of slavery its chief plank. But before I make further reference to the report it will not be amiss to refer briefly to the subject of slavery in its relations to the Church.

At the organization of the Church in this country, and for years thereafter, the testimony she gave against American Slavery was distinct and unequivocal. Both the Ministers and people were agreed that the Institution was, as Mr. Wesley was pleased to call it, "The sum of all villanies." Agreeing in this, they further believed that, as a relic of barbarism, it would soon pass away. Under this conviction they hardly deemed it necessary to enter up any very stringent enactments against it, save that it might be well as a temporary arrangement to provide that there should be no traffic in slaves. Under such a regulation matters passed on for a term of years. But in due time it was found that the tendency of events was not altogether satisfactory.

At the outset, the Church had been planted in the central portion of the Atlantic States, and had then grown rapidly southward, giving the balance of power to the Conferences where slavery existed. At this juncture, also, by a remarkable change in the commercial affairs of the country, the cotton crop of the South began to find an increasing demand and appreciate in value, thereby giving an increased value to slave labor. With this change came at once the multiplication of slaves and large returns. To own slaves and cultivate cotton now became the ruling inspiration of the people.

At the first the Church stoutly opposed the insetting tide, but as the waves of commercial life grew strong and swept around her, the power of resistance grew more feeble from year to year, until finally some of her own people began to plead extenuation and even tolerance. The conflict was now open, and the result seemed questionable. With the conscience of the Southern portion of the Church asleep or dormant, the anti-slavery side of the issue came finally to depend upon the Church in the North for statement and defence.

At this stage of the conflict the controversy became sectional, the South upholding and the North seeking to remove the evil. Thus the contest raged for years, until the South, growing strong on her ill-gotten gains, and arrogant from her success with the supple-kneed politicians of the North, put the Church in the North upon the defensive by demanding toleration, if not actual adoption. The issue was made in trying to foist upon the whole Church a slave holding Episcopacy. This last act was the feather, if such it might be called, that broke the camel's back.

The effort was thwarted by the North only through the timely aid of a few of the Central Conferences. At this the South took offence, as is well known, and seceded, carrying with them more than half a million of members and a portion of the Church property. To secure the latter, it is true, long and bitter litigations followed the separation. And it is generally accepted in the North that the decision which gave it to the South took its shape from the political complexion at the time of the Supreme Court of the United States.

It was now thought that the question of slavery was put to rest. But alas! for human foresight. It still remained that the General Rules, which permitted members to hold slaves, provided they did not "buy or sell," had not been changed. And it was soon found that the awakened conscience of the North could not rest until the last vestige of the nefarious institution was swept from the Church. Agitations, therefore, followed, and each succeeding General Conference found this question to be still the troubler of Israel. Nor was the question left alone to the care of the General Conference. Each annual Conference was also agitated by it.

But it was evident to all that a serious embarrassment must be overcome to secure a change of the General Rules. The Constitution of the Church has a provision which, to effect a change, requires a two-thirds vote in the General Conference, and a three-fourths vote in all the Annual Conferences. To obtain the requisite vote with these provisions, it will be seen, can only be realized on such questions as can command great unanimity of sentiment. If the entire South had gone off in the separation, the trouble would have been at an end, but, as we have seen, the border Conferences remained with their brethren of the North, and aided them in fighting the first battle with the slave power.

But now, when the question of a change of rule was brought forward, they took the other side, and in doing so were able to furnish enough votes to defeat the proposed measure. And the question, which was now agitating the Annual Conference, was the framing of such a rule as would meet the approval of the great body of the Church, and pass it along the line of the Conferences to secure their favorable consideration before taking it to the General Conference.

At the preceding session of the Wisconsin Conference such a rule had been framed and sent on its way to the several Conferences to obtain their approval. This was called the "Wisconsin Conference Rule," and read as follows: "The buying, selling, or holding of a human being as a slave." This rule received very general favor among the Northern Conferences, but was rejected of course by those lying along the border.

At the Conference now in session in Racine, as before stated, a report was submitted touching this matter. And it was intended to so set forth the sentiment of the Conference as to make it a test of eligibility in the election. I subjoin an extract from the resolutions adopted:

"*Resolved,* That we contemplate with feelings of deep humility and sorrow before God, that the M. E. Church has any connection with the system of American Slavery, and that we will not cease our efforts for extirpation until the last ligament is severed."

"*Resolved,* That we record with gratitude, the favor with which the 'New Rule,' proposed by our Conference at its last session, has met in so many of the Conferences in which it has been acted upon, and we believe that the principle involved in it is the standard at which the Church should and will soon arrive."

"*Resolved,* That whether or not the next General Conference adopt it as a substitute for our present General Rule on Slavery, we earnestly request that body to so modify the Chapter on Slavery as to prevent the admission of any slaveholder into the M. E. Church, and secure the exclusion of all who are now members, if they will not, after due labor, emancipate their slaves."

This report was adopted with remarkable unanimity, but when the vote was taken for delegates, it so happened that at least two of the men who had been most clamorous in its support, failed to secure an election. This result, however, did not come from a real difference in sentiment on the main question, but from a desire to send to the General Conference a delegation that would not defeat the desired end by a manifestation of zeal without prudence. The Chairman of the Committee, however, was elected to lead the delegation. The Delegates were P. S. Bennett, I. M. Leihy, Edward Cooke, Elmore Yocum and Chauncey Hobart.

During the session of the Conference, a meeting of the principal members of the Church and congregation at Racine was held, to take into consideration the condition and wants of the charge. The deliberation had resulted in laying before the Presiding Bishop a request for the appointment of the writer. The appointment was accordingly made. But a removal to the charge was attended with no little difficulty.

During the latter part of the spring term of the Lawrence University, the typhoid fever appeared among the students, and in several instances proved fatal. To prevent the like result in other cases, the inhabitants opened their doors to receive sick students who could not be suitably cared for in the dormitories of the College. Four of these were taken by Mrs. Miller, and, in every case, it was believed that their lives were only saved through her kind intervention and care. This kindness to others, however, proved disastrous to her and the family. Before her charge was well off her hands, she was herself attacked by the same malignant disease. Then followed weeks of suffering on her part, and not a little interruption of my work as Presiding Elder, especially unfortunate in the closing part of the year. She passed down to the borders of the grave, and on two occasions the beating of the pulse seemed to cease, but in the good providence of God she was spared. Her return to health, however, was slow, and meantime her sister, now Mrs. Gov. C. K. Davis, of Minnesota, who resided with us at the time, was taken with the same disease. This latter case was also a severe one, and for several weeks delayed our removal to the new charge. But as soon as it would do to attempt the journey, we were on our way. Unable to walk, I was obliged to carry the invalid from the house to the carriage, and from the carriage at Menasha to the steamboat. We reached Fond du Lac in the evening and tarried for the night. The following morning we took the stage for Sheboygan. The roads were excellent and the coach comfortable, but it was necessary to carry the invalid literally in my arms the entire distance. On arriving at the shore end of the pier at Sheboygan, the steamboat, at the other end, gave a signal for her departure. Hastily leaving the coach and sending the family forward with all possible dispatch, I chartered a common dray, the only conveyance at hand, placed a trunk upon it, took the invalid in my arms, seated myself on the trunk, and bade the driver to put his horse on his best speed. The race was a most creditable one, and before the boat had time to get under way, we were nicely on board, to the great merriment of all concerned.

But out of one trouble, we were soon into another. We had hardly reached the open lake before the boat encountered a heavy sea, which brought sea-sickness to all of the company for the balance of the journey. But in this misfortune we were not alone. Rev. E. S. Grumley, the newly appointed Presiding Elder of the Racine District, and his family, had also come on board at Sheboygan, and were now our companions in travel, as also in misery. Tossing amid the waves, the progress of the steamboat was slow, and we did not reach Racine until after midnight. We were happy to gain a landing, but we found ourselves without a conveyance to the hotel. Not even the common dray was at hand. But, nothing daunted, we groped amid the darkness until we came upon the buggy of the Presiding Elder, which fortunately had been landed from the same boat. The invalid was soon placed in it, and, adopting a style of travel that might have seemed unusual by daylight, in due time we were at the hotel.

The following morning we were sought out by the good people and kindly cared for, being assigned to quarters with my late host and his obliging family.

CHAPTER XVII

The great centers from which the Church in Wisconsin has radiated were few in number and were fixed upon at an early period in the development of the work. These centers were Green Bay, Sheboygan, Fond du Lac, Aztalan, Racine, and Janesville. Of the first five a record has been made, and, following the line of my labors, Racine should next engage my attention.

At this place the first settlement was made in November, 1834, by Captain Gilbert Knapp, who came on horseback from Chicago. On the second day of January following, Stephen Campbell, Paul Kingston, and Messrs. Newton and Fay arrived, and, as far as I am able to ascertain, were the first Methodists who settled at Racine. At the same time William See and Edmund Weed came to the vicinity, the former settling at the Rapids, where he built a mill, and the latter making a claim on the lands which have since become the homestead of Senator Fratt. Alanson Filer came in November, 1835, and A.G. Knight in April, 1836. In his journey to Wisconsin, Brother Knight traveled on horseback from Wayne County, N.Y., to Chicago, and on foot the balance of the way. Jonathan M. Snow and Nathan Joy came soon after, the latter coming around the lakes in the first three-master that visited Lake Michigan. Rev. Daniel Slauson and William Bull came in September, 1837, traveling in their own conveyance from Detroit. The list of names thus given does not make a full record of the early arrivals, but furnishes, as far as I am informed, such as constituted, with the exception of the first named, the first Methodist Community.

The writer has been unable to ascertain where and by whom the first class was formed, or who constituted the first members. But it is probable that the place was included in Milwaukee Mission as early as 1835, and that the class was formed by Rev. Mark Robinson during that year, or by his successor, Rev. Wm. S. Crissey, the year following. And it is also probable that the gentlemen above named, who were there at the time, and their families, constituted the first members, with Brother Paul Kingston as Leader. The meetings were held in the log residence of the last named, located near the lake, at the foot of Seventh street.

Racine Mission was formed in 1837 and Rev. Otis F. Curtis was the first Pastor. The Mission, reaching from the Illinois State Line to Milwaukee, included appointments at Racine, Southport, Pleasant Prairie, Kellogg's Corners, Ives Grove, Caledonia and Root River.

In 1839 the charge took the name of Racine and Southport Mission, the Pastor being Rev. Salmon Stebbins. In 1840 Southport was made a separate charge, and the Pastor at Racine was Rev. L.F. Moulthrop. In 1841 the Root River portion was set off and made a separate charge, and Racine was left to be supplied. The following year the Sylvania circuit was formed, and Southport and Racine were again put together, with Rev. James Mitchell as Pastor. In 1843 they were again separated, and the Pastor at Racine was Rev. Milton Bourne. In 1844 the Pastor was Rev. G. L. S. Stuff, and in 1845, Rev. Julius Field.

As before stated, the meetings were at first held in a private house, but as the congregations increased, a public building was rented near the foot of Main Street. After the school house was built, the meetings were removed to it, and it was at this latter place the writer attended a service during his first Sabbath in the State. Soon after the first Church was built, to which we shall have occasion to refer hereafter.

Racine District was created in 1847, and Rev. Chauncey Hobart was appointed the first Presiding Elder. Dr. Hobart entered the Illinois Conference in 1836, the Conference then including Illinois, Wisconsin, Iowa and Minnesota. His appointments before coming to the District had been: Rockingham, Iowa, Monmouth, Macomb, Quincy, Rushville, Peoria, Jacksonville, Springfield, and Clark Street, Chicago. After leaving the District, in 1849, he was appointed Presiding Elder of Minnesota District. At the end of his term he was stationed at Spring Street, Milwaukee, and next served one year as Presiding Elder on the Milwaukee District, when, on account of the infirm health of his wife, he returned to Minnesota. Since his return, he has continued to labor on both stations and districts with great acceptability up to the present time.

Dr. Hobart is a man of superior abilities, and his labors have been in special demand. He has been elected five times to the General Conference, and has been seven times appointed to Districts. As a Preacher he is always acceptable, but at times he delivers extraordinary sermons. It requires a great occasion to take the full measure of the man. At such times he has been known to move audiences with overwhelming power. Especially was this the case under the sermon he delivered at a Camp-Meeting held two miles west of Big Foot Prairie, in 1849. On this occasion the tide of feeling rose to such a height that great numbers of the congregation unconsciously left their seats and stood entranced, while the saints shouted for joy, and sinners cried out in the anguish of their souls for mercy.

Having thus spoken of the Presiding Elder of the Racine District, it is fitting that we should now glance briefly at a few of the early charges.

Kenosha, as we have seen, was included in the Racine Mission in 1837, and shared the labors of Brother Curtis. The first class was formed during this term probably by either the Pastor or Rev. John Clark, the Presiding Elder, and consisted of Rev. Reuben H. Deming, Austin Kellogg, Hon. and Mrs. Charles Durkee, Mrs. Harvey Durkee, John W. Dana Martha E. Dana, and Susan Dana. The Presiding Elder, Rev. Salmon Stebbins, held a Quarterly Meeting in Kenosha, then called Southport, November 24th, 1837. The meeting was held in a small log school house standing near the present site of the Simmons Block.

During the following year a revival occurred, which resulted in the conversion of nearly the entire community. The meetings were held in a public building on the North Side, but the erection of a Church immediately followed. As before stated, Brother Stebbins became the Pastor in 1839, and remained also the following year. The succeeding Pastors up to 1845 were Rev. F.T. Mitchell, Rev. James Mitchell, Rev. Wm. H. Sampson, Rev. C.D. Cahoon and Rev. Warner Oliver. At this writing, Kenosha ranks among the leading stations of the Conference.

Brother Stebbins entered the New York Conference in 1822. When the Conference was divided he fell into the northern portion, which took the name of Troy. In this field he labored fourteen years, his charges covering the territory from Albany to the Canada line. At the solicitation of Rev. John Clark, he was transferred to the Illinois Conference in 1837, and appointed Presiding Elder, the District extending from the Illinois State Line to Green Bay. In 1839 he was appointed to the Racine and Southport Mission, as before stated, and remained on the Southport part the following year. After leaving Southport charge he was stationed at Platteville, Lake, Madison and St. Charles. Subsequently taking a location, he became a resident of Kenosha, in the vicinity of which place he still resides.

Brother Stebbins is a man of superior ability, and in his prime enjoyed considerable reputation as a Preacher. He is spending the evening of his life in quiet, trustingly awaiting the change that now cannot be long delayed.

Sylvania was settled by three Kellogg brothers and their families in the spring of 1837, the place being first known as Kellogg's Corners. Soon after their arrival the ladies, one of whom, Mrs. Seth H. Kellogg, was the daughter of Rev. Ebenezer Washburn, of New York Conference, organized a Sunday School. The neighborhood was connected with the Racine Mission, and a class was formed at an early period, with Seth H. Kellogg as Leader, but I cannot fix the exact date. Nor am I able to state at what time the first Church was completed. It was claimed, however, to have taken precedence in the State.

In the erection of the Church, which was built by Chauncey Kellogg, the young society was assisted by a donation of two hundred dollars from Sunday Schools in New York City. Rev. Julius Field, whose wife was a sister of the Kelloggs, secured the aid, he having been stationed in that city. The Church edifice cost six hundred dollars, and was the building in which I preached the funeral sermon of Mother Washburn some sixteen years later. The veteran, Father Washburn, was also buried at this place. Sylvania was made a separate charge in 1842, with Rev. Milton Bourne as Pastor.

Passing westward, the old Walworth circuit should next claim our attention. It will be remembered that this charge was formed in 1839, taking the south half of the old Aztalan circuit. The first Pastor was Rev. James McKean, who was an earnest and devoted laborer in the vineyard. But as his fields fell on the south side of the State Line at the end of his term, a record will doubtless be made of him elsewhere.

In 1840 the circuit was divided. The southeastern portion was called Burlington and Rochester, with Rev. David Worthington as Pastor, of whom a record has been made in a former chapter, and the name of the old charge was changed to Troy, on which Brother McKean remained as Pastor.

On the new charge there were two classes formed by Brother Worthington during this year. The first was formed in Puffer's school house on Spring Prairie in the summer of 1840, and included in its membership, Mr. and Mrs. John M. Cowham, Lansing Lewis, and Mrs. Lewis, his mother. Brother Cowham was the Leader.

The other class was organized in Lyonsdale, with Mr. and Mrs. Thomas Lyon, Mr. and Mrs. Fletcher Lyon, Mr. and Mrs. Ansel Waite, Mr. and Mrs. Marshall, and Mrs. Jones. Hon. Wm. P. Lyon, of the Supreme Court, subsequently became identified with the Society. Lyons, as the village is called, is at the present writing a charge of respectable standing, having a good Church and Parsonage. The writer had the pleasure to dedicate the Church during his Pastorate in Racine.

At Troy, a class had been organized by Brother McKean during the latter part of the former year. At this time the members were Daniel Griffin, Sen., Daniel Griffin, Jr., Dr. and Mrs. Brooks Bowman, Mrs. McCracken, Mr. and Mrs. John Spoor, and a Brother Jennings. Brother Spoor was a Local Preacher, the Leader and the S.S. Superintendent.

In 1841, Rev. L.F. Moulthrop was appointed to Troy circuit. He remained the second year and had as a colleague the excellent Rev. Henry Whitehead, so long and well known by the Preachers of the Northwest in connection with the Chicago Book Depository. The circuit at this time included Troy, Eagle, Hart Prairie, Round Prairie, Turtle Prairie, Delavan and Elkhorn.

At Eagle a class was formed consisting of Rev. William Cross, Local Preacher, Mrs. William Cross, and her sister, now Mrs. James Parsons, Mr. and Mrs. A. Hinkley, Mr. and Mrs. Thomas, Mr. and Mrs. Atwater, Mr. and Mrs. Long.

At Round Prairie a class was also formed. The members as far as ascertained were Rev. James Flanders, Local Preacher, Mr. and Mrs. Houghton, Mrs. Norcross, Father Cornice, and Mr. and Mrs. Nelson Cornice.

At Hart Prairie, the services were held in Father Worthington's log house, where a class was also organized. Father Worthington, his wife, and two sons, Elijah and Theodore, and Mrs. Lewis, were the first members.

At Delavan the meetings were held alternately in Mr. Bradway's log house in the village, and at the residence of Mr. Phoenix, on the prairie. The class at this place was small, and I am unable to insert in the record more than the names of Mr. and Mrs. Bradway. Delavan has since grown to the position of an influential charge, with an attractive Church and enterprising membership.

Elkhorn at this early day had no class, but, as the County Seat, the village commanded an appointment. For several years the cause moved slowly, but finally won its way to a position. At the present writing, the charge holds a respectable rank in the Conference.

Having thus briefly examined the early history of Racine and the other charges that constituted her immediate surroundings, it is now proper that we should return to the record of the writer's Pastorate.

Finding that there was no Parsonage, I proceeded to rent a respectable house in a pleasant part of the city, paying for the same an additional one hundred dollars out of my salary. Having settled my family, I adopted my usual method of devoting my mornings to my study, and afternoons to pastoral visiting. I soon passed over the entire membership of the station, making it a special point to secure, as far as possible, a faithful attendance upon the means of grace. The effort was successful beyond my expectations.

The congregation soon filled the Church. And as the interest continued to increase, the aisles and doors were thronged, while large numbers were utterly unable to obtain admission. With this manifestation of interest, it was deemed advisable to enter upon a protracted meeting without delay. We did so, and I preached every night for two weeks. But the result was not satisfactory. We found the spiritual condition was not on a plane with the demands of the work. The vast throng of people had brought upon us a tide of worldly influence that we were unable to withstand. Additional moral force was necessary, and, to secure it, we deemed it better to go into the lecture-room and rely upon the social meetings to develop the requisite spiritual power. With this change there came to the membership the spirit of consecration and a remarkable baptism of the Holy Ghost. Before the end of two weeks we were compelled to return to the audience room. The place was again thronged with people, but the good work went forward. I continued to preach nightly for four weeks. One hundred persons were converted and added to the Church.

With this large increase of members and a corresponding increase of attendants, it was necessary to enlarge the Church edifice for their accommodation. Accordingly the work was undertaken. The rear end of the building was opened, and the edifice was lengthened so as to accommodate nearly one-third more people. In doing this, it was thought advisable to still increase the length by adding twelve feet more for an orchestra, thereby providing for the removal of the organ from the gallery to the rear of the pulpit.

The enlargement, besides furnishing the necessary accommodations for the people, laid a broader financial basis to the charge, by bringing into the congregation a number of families who were able to take the new seats at a good rental. The year passed very satisfactorily.

The Conference of 1856 was held September 17th, at Appleton, Bishop Simpson presiding. As expected, we were returned to Racine. We retained the same house, and found our social relations with the people of Racine exceedingly pleasant. With not a few families a life-long friendship was established, and to the present hour the mention of Racine revives many pleasant recollections. Judge Lyon, who came into the Church this year, and his good lady, and Messrs. Knight, Yout, Adams, Langlois, Jones, Lunn, Slauson, Bull, Lees, Conroe, Kidder, Orr, Jillson, Brewer, Lawrence, with their families, and many others, will never be forgotten.

The labors of the year would afford many pleasing incidents were they permitted to appear in these pages, but their recital would unreasonably swell the volume.

The usual protracted meeting was held, continuing five weeks. The work was very satisfactory, strengthening the converts of the previous year, and swelling the list of accessions. The revival was especially fruitful in the Sunday School, leading many of the young people to Christ. But the labors of the year, as usual, came to a close when we were in the midst of our work, and we were compelled to sunder old associations and form new ones in other fields.

CHAPTER XVIII

The Conference for 1857 was held June 26th, at Spring Street, Milwaukee, Bishop Ames presiding. At this Conference I was stationed at Janesville.

Janesville, holding a central position in the southern portion of the State, was the initial point of settlement at an early period, and in after years, became the focal as well as the radiation center of Church operations.

On the 15th day of November, 1835, a company consisting of six men started from Milwaukee with an ox-team and wagon, the latter containing provisions, tools, etc., for the Rock River Valley. On the 18th they arrived where Janesville now stands, and immediately proceeded to build a log cabin opposite of what is called the "Big Rock." This was the first settlement in Rock River Valley. Two of their number, however, had explored the southern portion of the Territory in the preceding July. At that time there were but two white families in Milwaukee, and only one between that place and Janesville, that of Mr. McMillen, who lived at what is now called Waukesha.

On the 23d of April, 1837, the first United States Mail entered Janesville. It contained one letter, and this was for the Postmaster, Henry F. Janes. The mail was brought by a man on horseback, whose mail route extended from Mineral Point to Racine. The post-office at Janesville for several months consisted of a cigar box, which was fastened to a log in the bar-room. Small as it was, it was found to be amply sufficient to contain all the letters then received by the citizens of Rock County.

The first sermon preached in Janesville was delivered by Rev. Jesse Halstead in September, 1837. Brother Halstead, then on Aztalan circuit, on coming to this place found a small log house, which enjoyed the appellation of a tavern. He accepted entertainment in common with other travelers, but, it being soon known that he was a Minister, he was invited to preach. He consented, and the services were held in the bar-room. The liquors were put out of sight, and the Minister made the bar his pulpit. The audience consisted of a dozen persons.

The next religious services of which I can obtain information, were held in the summer of 1838. They were held in an oak grove on one of the bluffs east of the village. I am not able to find any one who can furnish me the name of the Preacher, but am assured that he was a Methodist, and that he did not neglect that special feature of a Methodist service, the collection. This last part of the exercises, I am assured, made a vivid impression on the mind of the party to whom I am indebted for this item of history. And it came in this wise: When the hat was passed he threw in a bill, an act so generous that it could not fail to call attention to the contributor. The next day he received a call from the Minister, who desired him to replace the "wild-cat" bill by one of more respectable currency, as those kind of bills were beginning to be refused throughout the Territory.

In 1839 Rev. James F. Flanders made an occasional visit to Janesville and preached to the people. His first sermon was delivered in the bar-room of the public house, which stood on the present site of the Myers House. Subsequently he preached in an unoccupied log house opposite where Lappin's Block now stands. The services were next held in school houses, some log and others frame, until the erection of the Court House in 1842. Thereafter the court room was occupied and used alternately by the different religious denominations.

The Rev. James McKean was the first Minister who preached regularly in Janesville. The place was taken into the Troy circuit in 1840, and Brother McKean visited it once in four weeks. This year Rev. Julius Field held the first Quarterly Meeting in Janesville.

In the spring of 1841, Brother McKean formed a class and appointed J.P. Wheeler Leader, but during the following winter the members all left the place.

Janesville appears first in the Minutes as the head of a charge in 1841, with Rev. Alpha Warren as Pastor. At this time it was connected with Platteville District, and the Presiding Elder was Rev. H.W. Reed. Brother Warren was succeeded by Rev. Boyd Phelps, who organized a class in the spring of 1843, consisting of nine or ten members, with John Wynn as Leader.

Rev. Lyman Catlin, who came in 1844, was the first resident Pastor. He was formerly a Professor in Mt. Morris Seminary. During the winter his wife, who was a lady of fine culture, taught a select school in the village. Brother Catlin preached in Janesville on the morning of each Sabbath, and in the afternoon alternated between Union and Johnstown.

The following year, Rev. T.W. Perkins was appointed to the charge, but in consequence of ill health, he was soon obliged to resign. His place was supplied by Rev. Stephen Adams, of Beloit. In 1846 Rev. John Luccock was the Pastor, and was followed the next year by Rev. Wesley Lattin, who remained two years. Brother Lattin was very popular with all classes, and his labors were blessed with an extensive revival. During his Pastorate the Society erected a small frame church, 35 by 25 feet in size. It was opened for worship in the fall of 1848. The location was on the opposite side of Centre Street, and a little west of the present edifice. A Parsonage was also erected the same year. Both of them, however, were sold when the grounds were purchased for the new Church. It was during the Pastorate of Brother Lattin that the first donation party ever held in Janesville, was given. The company assembled at the residence of Mr. and Mrs. John Wynn, where Brother Lattin boarded. The ladies furnished the table with all the luxuries the village afforded, and the affair was considered a grand success.

Brother Lattin was followed successively by Revs. J.M. Snow, O.F. Comfort, and Daniel Stansbury. During the winter of 1852 Brother Stansbury held a series of meetings, assisted by Rev. C.C. Mason, which resulted in a considerable addition to the membership of the Church.

Finding that the little Church was now becoming too small to accommodate them, the Society decided to build a more commodious house of worship. It was commenced in the spring following, and was located on the corner of Jackson and Centre Streets. This is the edifice now occupied by the first charge, is built of brick, and is 75 by 45 feet in size. The building was not fully completed until during the Pastorate of Rev. Henry Requa, in 1855, but it was so far advanced that it was dedicated in July, 1853, by the pioneer veteran, Rev. John Clark, of the Rock River Conference.

The severe labors of Brother Stansbury overtaxed his strength, and he was compelled to seek rest. Brother Mason was employed to fill out the balance of the year. Brother Mason was a Local Preacher from England, had lost one limb, and though somewhat eccentric, he held a high rank as a pulpit orator. He was often not a little surprised with the queer ways of this country. I remember to have met him at the Janesville Conference several years later. He was put up to preach, as usual on all great occasions, and delivered a grand sermon. The following evening the Missionary Anniversary came, and at the close of the speeches, the meeting proceeded to constitute Life Memberships. This was a new role to the old gentleman, but, soon comprehending the movement, he launched into it with all his soul. The good Bishop was made a Life Member, then his wife, then the Missionary Secretary, and so on in a spirited manner. As each proposition was made, the good brother planked his dollar, little dreaming of the length of the road upon which he had entered. But as the memberships were multiplied, his purse fell under the law of subtraction, until it contained but one dollar more. Just at this moment some zealous brother proposed to be one of ten to make the Presiding Elder of the Janesville District a Life

Member of the Conference Missionary Society. It was no time for parley about that remaining dollar, for the Janesville District must not be outdone by the other Districts in gallantry, so down went the last dollar. But it had hardly reached the table before the giver was hunting for his crutches. Such was the generous nature of the man, however, that he would have stood his ground to the coming of the morning if he had been advised in advance of the character of the Anniversary exercises.

In 1853 Rev. J.W. Wood was stationed at Janesville, and Rev. Henry Requa in 1854 and 1855. Brother Requa was very popular, drew large audiences, and realized an accession of fifty members. At the Conference of 1855 a new charge was formed on the east side of the river, and Rev. C.C. Mason, who had been received on trial, was appointed as its first Pastor.

In 1856, Rev. A. Hamilton was appointed to Janesville, and Rev. D.O. Jones to East Janesville. Brother Hamilton came to the Conference this year by transfer from the Oneida Conference, where he had done effective work for several years. At the close of the year in Janesville he was made Presiding Elder of Watertown District, where he remained two years. In 1859, by a reconstruction of the Districts, he was assigned to Beaver Dam District, where he remained the other two years of his term. For a number of years thereafter he served on circuits and stations. His health now failed and he took a superannuated relation. Brother Hamilton was a good and true man, of a metaphysical turn of thought, well versed in theology, and an instructive Preacher.

Brother Jones entered the Conference in 1851, and had been stationed at Elk Grove, Richland City, Muscoday, and Green Bay. Since he left Janesville, he has taken a respectable class of appointments, filling them creditably to himself and acceptably to the people. He is genial in spirit and warm in his attachments. He is still in the enjoyment of good health, and promises years of efficient service.

This brief record brings us to the date of my appointment. At the recent session of the Conference, the charge on the east side of the river was left to be supplied, and as it had, up to this time, developed but little strength, twenty-six members only, it was deemed best to let it go back to the old charge.

I found the Church edifice in good condition, but without class or prayer-rooms. The external appearance was decidedly respectable, and the accommodations within, both in respect to size and furnishing, equal or superior to any other Church in the village.

The Parsonage, a small and inferior building, had been recently sold to liquidate in part the indebtedness remaining on the Church, and this involved the necessity of renting a house for my family.

After becoming settled in our new home, the first special work was to complete the payment of the Church debt. This was soon arranged, and I was at liberty to direct my attention more particularly to the spiritual interests of the charge. My first labor in this direction, as in all my former charges, was to look well after the people at their homes, and the second, to see that the social means of grace were well arranged and properly sustained. And I soon found in Janesville, as I have always found, that they are the key to successful labor. It is possible by corresponding adjustment of pulpit labor to excite the attention of the community, and thereby secure large congregations, but such a result is not a certain index of true success. In the forum, as on the platform, it may be otherwise, but in the building up of Christ's kingdom, there must be a spiritual basis; for his kingdom is a spiritual kingdom. In these days of special clamor for superior pulpit attractions to draw the crowd, there is a strong temptation to court popular favor by adjusting both the themes and style of address to the pulpit in such a way as to withold from the people the only spiritual food that can give life to a dead soul. Such a Ministry in the eyes of the world may be deemed a great success, but to such as judge not after the outward appearance, it is known to be a dead failure. While it utterly fails to bring souls to Christ, it is also disastrous to the Church itself. The mighty adhesive forces, which bind the hearts of Christians to each other, can only subsist on the marrow of Gospel truth, and if this is wanting, dissension will soon appear, and the Church suffer disintegration. Holding these views, strengthened as they had been by my former experience and observation, I resolved, at whatever cost of reputation, to adhere to them in Janesville.

The result proved their wisdom. With the revival of the prayer and class meetings, and the utterance of plain Evangelical truth from the pulpit, came a speedy manifestation of spiritual interest and growth. And so marked had this indication of the presence of the Spirit become, that I felt justified in opening a protracted meeting with the watch-night services. The meeting grew in interest from night to night, and in a short time the Altar was filled with penitents. Thus opened a meeting that continued four months, resulting gloriously to the charge. Nearly three hundred persons professed to be converted, and near two hundred of them were received on probation.

During the meeting I preached nearly every night, and sometimes in the afternoons. But I was greatly assisted in the meeting by Revs. J.B. Cooper and I.S. Eldridge, of whom mention will be made in another chapter. Rev. A.B. Bishop, now a valuable member of Minnesota Conference, was also, though young, a good laborer in the meeting. Among the laymen who rendered special service was Brother J.L. Kimball, who, with his daughter Emily, had been for years the principal reliance in the singing, both in the choir and social meetings. Referring to this good brother brings up an incident of the meeting. Brother K. had long been recognized as the financial man and the singer of the Church, but could never take a part in the social services with any comfort to himself. In one of the meetings I suggested that in these matters as in others, practice would relieve the case. He concluded to try it, and for two weeks spoke a few words as opportunity offered. But he finally told the congregation that my recipe would not work. Others might be able to talk their way to Heaven, but he was satisfied that, as for himself, he would have to pay his way, if he ever got there. The pleasant remark seemed more in keeping, when it was remembered that he was always a generous contributor to every good cause.

While many of the converts were from among the young people, not a few were persons of mature years, and some of them in affluent circumstances. The large increase of members rendered it necessary to reconstruct the classes, but the want of class rooms retarded this branch of our work. Several of the classes were assigned to meet during the week at private houses, and four of them met in the audience room at the close of the morning service. By placing a class in each corner, with the understanding that when one of them commenced to sing, all the others should join, the plan worked very well. After the singing each class took up the thread where it had been dropped, and proceeded with the service. Usually the Pastor sat in the Altar to give the responses to the exercises of each as they seemed to require them. Sometimes not a little confusion occurred, but it was taken in good feeling by all, and the meetings were profitable.

We also organized meetings outside of the village. School houses and private dwellings were used for this purpose, and these meetings not only accommodated the people of the several neighborhoods adjacent to the village, but gave the needed religious employment to the Local Preachers and other members of the Church. The meetings were held in the afternoons of the Sabbath, and sometimes, to hold the plan in countenance, the Pastor himself would go out and deliver a sermon. At first it was feared by some of the good brethren that these side meetings would detract from the regular services of the Church, but the result proved that, on the contrary, they gave an increase of both interest and attendance. For the people, thus edified and interested, came into the village and thronged the Church.

But the year was now drawing to a close. By request of the preceding Conference, the Conference session had been changed to spring. The year had been one of severe labor, but its compensations were abundant. I was able to report a membership, including probationers, of three hundred and six. Two events in my own family clothed the year with special interest. The one, the conversion of our eldest daughter, then nine years old, and her reception into the church, the other, the birth of our son. They were both occasions of devout thanksgiving to God.

During this year I made a visit to Evansville, a charge that seems to hold a central position in the Conference west of Janesville. The first settlement was made in this vicinity in the fall of 1839, when six families came into what was then called the town of Union. These early settlers were Rev. Boyd Phelps, Rev. Stephen Jones, Erastus Quivey, Samuel Lewis, Charles McMillin, and John Rhineheart. During the winter and spring religious meetings were established in private houses, Rev. Boyd Phelps preaching the first sermon. In the following spring and summer, the settlement was enlarged by the arrival of Ira Jones, Jacob West, John T. Baker, Rev. John Griffith, Hiram Griffith, David Johnson, John Sale and their families. The heads of all these families being members of the Methodist Episcopal Church, they applied to Rev. Samuel Pillsbury, in charge of the Monroe circuit, for recognition. He visited them, established an appointment and formed them into a class in August, 1840. The class was organized at the residence of Hiram Griffith, located about one mile northwest of the present site of Evansville. At the first organization the members were: Jacob West, Leader, Margaret West, Boyd Phelps, Local Preacher, Clarissa Phelps, Stephen Jones, Local Preacher, Isabel Jones, John Griffith, Local Preacher, Belinda Griffith, John T. Baker, Jemima Baker, Ira Jones, Sarah J. Jones, John Rhineheart, Deborah Rhineheart, Alma Jones, Samuel Lewis, Sarah Lewis, Charles McMillan, Miriam McMillan, Jane Brown, Erastus Quivey, Sally Quivey, Hiram Griffith, Sally Griffith, David Johnson and Kizziah Johnson. Soon after John Sale and Jane Sale also became members.

Of this number, at least two became Itinerant Preachers. The first, Rev. Boyd Phelps, filled several appointments in the Conference, and was Presiding Elder of Beaver Dam District. He then removed to Minnesota, where he has also rendered effective service. The second, Rev. Stephen Jones, was my predecessor at Watertown, but only continued a few years, when he entered secular pursuits. At one time he was a member of the State Legislature.

Rev. James Ash was sent to the Monroe Circuit in 1840, and his work embraced Union. He remained two years, and was very successful in his work. The first Quarterly Meeting was held in the house of Brother Jacob West, by Rev. H.W. Reed, in the fall of 1840. In 1842 Union was attached to the Madison circuit, and the Pastor was Rev. S.P. Keyes. During this year a log school house was erected on the present site of Evansville, for the double purpose of school and religious meetings. This building was used for public worship until the summer of 1847. From 1843 to 1845 Union was connected with the Janesville circuit. In 1845 the Union circuit was formed, with Rev. Asa Wood as Pastor. It was assigned to the Platteville District, with Rev. Henry Summers as Presiding Elder.

Brother Summers was a veteran representative of the Methodist Preacher of the olden time. He entered the work when Illinois was yet in her maidenhood, and from the first was a recognized power in the land. Genial in spirit, full of anecdote, abundant in labors, an able Preacher, a faithful administrator, and a devoted servant of the Master, he enjoyed the esteem of all. But I need not enlarge, as doubtless a record will be made of his labors in Illinois, where his fields of labor were principally located.

Under the labors of Brother Wood, a frame church, 45 by 30 feet in size, was erected, the location being in the block now occupied by J. R. Finch as a store in the village of Evansville. The building was dedicated by Brother Summers in June, 1847. But it will be necessary to omit further details of these early years.

Old Union, the mother of charges west of Janesville, has been well represented in the Itinerant ranks. In addition to Brothers Phelps and Jones, to whom reference has been made, she has sent into the field Revs. James Lawson, J.H. Hazeltine, George Fellows, and A.A. Hoskins.

In 1855, Evansville Station was created, with Rev. E.P. Beecher as Pastor. The Janesville District was also established this year, with Rev. J.W. Wood as Presiding Elder.

Under the Pastorate of Rev. George W. De Lamatyr, which begin in 1864, the new Church was erected, costing some six thousand dollars. It was dedicated by Rev. Dr. Fallows in the fall of 1867. At the present writing Evansville is recognized as a charge of excellent standing.

The Conference of 1858 was held May 12th at Beloit, Bishop Morris presiding. At this Conference the writer was elected Secretary, and Revs. S. W. Ford and George Fellows Assistants. The session was brief and harmonious.

Beloit is located on the line between the States of Illinois and Wisconsin, and was at first connected with Roscoe Circuit, a charge lying on the Illinois side. The class was probably informally organized by Brother Thomas McElhenny, the first Leader, in 1839. The following year Rev. Milton Bourne, Pastor of Roscoe Circuit, established an appointment and recognized the infant Society. The members, besides Brother McElhenny, were Tyler Blodgett, Mrs. M.M. Moore and Sister Lusena Cheney. The Pastors of Roscoe Circuit, during its supervision of Beloit, in addition to Brother Bourne, were Revs. James McKean, O.W. Munger, John Hodges, Alpha Warren, and Zadoc Hall.

Beloit was made a separate charge in 1846, with Rev. Joseph T. Lewis as Pastor, to whom reference has been made in a former chapter. During this year the Society entered upon a Church enterprise. The lot was purchased by Rev. Stephen Adams and Brother Thomas McElhenny. The Society was feeble, and the erection of the building, a substantial stone structure, required a great effort and many sacrifices. To purchase the lime, three hundred and fifty bushels, Brother Adams sold his only cow. Little can those who come after realize the sacrifices the early pioneers were called to make to render the later years happy and prosperous.

The Church thus begun under the Pastorate of Brother Lewis was not fully completed until 1849, when it was dedicated by Bishop Janes. The death of Brother Lewis in the midst of his second year, was a severe loss to the charge. But the good brethren were not discouraged, and pushed forward the work.

Beloit has been highly favored in her Pastors, among whom may be found such men as A.P. Allen, I.M. Leihy, J.M. Walker, P.S. Bennett, S.W. Ford, J.W. Wood, John Nolan, R.M. Beach, C. Scammon, W. Lattin, P.B. Pease, C.D. Pillsbury, W.P. Stowe, L.L. Knox, W.W. Case, C.R. Pattee, A.C. Higgins, and G.S. Hubbs.

At the close of the Conference we returned to Janesville for a second year. There still being no Parsonage I purchased a residence, thereby securing a pleasant home. The plan of supplying outside appointments was continued during the summer, and in some instances Sunday Schools were also opened. The religious interest continued, and the Church was filled with people. At the expiration of their probation one hundred of the converts were received into full membership, and, in the following fall and winter, many others. During the winter a revival again visited the charge, which greatly strengthened the converts of the previous year, and added to their number. The two years spent in Janesville to us were exceedingly pleasant, and gave us a goodly number of life-long friends. The Sunday School had become very prosperous, the charge was now out of debt, and the finances self-supporting. And more than all, we left a united and happy people.

Janesville has since enjoyed her full share of able and successful Pastors. Several years ago, she divided into two bands, and has now two good Churches, two good congregations, and two able Ministers.

CHAPTER XIX

The next Conference session was held April 20th, 1859, at Sheboygan Falls. The excellent Bishop Baker presided, and I was again elected Secretary. It was at this Conference the trial of Rev. J. W. Wood was had. He had been the Presiding Elder of the Janesville District, but, having obtained a divorce from his wife on the ground of desertion, instead of the one cause named in the New Testament, and married another, he had been suspended during the year. The trial resulted in his expulsion. The case was carried to the next General Conference on Appeal, and that body sustained the action taken by the Conference.

The disability thus hanging over the Presiding Elder of the Janesville District, rendered it necessary that some one should be appointed to represent the District in the Cabinet. The Bishop appointed me to this duty, thus imposing severe labor for the session. Since I was appointed to represent the District at the Conference, it was generally supposed that I would be continued the following year, my term having expired at Janesville. But on the contrary, I was assigned to the Milwaukee District.

This arrangement made Waukesha my place of residence, as the Milwaukee District had erected at this village a District Parsonage. The inevitable concomitant of the Itinerancy, the moving season, passed in the ordinary course of events, and left us comfortably located in our new home.

The District at this time included nineteen charges. The larger portion of them could be reached by railroad, but a sufficient number lay off the line of public conveyance to render it advisable to keep a horse and buggy, and hence they were obtained.

Soon after reaching my new field of labor, my attention was called to the financial condition of the District Parsonage. I found that a small debt had come down from the erection of the building, which had been increased from year to year by accruing interest and repairs, until at this time the entire indebtedness amounted to nine hundred and thirty-one dollars. Meantime there had been, during the preceding year of financial pressure, such a depreciation of property in the village, that the building was now worth but little more, if any, than the amount of indebtedness.

In looking the matter over, I saw at a glance that it would be much easier to build a new house in a desirable location than to pay an old debt of this magnitude. But there were other interests to be considered. The money for the erection of this Parsonage had been given in good faith by the people, and if it were now permitted to pass out of the hands of the Trustees, there would be a shock to the confidence they had reposed in the administration of the Church. And in the next place, this money had been borrowed of innocent parties, and it was but right that it should be returned.

With these views, I undertook to save the property, but I am free to say it was the most thankless financial task I had ever undertaken. I gave the first one hundred and fifty dollars, and then divided the balance among the charges of the District. In passing around to my Quarterly Meetings, the amounts in most cases were pledged, and the larger portion finally paid. Yet the collections were not fully completed before the end of my term.

Milwaukee at this time still retained its three charges, and they were now in charge respectively of Rev. J. M. Walker, Rev. E. Cooke, D.D., and Rev. A.C. Manwell. As stated in a former chapter, Brother Walker had served his full term on the Beaver Dam District, where he had been very popular. He entered upon his field with great spirit, but found himself greatly embarrassed by the unhappy financial condition of the charge. Besides the indebtedness remaining on the Church, there remained considerable arrears on the salaries of preceding Pastorates.

This paying a Pastor at the end of his term in notes, that shall come back to haunt his successor, is not in keeping with the financial genius of the Church. I once had some sad experience in that line, and since it was not in Milwaukee, I will take occasion to refer to it in this connection. It was at a time when the slip rents were not large, averaging only about two hundred dollars a quarter. In the case referred to, the two hundred dollars of the first quarter of my year, had been absorbed to meet the claims of the outgoing Pastor. And then, as he was still behind two hundred dollars, a note was given him for the balance. By this arrangement, the first half year of my term had been anticipated, and had not the people, finding out the state of the case, come to my aid with a good donation, I must have been greatly embarrassed.

Nor does such mismanagement affect the one man alone. The system entails disaster upon the successive Pastors of the charge. Each man feels that his predecessor has done him a great wrong, when the case may be, the wrong was done by one man several years before, and afterwards his successors have only been carrying it over from year to year. But, however long it may be carried, it still remains as the plague of both the Pastors and the Church.

But in the person of Brother Walker, the system was squelched. Though at the end of his term, owing largely to this irregularity, he was largely deficient in his claim, he balanced the year.

Brother Manwell, the Pastor of Asbury, entered the North Indiana Conference in 1853, was transferred to the Wisconsin Conference in 1857, and had served Green Bay two years, before coming to this charge. The Church accommodations were limited, but he made two good years at Asbury, and was able at their close to report considerable progress. After leaving the city, Brother Manwell served a good class of appointments, and among them Racine, Janesville, Whitewater and Ripon, until 1873, when he was transferred to Upper Iowa Conference. He was a man of kind spirit, pleasant address, and specially successful in leading the social meetings in his charges.

Reference is made to Dr. Cooke in a former chapter, and I need only say in this connection that under his Pastorate Summerfield had a prosperous year.

At Wauwatosa, I found Rev. N.J. Aplin, of whom mention is made in a former chapter. His assistant was Rev. Edward Bassett, a promising young man, who had been converted in the revival at Janesville. The two men worked admirably together, and the year was one of great prosperity to the Circuit. The Circuit was in a flame of revival. And during the year, the beautiful brick Church at West Granville was erected.

The Brookfield class, it will be remembered, was formed by Brother Frink in 1840. The members were: Robert Curren, Leader, Sarah Curren, T.M. Riddle, Adeline Riddle, Gideon Wales, Polly Wales, Mark Johnson, Ann Butterfield, Margaret Underwood, Charles Curran, Frank Morgan, Mrs. Frank Morgan, and Mrs. Fellows. To these were soon added, Mr. and Mrs. Carlton, Mr. and Mrs. Raymond. This Society had already erected a comfortable frame Church, and the neighborhood had become famous as the locality in which the Milwaukee District Camp-Meetings were held.

West Granville Church was located in the neighborhood that was known in the early times by the name of Menomonee. And it will be recollected that Brother Frink organized a class at this point also in 1840. The members of the class were: William Coates, Leader, Sarah Coates, T.J. Rice, Cynthia Rice, Edward Earl, Hannah Earl, Lyman Wheeler, Bigelow Case, Alvira Case, Mrs. Martin M. Curtis, Nathan Wheeler, Jr., William Hudson, Susan Hudson. At the first the class at Menomonee included all the members in that region, but as the country became settled other classes were organized, and among them those at the Haylett, Nelson and Coates neighborhoods. Subsequently these classes concentrated at Menomonee Falls and erected a Church. A new Church has since been built, and at this writing the village constitutes a respectable charge.

At Wauwatosa there was no Church, and Brother Aplin held his meetings in a school house. But in 1869 a fine brick edifice was erected under the Pastorate of Rev. John P. Roe.

Brother Roe resided, at the time of my appointment to the Milwaukee District, on the New Berlin Circuit. During the war he went to the army and served as Chaplain with great acceptability. On his return he rendered effective service as a Local Preacher until 1869, when he entered the Conference and was appointed to Wauwatosa. At the end of two years he was elected Agent of the Lawrence University, and continued two years, performing prodigies of labor, and achieving a grand success in raising an Endowment Fund. But his health finally failed, and he was compelled to retire from the work. At this writing, he is traveling in Europe.

At Waukesha, the Pastor was Rev, Wesley Lattin, who had been returned for a second year. This noble and true man was received into the Conference, as before stated, in the same class with the writer. His first appointment was Sycamore, Ill., with Rev. Stephen R. Beggs as Preacher in charge.

Brother Lattin had been stationed in Waukesha in 1852, and had now returned in 1858 and 1859. The year was a prosperous one. A good revival crowned his labors, and all the interests of the Church were kept in a healthy condition. In the department of Pastoral labor Brother Lattin was not inferior to any man in the Conference. Filled with the spirit of charity himself, he was always able to diffuse the same kindly feeling among the people. Nor is it too much to say, he was universally beloved. Of an easy and graceful delivery, and plain, practical thought, his Ministry was always agreeable and useful.

After leaving Waukesha, he was stationed successively at Beloit, Fond du Lac, Waupun, Ripon, Appleton, and then returned again to Waukesha. But here his health failed and he retired from the work for two years, but having removed to Kansas where his health rallied again, he was transferred to the Kansas Conference in 1872. Since going to Kansas, our dear brother has had the misfortune to lose his wife and son. They were traveling to a neighboring town with a horse and buggy. In trying to ford a river the waters proved too strong for the faithful horse, and they were all swept down the stream together, and were drowned. In this great sorrow Brother Lattin has the sympathies of all his brethren of the Conference.

Oconomowoc was at this time under the Pastoral charge of Rev. Thomas Wilcox. It will be remembered that a class was formed at this place by Brother Frink, in connection with his labors on the Watertown Circuit. The members were: George W. Williams, Leader; Mrs. George W. Williams, Jonathan Dorrity, Mr. and Mrs. Day Dewey. In 1840 it was connected with Summit, and retained Brother Frink as Pastor. In 1843 it was connected with Prairieville Circuit, and shared the services of Revs. L.F. Moulthrop and S. Stover. Before the erection of the Church, the meetings were held in a hall over a cooper shop. The Church enterprise was commended under the Pastorate of Rev. S.W. Martin, a lot being donated for the purpose by John S. Rockwell, Esq. Under the Pastorate of Rev. A.C. Pennock, the Church was put in condition for use, and on the 3d of February, 1850, the writer was called to dedicate the basement.

The second Church enterprise was commenced in 1867, tinder the labors of Rev. George Fellows, and was completed during the Pastorate of Rev. Wm. R. Jones in 1868. It was dedicated by Bishop Thomson. Oconomowoc has grown to be one of the strongest and most desirable appointments in the Conference.

At the time of my visit in 1850 the charge had been divided, giving to Rev. A. C. Pennock the Oconomowoc portion, and Rev. Job B. Mills the northern appointments.

Brother Pennock entered the Conference in 1848, and was appointed to West Bend. The following year, as above stated, he was sent to Oconomowoc, but here his health failed, and he was compelled to rest a year. In 1852 he was re-admitted and again appointed to Oconomowoc, with Rev. T.O. Hollister as Assistant. During this year he was greatly afflicted in the loss of his wife, and before the expiration of the year he was sent to Waukesha to supply the place of Brother Lattin, whose health had failed. In 1853 Brother Pennock was stationed at Asbury, Milwaukee, but, his health again failing, he decided to go to Minnesota at the end of the year. He remained in Minnesota, doing effective work until 1864, when, becoming satisfied his health was unequal to the Itinerancy, he located. At the present writing he is residing in Madison. He has a clear head and a warm heart.

Brother Mills came to Wisconsin from Washington, D.C., in the Spring of 1848. After stopping in Milwaukee a few months, and receiving license to exhort from Spring Street Station, he removed to Oconomowoc, where he was granted a Local Preacher's license. Being employed, as before stated, on the north part of Oconomowoc charge, he found ten appointments and seven classes committed to his care, which gave him abundance of labor.

He was admitted into the Conference at its next session, and returned to his former field. His subsequent appointments in Wisconsin were Bark River, Palmyra, and Root River. In 1854 he was sent to Minneapolis Mission in Minnesota, having Rev. David Brooks as his Presiding Elder.

In this place, now so flourishing a city, he was compelled to hold his meetings in a loft over the Post Office. But, notwithstanding these disadvantages, he formed a class, and his good wife organized a Sabbath School. In 1856 Brother Mills took a transfer to the Peoria Conference, now Central Illinois, and in 1864, on account of blindness, was compelled to take a superannuation. At this writing he is residing at Oconomowoc, but, on invitation, often goes abroad to assist the brethren in their work. He is a grand, good man, and his labors are always appreciated.

The next charge visited was Hart Prairie. This Circuit had once formed a part of the old Troy charge of the early times, but, after undergoing various changes, it was now a charge by itself. It had a small Church and a most interesting congregation. Here I was the guest of Rev. Richard Fairchilds, a Local Preacher of large intelligence and extensive influence.

The Pastor was Rev. Delos Hale, who entered the Conference in 1854. He had shirked duty for several years, and had been known as a reliable business man at Summit. But finally, accepting his responsibilities, he was appointed first to Oak Creek, and then West Bend. He was now on his second year, and was in the midst of a revival.

At my visit in the following summer, I attended a Camp-Meeting on grounds a short distance east of the Church. The meeting was largely attended, and many souls were brought into the Kingdom.

I was greatly pleased with my visit to Watertown. The Church I had left in an unfinished condition in 1848, was completed by Rev. David Brooks two years later, when I returned and performed the dedicatory service.

Brother Brooks entered the Rock River Conference in 1844, and was stationed at Dixon, Illinois. On coming to Watertown, he entered upon his work with spirit, and success crowned his efforts. After leaving Watertown, he rendered effective service in the regular work until 1852, when he was elected Agent of the Lawrence University. In 1853 he was appointed Presiding Elder of the Minnesota District, since which time he has continued to labor on both stations and Districts in that field with great acceptability.

Brother Brooks is a man of sterling qualities. Sound in the Faith, circumspect in demeanor, faithful in his work, and true to every interest of the Church, he could not fail to make a good record.

I found Rev. A.C. Huntley the Pastor at Watertown. Brother Huntley entered the traveling connection in Western New York, and came to the Wisconsin Conference by transfer in 1858. He had already held a protracted meeting, and a large number had professed conversion, giving considerable additional strength to the charge. The Church edifice had now become too small to meet the demands of the charge, and Brother Huntley had entered upon the labor of enlargement. In this good work he had not only planned and superintended, but had also put his own hands to the actual labor. He succeeded so well in the enterprise, that he finally decided to make the extension large enough to furnish also a good Parsonage in the rear of the Church edifice. The dedicatory services were conducted by the writer on Saturday, July 16th.

The Brookfield Camp-Meeting was held in the latter part of June. The grove on the farm of Robert Curren, Esq., was secured for a term of years, and through the assistance of Brothers Aplin and Bassett, and the brethren on adjacent charges, it was well fitted up for the purposes of a Camp-Meeting. At this meeting we adopted the plan of making our Camp-Meetings self supporting. Instead of relying upon the brethren in the neighborhood to do all the work and keep open doors for the week, we determined to pay our own bills, and thus permit the good people in the vicinity to enjoy the meeting, as well as those who came from abroad. The change was deemed a great improvement. There was a good show of tents, and the attendance was large. The preaching was excellent, as the good brethren were more intent upon saving souls than ventilating their great sermons. The meeting resulted in the conversion of many souls, while the membership was greatly quickened.

In these latter days the question is sometimes raised, "Of what advantage are these Camp-Meetings, now that we have good Churches in which to worship God?" The question might be answered by another, "Of what advantage is it to have picnics and other excursions in the open air, and pleasant groves, since we have houses to dwell in and restaurants to supply the cravings of the appetite?" The fact is, Camp-Meetings are as thoroughly in harmony with the laws of Philosophy as they are in keeping with the principles of Religion.

To intensify either the mental or spiritual forces, it is necessary to break up, at times, their monotonous habits, and send them off into new channels of thought and feeling. A lesson may be learned in this direction from the picnic excursion. It is not the little ones alone who, relieved of the confinement of the parlor, gambol in half frantic ecstasy, but the sedate matron and the grave sire renew their youth, and in their exhuberance of spirit, join in the recreations with the zest of childhood. The same law obtains in Camp-

Meetings. Why not go out into the woods, beneath the spreading branches of the trees, or even under the uncurtained canopy of Heaven, and enjoy a grand unbending of the spirit? With the shackles thrown off that have so long fettered the soul, what a Heaven of felicity there is in its conscious freëdom. The eagle, long confined in a cage, after stretching his wings to satisfy himself that he is really free, gambols in the air with an indescribable ecstasy. So there are thousands of Christians shut up in the Churches who are dying for a little spiritual freedom. Their poor souls need a holiday. Let them go out to a good thorough-going Camp-Meeting, and obtain a new lease of life. And in saying this, I am not advocating undue license. I am only pleading for the inalienable rights of a human soul. Such freedom of spirit is entirely consonant with the highest culture and absolute decorum. Communing thus with nature in her purest and most lovely moods, the soul is dwelling in the vestibule of God's own sanctuary. No wonder that prayer and song find such grand perfection in the Camp-Meeting. It is there they find their highest inspiration.

But another advantage of the Camp-Meeting lies in the unbroken chain of religious thought and feeling which it affords. In the ordinary experiences of life, the secular and the religious strongly mingle and intercept each other. But in the tented grove the secular is shut away from the mind, and the religious holds complete mastery. One service follows another, and one religious impulse succeeds another so rapidly that the soul finds no interval for communion with the world. And as the ore, by long tarrying in the furnace, where no breath of cooling currents can reach it, flows as a liquid and is ready to take any form, so the soul, held in hallowed communion with the Divine spirit, is prepared to receive the perfect image of God.

To the soul who has no knowledge of these delightful experiences, there hangs a mystery around the Camp-Meeting, but to Christians the whole subject is as clear as the noon-day. Like the disciples on the mount of transfiguration, they are prepared to say, "Master, it is good for us to be here." With them Christ is the central figure, and it is his presence that hallows the temple in the wilderness.

It is sometimes objected that the exercises at Camp-Meetings are too boisterous, and lead to extravagances. To this objection there are two replies. First, it must be conceded that Camp-Meetings are not the only meetings that may be denominated boisterous. At political meetings, and on other occasions, I have witnessed the equal, at least, of anything I have seen at Camp Meetings.

But the other reply is more to the point. No one can well deprecate the boisterous and extravagant in religion more than I do, and yet I accept both as a necessity. To move men to right action, they must be swayed by right influences. If men were susceptible to the good, then gentle influences might sway them, but as they are steeped in evil, and largely lost to the better influences, the sterner only can reach them. If this shall be found to be true in the individual, then certainly it is more emphatically true of men in the aggregate. To move a multitude, then, to the acceptance of Christ, the congregation must be put under an intense moral pressure. And it will be found that the measure of pressure that will move the great mass, will sometimes move individuals of peculiarly sensitive temperament over into the extravagant. Now in such cases, one of two things must be accepted. We must be content to leave the great aggregate unmoved, or we must endure the irregularities that are sometimes seen, not only at Camp-Meetings, but in all revivals of religion. We cannot accept the former, for it involves the ruin of perishing souls. Then, accepting the latter, we may not condemn what cannot be avoided, if the great end of Christian effort shall be realized. Human nature is a very strange combination, and it must be taken as it is. The religion of Christ proposes to save men, and to do so it must take us as we are. The wonder is not that it can make so little out of us, but rather, that it is able to make even a few fair specimens, while the balance of us are only indifferent ones. Yet I rejoice to know that even the poorest of us are vastly better than we would have been had it not been for the revelation of Christ in us.

CHAPTER XX

The thirteenth session of the Wisconsin Conference was held Oct. 13, 1859, in the village of Whitewater, and was presided over by Bishop Ames. The year had been of less than seven months duration, as by request of the Conference, the time of holding the sessions had been changed back to the Fall. When the change was made in the first place, from Fall to Spring, it was believed by many that such an arrangement would be a benefit to the Preachers, by giving them, for the winter, the products of their gardens. But, after a trial, it was found that the roads were generally much worse in the Spring than in the fall, and if the Conferences were delayed so as to find good roads for moving, the Preachers would reach their new fields too late to plant their gardens. Hence, after trying the experiment, it was thought best to return to the Fall.

At this Conference the election of delegates to the General Conference again occurred. The slavery question was now rife, and of course this election could not be held without making it an issue. During the early part of the Conference this subject became the general theme of conversation, and, I might add, the discussions and the prayers. In short, every man who was in danger of being struck with a vote must certainly show his colors on the slavery issue. An able Committee was formed, and a careful report rendered. And when the vote was taken on the report, all eyes were on the alert to see how each candidate voted.

As the Report on Slavery is not lengthy, I will insert it as taken from the Conference Minutes:

1. That the assertion that the M.E. Church is constitutionally pro-slavery, whether that assertion be made by our professed friends or by our enemies, is a base slander.
2. That we recommend to the next General Conference so to change the General Rule on Slavery as to prohibit the buying selling or holding a human being as a slave.
3. That we concur with the Providence Conference in recommending to the next General Conference so to

change the General Rule on Slavery as to read: 'Slavery, the buying or selling of men, women or children, with an intention to enslave them.'

4. That we concur with the Erie Conference in recommending to the next General Conference so to change the General Rule on Slavery as to read: 'The buying, selling, holding or transferring of a human being, to be used in slavery.'

It will be observed that the Wisconsin Conference preferred the wording of her own proposed Rule, yet such was her anxiety to secure action by the General Conference, that she was willing to adopt any other form of words, if the same sentiment should be explicitly incorporated. And by concurring in those sent from the Providence and Erie Conferences, and at the same time re-affirming her own, which was going the circuit of the other Conferences, she hoped to see some one of them reach the approaching General Conference, with the recommendation of a sufficient number of the Annual Conferences, to make it a law at once on the action of that body. With this intense interest thrown around the subject, it is not a matter of surprise that the votes of the candidates, on the adoption of the report, were carefully watched.

But in some cases even a fair and unequivocal vote was not enough. Committees were self-constituted, or perhaps caucus-constituted to interview candidates, much after the modern style, to see whether they were sound on the main question. And as I had now become sufficiently advanced in years to be considered a candidate, I was waited on by such an inquisitorial body. I told the good brethren that I was not a little surprised to find any one in doubt as to my position. "Oh," said they, "we are not really in doubt as to your position, but we would like to understand how strong your convictions are, as you have not attended our meetings." "Yes," said I, "and perhaps you will say that by neglecting your meetings, I have shown a want of zeal for the cause. If so, I wish to state my position. In the first place, I have never felt it to be my duty to make a great show of valor, as long as the enemy is out of reach. And in the second place, I am in a different position from many of our present abolitionists, and should bear myself accordingly. They are young converts, and having just come into the kingdom, they must get up a tremendous shout, so as to satisfy their new associates that their conversion is genuine. But as to myself, I was always an abolitionist. I have never uttered a word, written a sentence, or cast a vote that did not look in that direction. Why, then, should I go into a spasm on the eve of an election?" Whether my little speech had anything to do with the result of the ballot which placed me at the head of the delegation or not, it is impossible to divine. But of one thing I felt assured. I had "freed my mind," as the old lady said, and felt better. The balance of the delegation were I.M. Leihy, S. C. Thomas, E. Cooke, and P. S. Bennett. At this Conference, I was also appointed the Chairman of a Committee "To Collect Historical Facts." Thus early did the Conference indicate a desire that the record of her devoted and pioneer men should not be lost.

Whitewater, the seat of the Conference, was a thriving village of two or three thousand inhabitants, and gave the Conference a most hospitable entertainment. This place was settled April 1st, 1837, by Mr. William Barren, who was joined by Mr. Calvin Prince in the middle of the same month.

The first sermon was preached in the fall of the same year by Rev. Jesse Halstead. Whitewater became a separate charge in 1843, with Rev. Alpha Warren as Pastor. During this year a class was formed. The members were: J.K. Wood, Leader; Mrs. J.K. Wood, Henry Johnson, A.R. Eaton, Mrs. A.R. Eaton, Mrs. Dr. Clark, Mrs. J.J. Stearin, Roxana Hamilton, and Miss Whitcomb. The meetings were held in private houses until the new brick school house was built. They were then held in the school house until the Church was erected. The first Church was commenced under the Pastorate of Rev. J. Harrington in 1849, and was completed under that of Rev. J.M. Walker in 1852. It was dedicated by the last named, Feb. 5th, 1852. The Church was enlarged under the Pastorate of Rev. A.C. Huntley.

Whitewater Station erected a new brick Church, one of the finest in the interior, under the Pastorate of Rev. C.N. Stowers, which was dedicated by Bishop Merrill Oct. 19th, 1873. At this writing, Whitewater ranks among the leading stations of the Conference, having a good congregation and a most enterprising Society.

At the close of this Conference I was returned to the Milwaukee District. There were only a few changes made in the appointments of the Preachers. At this Conference the name of Rev. Henry Bannister, D.D., Professor in Garrett Biblical Institute, was transferred from the Racine to the Milwaukee District, and he was made a member of the Summerfield Quarterly Conference.

Dr. Bannister entered the Oneida Conference in 1842, and for two years served as Professor of Languages in the Oneida Conference Seminary. At the Conference of 1844, he was appointed Principal, and held that position with distinguished honor until he was elected to a Professorship in the Garrett Biblical Institute. At the present writing he is still at the Institute, doing efficient work. Nearly a third of a century he has devoted to teaching, dividing his time almost equally between the Seminary and the Institute.

Dr. Bannister is one of Nature's noblemen, and his membership in any Conference is an honor to the body. The Wisconsin Conference has recognized his worth, and has sent him three times as one of her delegates to the General Conference, and on one occasion was pleased to put him at the head of the list. But he is not the property of a Conference; he belongs to the whole Church, and is the peer of his brethren in any convocation she may assemble.

The General Conference met in Buffalo, N.Y., in May, 1860. The agitation known as the Nazarite movement was then raging through Western New York, and it was understood that several cases would come before the General Conference on appeal from the expelled members of the Genesee Conference. I was requested to go down to the troubled District and look the ground over before the opening of the Conference. I did so, but found the movement too far advanced to avoid a rupture of the Societies in many of the charges. Several of the men who had taken an appeal had stultified themselves and vitiated their appeals, by forming Societies on the basis of the new movement; and though they disclaimed all intention to establish another Church, the formation of these Societies, it was held, could be interpreted in no other way. Having thus become members of another Church their appeals, which contemplated their restoration to the former Church, could not be entertained.

But the great question before the body was the new Rule on Slavery. At the beginning, the subject was given to one of the large Committees, of which the writer was a member. The late Bishop Kingsley was the Chairman, and the Committee met almost daily for three weeks. The report to the General Conference was made to cover the whole ground, and accepted the basis which had been advocated so long by the Wisconsin Conference. On its presentation a long discussion followed, and it was believed that the requisite two-thirds vote would be obtained. But judge of our surprise when, on taking the vote, we found the measure had been lost by a few votes, and these had been mostly given by the delegation of the troubled District in Western New York.

But though the majority were thus defeated in their effort to change the General Rule, they passed a chapter that declared it to be unchristian to hold slaves, as well as to traffic in them. The war, however, soon followed, and the "logic of events," disposed of the Slavery question. At this Conference I was elected a member of the General Mission Committee at New York, which rendered it necessary for me to visit the city annually for four years.

The Conference of 1860 was held Sept. 26th, at Janesville, Bishop Scott presiding. At this session the Conference received Rev. I.L. Hauser, and he was sent as a Missionary to India.

Brother Hauser is of Austrian, German and French descent. His mother's family were German, and the Hauser name is over six hundred years old in Vienna, Austria. His grandmother on his father's side was directly descended from one of the Huguenot families driven out of France by the revocation of the edict of Nantes. Coming to America, the family settled in Pennsylvania, where Brother Hauser was born, in 1834. His family came to Wisconsin and settled at Delavan in 1850. He graduated from Lawrence University in 1860. During his senior year he was President of the College Missionary Society, and when writing to Rev. Dr. Durbin, requesting him to preach the annual sermon at Commencement, he stated that he would soon be through College and be ready for duty, but he did not know just what it was, and wished advice. The reply came for him to send the name of the Pastor of the Church. The names of Rev. M. Himebaugh, Pastor, and Rev. Dr. Knox, one of the Professors, were sent. Three days after his graduation, having reached his home, he received a letter from Bishop Simpson, asking him to come at once to Evanston. From there the Bishop sent him to the Erie Conference, then in session at Erie, Penn., where he was ordained and appointed to the Mission in India.

Returning to Wisconsin, he was united in marriage with Miss Jeannette Shepherd, of Kenosha, Sept. 13th. Starting for their field of labor, they sailed from Boston on the vessel Sea King, and after a tedious and stormy voyage of one hundred and thirty-eight days, they reached Calcutta. From there, after an eleven days' journey of one thousand and three miles up the valley of the Ganges, they arrived at Bijnour, forty-five miles from where the river Ganges flows out of the mountains into the plains of India. Here they labored six years, their field comprising a District of nineteen hundred square miles, with a population of nearly one million, being fifty-four miles from the nearest Mission Station.

Four schools were organized, in which twenty teachers were employed, and six languages were used in the various studies. When the schools were first started not two natives in the District could speak English, but after six years nearly six hundred had been taught in the schools to both read and speak it. Regular services in the Chapel, such as preaching, Sunday School, class and prayer meetings, were held in the Urdu language for the native Christian Church. Brother Hauser also conducted the Church of England service each Sabbath morning for five years, for the few English residents stationed there, as they had no Chaplain.

Besides studying the several languages of the country, preaching in the bazaars and other public places to tens of thousands of people, instructing the native preachers and teachers, looking after and giving employment to the native Christians, he was appointed by the Publishing Committee of the Mission to translate the Discipline into the Urdu language, having the honor of making the first translation of that book into any Eastern tongue. But in the midst of his labors, sickness fell upon himself and family. Diptheria attacked himself, his wife, and two of his children. One little girl died of that disease, and shortly after another from fever. Brother Hauser's throat became seriously affected, and he was compelled to retire from the work. With his family, he made a tour of several months through the Himalaya Mountains, to within eight miles of the borders of Thibet. In this tour he was not unfrequently twenty thousand feet above the sea, but failing to recover his health, he, in 1868, returned to the United States, after an absence of eight years.

Since his return, he has devoted his labor to the publication of the Christian Statesman, the only Protestant religious paper published in Wisconsin. Being undenominational, the paper, patronized by all the Protestant Churches, has attained a wide circulation. Brother Hauser is a man of great energy, and is doing a grand work for the Churches of Wisconsin.

Mrs. Hauser is a lady of very superior talent. In their Mission field she took her full share of the work, and since her return, she has not only been one of the best contributors to the Statesman, but has largely identified herself with the Woman's Foreign Missionary Society work in the State. Both on the platform, and in the general work of the Society, she holds a high rank. And in addition to this work, she is now preparing a volume of sketches of Women in Heathen Lands.

At the close of the preceding year, the Summerfield Quarterly Conference requested my appointment to the Pastorate of that station. The Bishop at first was inclined to grant the request, but finally came to the conclusion that I ought to remain on the District. This left the charge to be supplied, and I secured the services of Rev. J.E. Wilson, then of Ohio, but who had formerly served Milwaukee, as stated in a preceding chapter.

Summerfield was just in the midst of her financial embarrassment. The indebtedness was about fifteen thousand dollars, and threatened to overwhelm the charge. But the good brethren were steadfast, and through great labor and sacrifice, aided by Rev. S.C. Thomas, succeeded in meeting their obligations. Brother Wilson rendered effective service, but at the close of the year returned to his home in Ohio.

Rev. J.C. Robbins was appointed this year to the Spring Street Station. Brother Robbins entered the North Indiana Conference in 1844. His appointments were Winchester, Plymouth, Clinton, Hagerstown, Williamsburg, Knightstown, Doublin and Lewisville. He was transferred to the Wisconsin Conference in 1855, and stationed at North Ward, Fond du Lac. His subsequent appointments were Waupun, Berlin and Empire. The year opened finely, and during the winter Brother Robbins held a protracted meeting, which resulted in the conversion of many souls. But the Society met with a severe loss this year, in the destruction of their Church by fire.

Brother Robbins remained a second year at Spring Street, and again enjoyed a good revival. After leaving the city, he has been stationed at Racine, Waukesha, Sheboygan Falls, Waupun, Berlin, Green Bay, Hart Prairie, Sharon and Footville. At the present writing, he is at the last named place, seeking to gather sheaves for the Master.

This year intense excitement prevailed throughout the country. The Presidential election, which placed Abraham Lincoln at the head of our national affairs, occurred in November. And during the following months, the rebellion was taking form in the Southern States, but did not culminate in open rupture until the middle of April. But before stating the position of the Conference and Church in the pending struggle, it will be proper to refer to the causes which produced the conflict.

In the settlement of the United States, two distinct types of society planted themselves in the two great centres of the Atlantic Coast. The one made New England the theater of development, and the other the Eastern cordon of the Southern States. From the first center, the population moved westward through New York, Pennsylvania, and the Prairie States, to the Mississippi. From the other, the settlements extended through the savannahs of the South to the Gulf.

The emigrants in the North were mainly those who came to the Western world to find an asylum from the religious persecutions to which they had been subjected at home. In the South, society was largely established under the sanctions of royalty. These two facts will account for the radical differences existing between the people of the two sections. In the North, society very naturally accepted the political doctrines of personal equality and universal freedom. In the South, the people as naturally adhered to their aristocratic ideas, and held to the doctrine of privileged classes.

The two types of society, thus placed side by side, were now given an open field, in which the contest for supremacy could not long be delayed. In geographical position, it would seem that the advantage was decidedly with the South. And the same may be said of the patronage bestowed by the home governments. But notwithstanding the high mountain ranges, the deep forests, and the sterile coasts of New England, her people cut their way through every obstacle, and soon stood face to face with their aristocratic neighbors. A collision of ideas was now inevitable. The South, quick to discover the unheralded force of Yankee character, took the alarm and declared that "Mason and Dixon's line" should divide between her and her neighbor. Here was deposited the first egg in the nest, from which has been hatched the terrible brood of vipers which, under the name of "State Rights," has involved the country in a most desolating war. It was on this line that Calhoun planted his standard when he sought to inflame the South against the North. And it was on this fatal line that his followers, thirty years after, sought to overturn the decisions of the ballot-box, and establish a Southern Confederacy. With what result, the record of the conflict affords an answer.

On the 13th of April, 1861, the rebels opened fire on Fort Sumter, and on the 14th Major Anderson and his brave men were compelled to surrender their stronghold. As the news of this attack and surrender swept along the telegraphic wires throughout the North, a most intense patriotism awoke in the heart of every loyal citizen. The people assembled on the corners of the streets, in halls, in places of business, and in short, at every convenient place of resort, to discuss the situation, and feed the flames of patriotism. Everywhere men and money were offered to support the government, without stint. The press teemed with burning words, and the pulpit was outspoken in characterizing the rebellion and vindicating the government.

The writer was in Milwaukee when the news of the surrender of Fort Sumter reached the city. On Sabbath, April 21st, I preached a sermon, from which the following extract is taken. I quote from Rev. Mr. Love's "History of Wisconsin in the War."

> "But, Ladies and Gentlemen, the war is inevitable. Its coming may be hastened or retarded by the shaping of events during the next thirty days, but that war is upon us, and a civil war, of a most frightful character and most alarming proportions, is to my mind no longer a question. You can no more prevent it than you can stay the leaping floods of Niagara, or quench the king of day in the palm of your hand. It is the legitimate offspring of an 'irrepressible conflict' of ideas as antagonistic as light and darkness, as diametrically opposed to each other as right and wrong, truth and error. The Bible declaration, that God hath made of one blood all the nations of men to dwell on all the face of the earth, so beautifully set forth

in our Declaration of Independence, and teaching the great lesson of universal equality and universal freedom, forms the corner-stone of our institutions. But a plague spot is found in the opposing doctrine of caste and privileged classes, which finds illustration in American slavery. This war of principles has already culminated in a collision at Fort Sumter, and it would be contrary to all history to arrest the tide of war at this stage. The antagonism is too direct, and the conflict too heated to quench the flame till rivers of blood shall pass over it. The act of the South in firing on Sumter is none other than a rebellion, and that of the most inexcusable and wicked character, against the best government on earth; and I am free to confess that I am filled with horror when I contemplate the result of this suicidal act on their part, an act that must lead to years of war, as far as human ken can see, and the most fearful desolations in its train. But, gentlemen, there is no alternative. The glove is thrown to us, and we must accept it. If our principles are right, and we believe they are, we would be unworthy of our noble paternity if we were to shrink from the issue. Let there, then, be no shrinking from the contest. The battle is for human liberty, and it were better that every man should go down, and every dollar be sacrificed, than that we should transmit to the coming millions of this land other than a legacy of freedom. Were it not that good men have gone down into the dust and smoke of the battle, there would not be to-day a government on the face of the globe under which a good man could well live. And since God in his Providence has brought us to this hour, I trust that by his help we shall not prove unworthy of the trust--the noblest ever given to man--committed to our keeping. There can be no question as to the result. We shall triumph, and with the triumph we shall win a glorious national destiny."

The next Conference session was held in Fond du Lac Sept. 18, 1861, Bishop Baker presiding. The session was one of unusual excitement. The war had been begun, the terrible Bull Run defeat had occurred, and already seven regiments of our brave boys had gone to the front. And with the seventh, one of our own members, Rev. S.L. Brown, had gone as Chaplain, while several others were either in the ranks or looking in the same direction. In the matter of furnishing men, Wisconsin was already ahead of the call made upon her, but such was the devotion of her people to the Old Flag, that ten other regiments could have been sent during the year.

At this session, the Conference adopted a very able Report, written by Rev. J.H. Jenne, on the state of the country, showing a deep interest in the issue before the Nation, and pledging her unwavering support to the Government.

Brother Jenne entered the traveling connection in Maine, and came to the Wisconsin Conference by transfer in 1856. His first appointment was Agent of the Lawrence University. His next appointment was Presiding Elder of Appleton District, where he remained four years. His subsequent appointments have been Janesville, Janesville District, Lake Mills, Hart Prairie, Allen's Grove, Union Grove, Lyons, and Waupun. At the present writing he is on his second year at the last named place.

Brother Jenne is an able Minister of the New Testament. He is a man of large brain and profound research. Well versed in all the questions of the day, as well as in the writings of the Fathers, he is able to furnish a high standard of pulpit labor. He is a, true man, has a genial spirit, and to persons who can strike his plane of thought he is companionable.

At this Conference I was returned to the District for a fourth year, and Rev. S.C. Thomas was appointed to the Summerfield Church.

Brother Thomas entered the Erie Conference in 1842, and, before coming to Wisconsin by transfer in 1851, had been stationed at Conneautville, Geneva, Ravenna, Willoughby, and Fredonia, besides serving two years as Agent of the Alleghany College. After coming to Wisconsin, he had served Spring Street, Platteville, Jackson Street, and had been Agent of the Lawrence University for five years. He now remained two years at Summerfield, when he returned again to the Agency of the University. In 1864 he was made Presiding Elder of the Milwaukee District, where he remained four years. He next served four years as Presiding Elder of the Janesville District, when he was appointed to Fort Atkinson. At the present writing he is at Lyons. This outline completes a record of nearly a quarter of a century of labor in Wisconsin.

Brother Thomas is a man of good business habits, a careful administrator, and a good Preacher. He loves the theology and economy of the Church for which he has so long expended his energies. He is wise in counsel, closely attentive to all the trusts committed to his keeping, and has a host of friends.

Rev. George C. Haddock, Pastor at Waukesha, was received into the Conference the previous year, had been at Port Washington one year, where he had been a supply a part of the previous year, and was now appointed to

Waukesha. He remained two years, and did a good work. During the first year, the new stone Church was built in the place of the old frame building that had been burned during the former year. And during the winter following, the charge was blessed with a good revival, and among the fruits gathered into the Church, was our second daughter, then ten years of age.

After leaving Waukesha, Brother Haddock's appointments have been Clinton, Oshkosh, Ripon, Appleton, Division Street, Fond du Lac; Fond du Lac District, and Racine, where he is laboring at this writing.

Brother Haddock is a man of mark. Early in life he acquired the printer's trade, and subsequently devoted several years to the business of editing and publishing secular papers. Soon after his conversion he entered the Ministry, and in less than two years he was received into the Conference. During the fifteen years of his connection with the Conference, he has been an earnest and successful laborer, making full proof of his Ministry. Brother Haddock has a large intellectual development, a warm heart, an eloquent tongue, and an intense spiritual activity. What he does must be done at once, and done thoroughly. He has an ardent hatred of shams, and despises all clap-trap. Both in sermons and debate, he strikes home, and woe be to the luckless pate that has the temerity to dash under his well-aimed strokes. And yet under all this seeming severity, there dwells a spirit as kind and manly as ever throbbed in a human bosom.

During this, the closing year of my term on the District, my labors were very extended. Besides the regular duties of a large District, I added that of aiding in raising regiments for the war. At all suitable times and places, I held war meetings, as they were called, and addressed the people, often finding immense crowds congregated in groves and other convenient localities.

It was in connection with these services that I was nominated for the Colonelcy of a religious regiment, to be raised out of the Churches of the city. But such were my responsibilities at home, where the Government needed all the support it could obtain, it was deemed inadvisable for me to accept. And on further thought it was considered better for the service to avoid such distinctive organizations.

During my term on the District, the annual Camp Meeting at Brookfield greatly prospered. Permanent tents were erected, and the Meeting gave considerable promise of stability. And on these grounds from year to year many persons, were brought into the liberty of the Gospel.

CHAPTER XXI

The Conference of 1862 was held Oct. 1st at Kenosha, Bishop Janes presiding. The country was now in the full tide of war. During the year several members of the Conference had gone out as Chaplains, Rev. H.C. Tilton with the Thirteenth Regiment, Rev. C.D. Pillsbury with the Twenty-Second, and Rev. Samuel Fallows with the Thirty-Second.

This was the hour for brave words, and the Wisconsin Conference had them to give. Nor was it in words alone that she was prepared to sustain the Government. Such was the patriotism of the body that her ranks might have been seriously depleted at any time, if it could have been done with safety to the interests of the country. But it was conceded that the Government must now have a vigorous support at home. Partisan feeling in the late canvass had greatly demoralized the people, and a strong moral influence was needed to rightly shape the tone of public sentiment. In fact, it was necessary throughout the struggle that the Churches, under the lead of the clergy, should act the part of Aaron and Hur, in sustaining the Government.

The Report adopted by the Conference on the state of the country gave no uncertain expression of sentiment. Assuming the position dictated by the most lofty patriotism, she pledged the country an unwavering support until the flag of the Commonwealth should again wave in peaceful triumph over the entire land. Recognizing human freedom as the issue in the conflict, she deemed it alike the duty of the citizen and the Christian to prosecute the war.

At this Conference the death of Rev. Jonathan M. Snow was announced, and his obituary placed upon the Minutes. Brother Snow, after spending a short time in Racine, entered the Illinois Conference in 1838. His appointments were Elgin, Princeton, Mount Morris, Geneva, Washington, Sylvania, Troy, Janesville, Mineral Point and Madison. At the close of his labors at Madison, in 1852, he retired from the active work, but in 1859, he was re-admitted and granted a superannuated relation. Brother Snow was a decisive man, earnest, energetic and persevering. He performed his full share of pioneer work, and deserves an honorable mention among the Fathers of the Conference,

In compliance with the request of the Spring Street Station, Milwaukee, I was this year appointed to its Pastorate, my term on the District having expired. At the earliest possible moment, I entered upon the work of my new field. But at the opening of the year we were called to pass under a cloud. I refer to the death of Dr. Bowman, the father of Mrs. Miller. The Doctor had been compelled, through illness, to surrender his practice in Iowa, and had now been with us three years. His death was peaceful, and his assurance triumphant.

Dr. Bowman came to Wisconsin in 1840, residing, as we have seen, first at Troy, and subsequently at Waupun. In early life he was a skeptic, and continued in unbelief, until after his elevation to a Judgeship in Michigan. He was converted through the influence of his wife, and united with the Methodist Episcopal Church. Distinguished in his profession, reliable in his religious convictions, and devoted to the Church, he was an arm of strength to the cause in its early struggles in the West.

During the interval since my former Pastorate in 1851 and the present, various changes had occurred at Spring Street. The Society had lost two Churches by fire, and Summerfield charge had been formed. The successive Pastors had been Revs. S.C. Thomas, Chauncey Hobart, P.S. Bennett, Milton Rowley, C.S. Macreading, E. Robinson, J.M. Walker, and J.C. Robbins. To several of them reference has been made in former chapters. We will now refer to others.

Rev. P.S. Bennett entered the Black River Conference in 1838, and remained a member of that body until 1849, when he was transferred to the Wisconsin Conference. Among the several charges he filled in his old Conference, were Norfolk, Bangor, Brownville, Salina, Cleveland, Van Buren and Red Creek. In Wisconsin he had been stationed at Platteville, Beloit, and Waukesha.

After leaving Spring Street, he was made Presiding Elder of the Milwaukee District, where he remained four years. His subsequent appointments were Racine, Appleton, Agent of Lawrence University, Green Bay, and Appleton District. At the close of his term on this District, he retired from active labor, having given to the Church a long, devoted, and efficient service.

Brother Bennett is well read in the literature of the Church, and loves her doctrines with a "true heart, fervently." During his active labor he was faithful to every trust confided to his keeping, was a good Pastor and a successful Presiding Elder. And at the present time, it needs only an attack upon the doctrines or usages of the Church to bring him to the front in their defence. He is emphatically a true man.

Rev. C.S. Macreading came from New England, where he had held leading appointments in the Providence and New England Conferences for many years. He had located, and had come West, seeking a field of labor. Coming to Milwaukee, he found the charge vacant, by the removal of the former Pastor on account of affliction in his family, and was employed by the Elder. He served his full term, and at its close the people were reluctant to part with him.

Brother Macreading was a man of superior preaching talent; had an earnest spirit, and a warm heart. At Spring Street, the Lord greatly blessed his labors in the conversion of souls, several of whom remain to this day to bless the Church with their wise counsel and devoted services.

In entering upon the labor of the year, it was my first concern to retrieve, if possible, the disaster which had befallen the Society in the loss of the Church. But to do this, it was deemed important to put every branch of the work in the best possible condition. In this endeavor I had the earnest co-operation of the Official Board, composed at this time of Rev. T.T. Greenwood, Rev. Edwin Hyde, and Messrs. John H. Van Dyke, J.B. Judson, A.J.W. Pierce, Walter Lacy, Cornelius Morse, Daniel Petrie, Jonathan Crouch, James Seville, H.W. Goodall, Thomas Greenwood, O.H. Earl, J.R. Cocup, James Cherry, and Lawrence Harrison.

The spiritual condition of the Society was excellent, and the class and prayer meetings were in a flourishing condition. The next thing to be done was to organize the financial department. In doing this I submitted a new plan, called the "Card System," for raising the current expenses. The plan provided for monthly payments, and was operated through the use of cards. These were so prepared as to contain a subscription on one side, and rulings for entering the payments monthly on the other. The subscriptions were to be made at the beginning of the year, and each subscriber was expected to hand to the collector the several amounts promptly. The plan worked admirably, and placed the finances in a healthy condition.

During the winter we held a series of meetings, which resulted in a considerable accession to the membership. But this success was only preparatory to the Church enterprise before us. The hall that had been used as a chapel was small and inconveniently located. Better accommodations must be had. By the middle of the year the necessity became so urgent that the Pastor could hardly preach, pray or visit without making this subject his principal theme. Finding that the financial basis was quite limited, it was decided to erect a business block, thereby providing for a subsequent income, should the enterprise entail an indebtedness upon the Society. The precaution, however, was unnecessary, as the unparalleled liberality of the people not only met the demands of the enterprise, but provided for a former indebtedness. Ground was broken for the new edifice on the fifteenth day of July, and the Church was dedicated by Rev. Dr. Eddy on the twenty-third of January following.

The Juvenile Missionary Society was formed this year, and thereby the Sunday School became an efficient agency in raising Missionary money. In our plan, each class in the School constituted a Missionary Society, taking a distinctive name. The gatherings of the class for a month went into a common fund, and was reported at the monthly meeting. This meeting was held on the last Sabbath of each month, and was usually made an occasion of special interest.

The year now closing had been full of work. Besides my regular labor, and the responsibilities of the Church enterprise, I had rendered considerable service in raising regiments for the war, by delivering addresses in various portions of the State.

From the beginning of the conflict, I greatly desired to go forward with the brave boys and share with them the burdens and perils of the camp and field. But it was the view of many of my friends, and especially of the Central War Committee of the State, that I was doing a better service for my country at home, in seeking to shape public sentiment, than I could render by leading a regiment in the field. Accepting their judgment, I endeavored to fulfil my mission to the best of my ability in the field to which I seemed to be specially called.

The Conference of 1863 was held Oct. 1st, at Waukesha, and was presided over by Bishop Scott. The body again adopted a strong report in support of the Government. At this Conference Delegates to the General Conference were again elected. They were H. Bannister, S.C. Thomas, C.D. Pillsbury and M. Himebaugh. At the close of the session I was returned to Spring Street. My fellow Pastors in the city were Revs. P.B. Pease and George Fellows.

Brother Pease entered the Wisconsin Conference at its session in Fond du Lac, Sept. 1st, 1852. His appointments had been Aztalan, Wauwatosa, Palmyra, Appleton, Kenosha, and Beloit. He remained two years at Summerfield. His subsequent appointments have been Spring Street, Appleton District, and Janesville District, where at the present writing he is doing a good-work.

Brother Pease has a clear head, a sound understanding, and positive convictions. His pulpit ministrations are impressive and practical, his administration wise and reliable, and his intercourse with the people agreeable and spiritual. Wherever he has labored he has left a record of ability and fidelity.

Brother Fellows entered the Wisconsin Conference in 1852, in the same class with Brother Pease. He was stationed at Wauwatosa, Grafton, Hartford, Oconomowoc, Beaver Dam, and Kenosha. He located in 1859, was re-admitted in 1862, and appointed to Asbury the same year. Here he had been engaged in the erection of a new Church. During this year the building was completed, and the old Church changed into a Parsonage. The Church was dedicated by Rev. Dr. Eddy, assisted by Rev. Dr. Tiffany.

In 1864 Brother Fellows located, and for two years served Madison Station. He returned to the Conference in 1866, and was appointed to Oconomowoc. His subsequent fields of labor were Waukesha, Neenah, Menasha, and Cotton Street, Fond du Lac. In 1872 he accepted a Bible Agency, and in 1874 was appointed Presiding Elder of Waupaca District. Brother Fellows is a man of energy, and will doubtless make an efficient Presiding Elder.

On the Spring Street charge the new year opened auspiciously. The accessions of the former year, in connection, with the better Church accommodations, had given to the work a broader basis, and afforded the promise of wider usefulness. From month to month throughout the year, the stakes were strengthened and the cords lengthened. And at its close there was a general feeling of grateful satisfaction.

In 1864 the Conference was held Oct. 5th at Oshkosh, Bishop Scott presiding. At this session Rev. Samuel Fallows was elected Secretary. Brother Fallows, after his graduation from the State University, devoted several years to the profession of teaching, in connection with the Galesville University, in the Northwestern part of the State. He came to the Wisconsin Conference in 1861, and was stationed at Oshkosh. Before the expiration of the year, however, he went out as a Chaplain in the army, in the service of the Thirty-Second Regiment, and at the Conference of 1862, he received his appointment to that post. Having returned from the army his next appointment, in 1863, was Appleton Station. He was reappointed to the same charge in 1864, but before the expiration of the year he became interested in raising a regiment of one hundred days' men, and went out as Lieutenant Colonel. He graduated to the Colonelcy while in the service, and was brevetted as Brigadier General on his return home. The war having closed before the expiration of the Conference year, he returned to the regular work, and received his appointment in 1865 to the Summerfield Station. After serving three years at Summerfield, he was appointed in 1868 to Spring Street. Here he drew to his ministry a large congregation, and had an extensive revival, thereby hastening the erection of a new Church. The building during the second year was enclosed, but was not completed until the close of the following year.

Brother Fallows enjoyed a successful Pastorate at Spring Street, but before the expiration of his second year, he was appointed by the Executive of the State to the position of Superintendent of Public Instruction. He remained in this position until his second term expired, Jan. 1, 1874, when having been elected President of the Illinois Wesleyan University, he was transferred to the Illinois Conference.

Brother Fallows was a man whom his brethren delighted to honor. Though still a young man comparatively, he had served his Conference as Secretary nine years, and had been sent once as a Delegate to the General Conference. He is a man of superior culture, pleasant voice, and entertaining address. His genial spirit is a perpetual sunshine, and his conversational interviews, the fragrance of summer. In his addresses and sermons, the beautiful predominates. He was born an orator, and he has never been able to shake off the enchantment. It is not his fault that he is generally popular.

At this session the Conference adopted another report of the state of the country. It was full of patriotism, pledging an unwavering support to the Government. The chairman of the committee was Rev. R.B. Curtis.

Brother Curtis entered the Maine Conference in 1845, and in that Conference and the East Maine he filled the following appointments: Bingham, Corinth, Onoro, Frankfort, Searsport, Brick Chapel, Bangor, Bangor District, and again Brick Chapel. He was transferred to the Wisconsin Conference in 1862, and was appointed to Janesville. His next appointment was Delavan, where he remained three years. While here his health failed, and at the ensuing Conference he was compelled to take a superannuated relation. He passed from the earthly to the heavenly home, in Appleton, May 21st, 1872.

Brother Curtis was a man of rare endowments and sublime piety. In his mental development, there was an almost absolute equipoise between the imagination and the logical powers. In his logical dissections of error and defence of truth, a keener blade has seldom, if ever, leaped from its scabbard. Under his masterly imagery his audiences were sometimes chained to their seats, as if held by the toils of an enchantment. With such extraordinary elements of popular address, it is not surprising that he held a high rank in the pulpit. Nor was he deficient in his other qualifications as a Minister of Christ. When Brother Curtis fell from the walls of Zion, it might have been truly said, "A Prince in Israel has this day exchanged the earthly for the Heavenly Crown."

During this year Rev. D.H. Muller was Pastor of Asbury Church. Brother Muller entered the Conference in 1861, coming from the Biblical School at Evanston. His first appointment was Menasha, and his second Oshkosh. And from the last named he came to Asbury. He remained two years, was successful and highly esteemed; but at the close of his term he took a transfer to the Genesee Conference. He has held leading appointments in that Conference up to the present, and has also graduated to the dignity of a Presiding Elder.

Brother Muller is a man of superior talent, genial spirit and fine conversational powers. His name is fragrant in all the charges he served in Wisconsin and the Conference regretted his transfer from the State.

I was again returned to Spring Street, and the salary was now placed at thirteen hundred dollars. With the new Church full of people, with every department of Church work thoroughly organized and in successful operation, I was now permitted to devote my labor to the regular pastoral work. As far as possible, the forenoons were given to my study and the afternoons to pastoral visiting.

In a city like Milwaukee, this last department of labor is absolutely indispensable. It is not intended in this form of expression to intimate that it can be dispensed with in any other field, for it cannot, but simply to indicate the impossibility of caring rightly for the souls of men in a great city, if this form of labor shall be neglected.

In a large city, the population is constantly changing, and unless the Pastor shall be on the alert in looking up the people, members of his own flock, to say nothing of others, will drop out of sight. Soon they will feel that the band of union between them and the Church has been severed, and they have become outcasts. The result of such a state of things, will be either recklessness of life, or a seeking of other Church alliances. In either case, the charge itself suffers loss. In addition to this class of cases that need the eagle eye of the Pastor, there is a constant influx of population. These coming people, in large numbers, will fail to find churchly affiliations unless there is some one who shall seek them out at their new homes, and invite them to attend the means of grace.

I know it will be said, "Let the members of the Churches do this." I grant that the open field for this kind of labor is inviting to the Church members, but suppose they do not enter it, what then? Shall the work be left undone? Besides, the work can be done effectively only, through systematic arrangement, and this feature can only be given to it through the supervision of the Pastor. He only can know the entire ground, and become the nucleus around which the membership will be able to rally.

It would greatly aid the Pastor in his work, if all new-comers would immediately report themselves at the Parsonage or the Church. But as all such are usually burdened with many cares and perplexities during the first weeks or months in making a new home, the only way to reach the desired result seems to be through the vigilant maintenance of pastoral visiting.

During the winter I held a protracted meeting, which gave an addition of forty-seven probationers. I felt the fatigue very much, and at the close of the meeting found it necessary for a time to abridge my labors.

In March following, the Official Board granted me leave of absence to engage for six weeks in the service of the Christian Commission. I was assigned to service at City Point, and along the lines of Gen. Grant's army, before Richmond and Petersburgh. Leaving Milwaukee March 14th, and passing through Chicago, Pittsburgh, and Philadelphia, I entered the James River at Fortress Monroe, and reached City Point on the 21st. After calling at the headquarters of Gen. Grant, and preaching once in the Chapel at the headquarters of the Christian Commission, I went along the line of the army, first to the north of Point of Rocks, twenty miles, and then to the south, twenty miles, as far as Hatch's Run, making forty miles in all. In these excursions I preached in the several Chapels as opportunity offered, and rendered such assistance as I was able, in making the necessary preparations for the forward movement of the army, which was expected to occur in a few days. But I soon found that the exposures along the front were too great for my system, in its enfeebled condition. I contracted a severe cold, which rendered it necessary to leave the lines. I returned to City Point, and was advised to leave at once for Washington, where I could obtain the desired medical treatment. I took the steamboat the very afternoon the army was put in motion. By the time Gen. Grant had taken Gen. Lee, I had taken Washington.

The physicians here believed that my lungs were seriously compromised, and advised me to go to the seashore. I went immediately down to Brooklyn, and became the guest of my cousin, Col. J.T. Hildreth. My family and friends at Milwaukee at once became alarmed, and Mrs. Miller came down.

But through skillful treatment, good nursing, and a kind Providence, the indications soon changed for the better, and at the end of two months I was able to return to my people. On reaching the city the friends gave us a reception, and left us over two hundred dollars. I was able to resume my labors soon after, and the balance of the year passed pleasantly. I had now completed my full term of three years. During this time I had received into the Church about two hundred members, and after allowing for removals and other changes, the net increase had been about half that number.

Though the people had been greatly taxed in building their new Church, it was found that the benevolent collections had considerably increased. The Missionary, collection advanced during the first year from seventy-five dollars to two hundred and twenty. The second year it was two hundred and sixty-two, and the third, three hundred and forty.

The Sunday School had now reached an aggregate of four hundred scholars, and the Library six hundred volumes. Among the accessions of the term, there were several who gave considerable financial strength to the charge.

CHAPTER XXII

The Conference of 1865 was held Oct. 4th in Summerfield Church, Milwaukee, Bishop Baker presiding, and assisted by Bishop Ames. Rev. Samuel Fallows was elected Secretary, and Revs. Wm. P. Stowe, E.D. Farnham and R.W. Bosworth Assistants.

The relentless war that had raged for four years had now closed. The clouds had lifted from the fields of conflict, and the Conference was now able to take note of the past and anticipate the future of the country. The report adopted at this session, presented by the Committee on the state of the country, was a masterly document. It recognized the fact that the Wisconsin Conference, since its organization, had exhibited a bold and manly opposition to American Slavery. That the recent rebellion, aiming its blows at the Government, bought by the blood of Revolutionary patriots, was the outgrowth of the institution of Slavery. And that the Conference, in common with the Laity, and loyal citizens of the North generally, had acquitted herself nobly, in standing by the Government in its hour of trial, and, having rendered this service as a Christian duty, she had nothing to take back. Looking out upon the future, she also anticipated the coming day when equal rights should be accorded to all, irrespective of color or nationality.

The question of Slavery and the frightful war it had entailed upon the country having passed away, the Conference now took up the subject of Lay Delegation. And since the subject is new to many, it may not be improper to devote to it a brief examination.

The question has been raised, "How came it to pass that in the organization of the Methodist Episcopal Church, the Laity were not associated with the Ministry in the Conferences?" The question is a legitimate one, and deserves a considerate answer.

It should be remembered that the establishment of the Church was rather a growth than an organization. This one fact accounts, doubtless, for the peculiar feature referred to. Had there existed at the outset a large body of Christians, including Ministers and Laymen, awaiting an organization, at the time Mr. Wesley began his labors, it is possible that he might have so combined them in appropriate relations as to secure a united responsibility. But such was not the state of the case. In the strict sense of the word, Mr. Wesley had no Church, and no people out of which to organize one. And it is possible that he began his labors without an expectation of organizing a Church. His great concern, overleaping every other consideration, was to save souls. In this work he was ready to call to his aid such instrumentalities as gave the best promise of the desired result. It was but natural that, whenever he met a congenial spirit, there should be an affiliation. In such case a unity of effort would necessarily follow.

In this manner there grew up around Mr. Wesley a company of men, who were recognized as his helpers. With the multiplication of these assistant laborers, it became advisable to reduce the co-operative effort to a systematic plan. To adopt a plan of labor and give it efficiency, the organization of Conferences became a necessity. The first Conferences were composed of Mr. Wesley and his helpers, and could not embody Laymen, as no Church had been organized. This state of things continued during the life time of Mr. Wesley in England, and as he gave the Church in the United States its first organization, the same system was introduced here.

Subsequently, as the work extended and the Conferences multiplied, it was but natural that they should all take the same character. Nor would there have been any special need for a change, perhaps, if there had been no changes in the character of the work to be done. But with the erection of Churches, the founding of schools, and the creation of the Book Concern and Church literature, the Conferences, having these interests in charge, need the presence and aid of Laymen.

At the General Conference of 1864, action had been taken inviting the membership to vote on the subject, and also to elect provisional Delegates to the General Conference of 1868. The action of the Wisconsin Conference fully endorsed the movement and the body faithfully complied with its provisions.

At this session the Conference made a record of the death, of three of its members, Revs. Henry Requa, George Chester and Romulus O. Kellogg. To the first named, reference has been made in former chapters.

Brother Chester came to this country in 1849, from England, where he had been converted under the labors of Rev. James Caughey. He was received into the Wisconsin Conference in 1851, and was appointed to Prairie La Crosse. His subsequent appointments were Willow River, Madison Circuit, Waterloo, Columbus, Burnett, Fox Lake, Footville, Evansville, and Shopiere.

At the last named place he was attacked with typhoid fever, and, after an illness of three weeks, passed away in holy triumph, with the words, "Glory! Glory! Glory!" upon his lips. Brother Chester was a true man, and a successful Minister of the Lord Jesus Christ.

Brother Kellogg came with his parents to Milwaukee in 1836. He prepared for College at Rock River Seminary, Mount Morris, graduated at the Wesleyan University, Conn., in 1849, and served as Professor of Languages in the Lawrence University for five years thereafter. He was received into the Wisconsin Conference in 1862, and was appointed to Fort Atkinson. He was reappointed the second and third years, but, during the latter, his nervous system gave way under his devoted and trying labors, and he passed to the bright beyond. Brother Kellogg was a man of fine culture, genial spirit, faithful to every trust, and universally beloved by all who knew him.

The Conference at this session was again called upon to send one of its members abroad as a Missionary. Rev. L.N. Wheeler was sent to China. He was presented at the Conference with an album containing the photographs of the donors as a token of remembrance. The writer was selected to make the presentation speech, as he had known him from his childhood.

Brother Wheeler, before he engaged in the Ministerial work, devoted several years to editing and publishing secular papers. He entered the Conference in 1858, and had been stationed at Two Rivers, Byron, Empire, Manitowoc, and Sheboygan.

Having been advised with by the Mission Board at New York during the year, as to his qualifications, I was prepared to expect the appointment, fully persuaded that it would prove both creditable to the Conference and profitable to the Mission field. While abroad Brother Wheeler had charge for some time of the Mission press. He rendered efficient service in the China Mission during the seven years of his absence. But, on account of failing health, he was compelled to return in 1872. He is now stationed again at Manitowoc. He is a man of superior talent, and is greatly esteemed.

I had now completed my term of three years on the Spring Street Station, and my next appointment was very much in doubt. I had been solicited to accept invitations to several stations, and also the Fond du Lac District, but in each case I assured the good brethren that I deemed it best to let the Bishop and his Cabinet decide without prejudice, and assign me work where they believed I could serve the general cause to the best advantage. Had I allowed myself a preference, it would have been some quiet station of moderate responsibility, where I could have rallied my enfeebled health. Besides, I had a doubt whether I ought to be put on a District so soon again, after having completed two full terms before I reached my fortieth year. But it is vain to speculate in advance. At the close of the Conference, I found myself appointed Presiding Elder of Fond du Lac District.

The appointment was a surprise to both myself and family. But accepting the situation as a legitimate feature of the Itinerancy, we entered at once upon the needed preparations for a removal to Fond du Lac. The removal, however, was to be preceded by an event that, by separating the family, would render the change exceedingly trying. I refer to the marriage of our eldest daughter to Capt. Frank P. Lawrence, of Racine, thereby breaking a link out of the chain that had so long and pleasantly bound us together in the family circle. But, having previously learned that life's difficulties are best overcome by turning towards them a brave bearing, we prepared for the nuptials.

On the morning of the 17th of October a few friends came in at the breakfast hour, and our daughter passed into the keeping of another. Though fully satisfied with the arrangement, the occasion imposed upon me the most difficult duty of my life. The ceremony was performed in connection with the family devotions, and quite unmanned me. Assembled in the parlor, I took my usual place to lead the devotions. The Scriptures were read, and my daughter presided as usual at the piano. Thus far everything maintained its accustomed order. But when we knelt in prayer, and I closed my eyes to all visible things, the invisible came trooping in throngs to my already burdened thought. Then came the vivid recollection of the many happy years we had spent together as a family, the many sweet hours we had spent together in that parlor, with music and song, in which our dear daughter had ever been the central figure, and the now sad fact of an immediate separation. The chain must now be broken, and its then brightest link snatched away to gladden another home, while our own circle must be broken forever.

With these thoughts rushing upon me, it is not a matter of surprise that I was quite overwhelmed with feeling, and found utterance almost impossible. How I passed through the prayer and the ceremony that followed, has never been quite clear to me, but I was told that nothing was omitted that could be deemed essential to the occasion. The wedding party was soon after dismissed with our blessing, and we at once began the preparations for our own trip to the cars, to occur in the afternoon of the same day.

We reached Fond du Lac at nightfall, and were kindly entertained by Rev. J.T. Woodhead and his family. The following day we were invited to the pleasant home of our old friend, C.O. Hurd, who, with his most excellent family, gave us a kindly greeting and cared for us until the arrival of our goods.

My predecessor on the District was Rev. Theron O. Hollister, a man "full of faith and the Holy Ghost." Brother Hollister was received into the Conference at its session in Baraboo in 1853, and his first charge was Summit. His subsequent fields of labor were Fort Atkinson, Lake Mills, Greenbush, Sheboygan Falls, and Fond du Lac, where he succeeded to the District. At the close of his term on the District he was appointed to Oconomowoc, next to Waukesha, and the year following to Hart Prairie. Here his health utterly broke down, and at the following session of the Conference in 1868, he was compelled to take a superannuated relation. He now removed to Salem, in Kenosha County, where he died March 13, 1869, aged forty-seven.

Brother Hollister was a man of robust frame, and, generally, good health. He was an earnest man, and whatever he did was done with all his strength, of both mind and body. With limited early opportunities, and too intensely occupied in after years with the practical labor of the Ministry, to retrieve the loss he had sustained, he did not aspire to a knowledge of books. But in all the active labor of leading souls to Christ, he was a workman who needed not to be ashamed.

He swept over the District like a storm, "instant in season and out of season," laying his strong hand on every part of the work, and pushing it forward. And no doubt it was the work that he did on the District that laid the foundation of the disease which terminated his useful life. An overtaxed brain fell a prey to mental disability, and our good brother went to his reward.

Fond du Lac was under the pastoral care of Rev. J.T. Woodhead. This excellent brother entered the Conference in 1858, and before coming to Fond du Lac, had been stationed at Greenbush, Berlin and Ripon. He was now on his third year in his present field.

Brother Woodhead's early opportunities were limited, but with great devotion to his calling, he had carefully improved his time after entering the Ministry. He was accepted by his people as a man of rare excellences, happily blending in beautiful harmony both Faith and Works. In the pulpit, his manner is not always graceful, but it is never disagreeable. His discourses abound with Evangelical truth, set off usually in fine delineations of Scriptural scenes and characters. He has extraordinary dramatic talent, and only needs the culture of the schools, in addition to his present gifts and graces, to place him in the front rank as a speaker. Brother Woodhead is one of the best Pastors I have ever known.

The Fond du Lac District at this time numbered twenty charges. To visit each quarterly on the Sabbath was impossible, unless I chose to hold two on adjacent charges, the same day. And this plan I did not deem advisable, believing that it tends to break down Quarterly Meetings altogether, by dividing the interest. I chose rather to visit each charge regularly semi-annually, and the feebler ones more frequently, if possible. The intervening Quarterly Meetings were held by the Pastors, except they chose to procure supplies.

My first Quarterly Meeting, held at Fond du Lac, was an occasion of rare interest. Having been granted license to preach, and sent into the Itinerancy by these brethren, they were disposed to assert a special interest in the Presiding Elder. Besides, the Society, under the ministrations of Brother Woodhead, was in a happy spiritual condition, a satisfactory pledge of a good meeting.

As it is my purpose to write up more particularly, as far as space will permit, the charges and Ministers of the Conference, than my own labors, I shall not undertake to follow in order my visits to the several charges. During the present year, as well as the three following, I shall simply refer to such items as will further this object, well knowing that the adoption of any other plan would involve the issue of several volumes instead of one.

Waupun came early on the list. Many changes had occurred at Waupun during the twenty years which had intervened since my Pastorate in 1845. I found a small frame Church and one of the best Parsonages in the Conference. The Society had become strong both financially and in numbers. I was happy indeed to meet old friends with whom I had labored in other years, and especially the converts of the early times, now grown to be pillars in the Church. But with our rejoicing there also came the shadows of sadness. Many had gone over the river. And since my visit, others still have gone, and among them, Brother and Sister William McElroy. But they were ready.

Rev. D.W. Couch was the Pastor at Waupun. He entered the Conference in 1857, and before coming to Waupun had been stationed at Bristol, Pleasant Prairie, Geneva, and had also served as Agent of the Northwestern Seaman's Friend Society. After leaving Waupun his appointments have been Janesville in the Wisconsin Conference, and Mineral Point in the West

Wisconsin. At the last Conference he was appointed Presiding Elder of the Madison District, where he is rendering effective service.

Brother Couch is a very useful man, having unusual ability to adjust himself to such work as requires special adaptations. He has a great fund of anecdote, and is able to make a draft on this reserve whenever needed. He has special control of the purses of the people, and hence is in great requisition wherever there is a call for funds, and especially at Church dedications. He is a pronounced success.

At Lamartine my Quarterly Meeting also revived old recollections. The charge now embraced Rock River, where I formed a class in 1845, and also the Society that held their services, at an early day, in Brother Stowe's Chapel. A Church had now been built at Lamartine, the centre of the charge, and also a Parsonage. The charge was now in a flame of revival. With the praying band at Rock River at one end of the Circuit, and Brother Humiston and his devoted laborers at the other, an almost continuous revival was but the normal condition. But in addition, I now found the circuit under the charge of Rev. I.S. Eldridge, one of my old co-laborers at Janesville.

Brother Eldridge entered the Conference in April, 1859, and before coming to Lamartine had been stationed at Utter's Corners, Palmyra, Wauwatosa, and Byron. He was now on his second year, the charge having enjoyed during the former one great prosperity. After leaving Lamartine, Brother Eldridge's appointments have been Horicon and Juneau, Fox Lake, Brandon, Sheboygan Falls, Burnett, and Eagle.

Brother Eldridge is yet in the vigor of his strength, and gives promise of many years of usefulness. While his great forte is revival work, he has mental and spiritual force enough to amply sustain every other department of a Minister's obligation. During the earlier portion of his work, his incessant labor in protracted meetings greatly abridged his opportunities for study, but I presume in later years he has endeavored to retrieve the loss sustained. At this writing he is again at Eagle, where his accessions are already climbing the second hundred.

At Horicon I found Rev. Walter McFarlane, Pastor of the Horicon and Juneau charge. This dear brother and his most estimable lady gave me a hearty welcome, and made me feel at home in a few moments. I found the charge in a prosperous condition, and the Pastor in high esteem among the people.

Brother McFarlane is a Scotchman by birth. He entered the Conference in 1856, and was stationed at Cascade. His following appointments were Oconto, Vinland, Two Rivers, and Empire. He was now on his second year in his present charge. After leaving Horicon, he was stationed at Byron. While on this charge he and his good lady took great interest in fitting up the Camp-Meeting grounds of the Fond du Lac District. A fine Preacher's stand was erected, comfortable seats were provided, and many permanent tents were built. The meetings during this period became far-famed and highly profitable. The great burden of looking after all local matters was sustained by this good Brother, as the Pastor of the charge, and the administration was always highly acceptable. After leaving Byron, his appointments were Winneconne, Bristol, Sylvania, and Granville. In this last named charge, he is at this writing doing effective work.

Brother McFarlane is well versed in Theology and Biblical criticism. He has a large fund of information on all subjects of general interest, and is able to make himself an interesting companion among the people. He has an intense dislike to the superficial, and is never satisfied with the examination of any subject until he can feel the firm foundation beneath him. In his sermons he seeks to give reliable information on specific subjects rather than spin glittering generalities. Firm as the Highlands of his native home, and balmy as her valleys, he is none other than a highly esteemed brother.

CHAPTER XXIII

The Conference of 1866 was held at Ripon, Bishop Clark presiding. The Secretaries were the same as the preceding year.

The Centenary of American Methodism occurred this year, and the month of October had been set apart for the purposes of a celebration. The writer had been designated to preach a Centenary sermon during the session of the Conference, but as I was called to Waupun to attend the funeral of my brothers's wife, on the day the services were to have been held, the good Bishop kindly consented to occupy the pulpit for me.

The collections during the Centenary year were mostly given to Educational purposes, the Lawrence University, the Garrett Biblical Institute, and the Evansville Seminary being the beneficiaries. The first named received perhaps fifteen thousand dollars.

The subject of Lay Delegation again engaged the attention of the body. While fully sympathizing with the general movement, the Conference anticipated the contemplated change by inviting the several District Steward's meetings to elect three Delegates from each District to visit the ensuing session of the Annual Conference, and co-operate with that body in its deliberations, as far as the polity of the Church would permit. The invitation was accepted, and at the next session the Delegates were cordially received.

At this time the question of the Ecclesiastical Reconstruction of the South was beginning to agitate the Church. The Conference, always radical on all the great questions of the day, took advanced ground, and consistently adhered to its positions throughout the discussion. The subsequent history of the Southern work has fully justified the action taken.

With this session of the Conference began the Cabinet work of my third term as Presiding Elder. Adhering to my former convictions, I favored only such changes in the appointments as were dictated by the law of the Church and stern necessity. In connection with the appointments, an effort was made to secure my assignment to the station in Fond du Lac, but when it was known that a Committee from the Official Board was in attendance upon the Conference, the Ministers and Laymen of the District entered a vigorous remonstrance.

The Bishop kindly enquired whether I had any suggestions to make. I answered, "I have never interfered in making my own appointments; and it is too late to begin now. As you and the Cabinet understand the case, having had a full representation from both sides, I will step aside and let you decide the matter." After an absence of an hour, I returned, and found my name still at the head of the District.

At the close of the session I returned to Fond du Lac and entered upon another year of taxing labor. The work was growing rapidly, and it was necessary to reconstruct and enlarge several of the Churches, and build others. In several localities we succeeded in a consolidation of the work, thereby making it possible to erect several Churches. Instead of maintaining feeble appointments at contiguous school houses, we found it better to combine two or more of them, and build a Church in a central locality. In this way the Mulleton, Hingham, Leroy, Markesan, Lake Maria, and several other Churches found an existence.

During the winter season of this year, I was largely engaged with the several Pastors in protracted meetings. And during the first half of the year, I preached on an average seven sermons a week. The Pastors were a band of devoted and earnest workers, and the year was one of remarkable success.

At Fond du Lac a charge of Pastors occurred, as the term of the former Pastor had expired. His successor was Rev. O.J. Cowles. a young man of excellent promise. He was a graduate of Cornell College in 1860, and of the Garrett Biblical Institute in 1863. He entered the Conference the same year, and had been stationed at Kenosha, Berlin, and Appleton. After his two years of service in Fond du Lac, he was stationed three years each at Racine and Oshkosh.

Brother Cowles is a man of superior talent and excellent spirit. He is one of the rising men of the Conference, and bids fair to take a front rank. At this writing he is stationed at Whitewater, where he is in the midst of a gracious revival.

Beaver Dam Station was added this year to the District. Beaver Dam was settled by members of the Presbyterian Church, and hence its earliest religious services were held by the Ministers of that denomination. The first Methodist appointment was established by Rev. A.P. Allen in 1846, being then Pastor of Waupun Circuit as my successor. Rev. Henry Requa, as before stated, was employed by the Elder as his assistant. During the year these earnest laborers held a protracted meeting, which resulted in several conversions. The first class was formed by Brother Allen, and consisted of L.H. Marvin, Leader, Mr. and Mrs. Peters, Bennett Gordon, and Mrs. Reuben Dexter. Brother Marvin still resides at Beaver Dam.

The meetings were held in L.H. Marvin's cabinet shop, until other provision could be made. The first Church, a frame building twenty-six by forty feet in size, was commenced by Brother Allen in the winter of 1846 and '47, and completed the following year by Brother Requa. The building was enlarged under the Pastorate of Rev. I.M. Leihy in 1859. Under the Pastorate of Rev. A.A. Reed in 1870 and 1871, a large brick Church was erected, the writer being invited to lay the corner-stone the first year, and preach the dedicatory sermon the second. During Brother Reed's Pastorate a great revival also occurred, under the labors of Mrs. Maggie N. Van Cott, which added greatly to the strength of the Church. At the present writing, the Pastor is Rev. Isaac Wiltse, of whom mention will be made in a subsequent chapter.

Fall River and Columbus were assigned to the District this year from the Janesville District. At the organization of the work they constituted one Circuit, but had now grown to be independent charges.

Fall River Society was organized in the log house of Clark Smith, on Fountain Prairie, by Rev. Stephen Jones in 1844, the locality being at the time connected with the old Aztalan Circuit. The members were Rev. E.J. Smith, of whom mention is made elsewhere, his wife, Martha Smith, Clark Smith, Sarah Smith, Mr. and Mrs. Aaron E. Houghton. Brother E.J. Smith was appointed Leader.

A log school house, the first built in the county, was erected soon after, and the meetings were transferred to it. The population grew rapidly, being attracted by the beautiful location, and in due time there was a strong society. Under the energetic and effective labors of the Leader and his talented lady, this society was instrumental in the conversion of many souls.

In process of time a mill was built on the stream at Fall River. A fine school house was soon after erected, and the meetings removed to it, as the locality had become more central than the one on the Prairie. At the present writing, Fall River holds a most respectable rank as a charge, has a good Church, and a convenient Parsonage.

Columbus was visited by Rev. Stephen Jones in 1844, he having been appointed to Aztalan Circuit the preceding autumn. He preached the first sermon in the log dwelling house of Brigham Campbell, but I am unable to fix the date. Nor am I able to give the organization of the first class, but it is probable that during the early years the members in this locality were connected with the Society on Fountain Prairie.

In 1859 Columbus was made a station, and Rev. Henry Colman was appointed Pastor. The Society built their first Church, a frame structure, in an unfortunate location, but have now displaced it by a fine brick edifice, which they have placed in the central portion of the village. It is one of the best Churches in the interior of the State.

The present Pastor is Rev. Henry Sewell, who entered the Conference in 1858. His appointments have been Porter, Edgerton and Stoughton, Orfordville, Utter's Corners, Emerald Grove and Maxonville, Sun Prairie, Lake Mills, Oconomowoc, and Columbus. Brother Sewell is one of the most efficient men of the Conference. At Sun Prairie, he built a ten thousand dollar Church, and has succeeded in completing the enterprise at Columbus. In revival work Brother Sewell has met with rare success, usually increasing the membership of his charges at least one hundred per cent.

The Conference of 1867 was held Oct. 2d at Beaver Dam, Bishop Simpson presiding, and the same Secretaries were re-elected.

The action of the Conference on the subject of Lay Delegation will appear in the following resolutions:

"*Resolved,* That we are in favor of the representation of the Laity in Annual and General Conference."

"*Resolved,* That our Delegates to the next General Conference be instructed to use their influence in favor of such representation."

Having thus laid down the platform, the Conference next proceeded to elect the Delegates to the General Conference, resulting in the choice of G.M. Steele, W.G. Miller, Samuel Fallows, Henry Bannister, and C.D. Pillsbury.

Two other subjects specially engaged the attention of the Conference at this session. I refer to the "Sabbath Question," and "Ministerial Education." Appropriate resolutions were adopted, and measures taken to give efficiency to the timely expression of sentiment.

My work on the District opened at Cotton Street, Fond du Lac. This charge, under the name of Arndt Street, or North Fond du Lac, had been merged in the Division Street Station, and was now re-organized with Rev. M.D. Warner as Pastor. A new Church had been commenced during the preceding year, and it was now completed. The dedicatory services were conducted by the lamented Dr. T.M. Eddy.

Brandon was the next charge visited, the Pastor being my old friend Rev. R.S. Hayward, whose acquaintance, it will be remembered, I made as an Exhorter at Brothertown.

Brother Hayward entered the Conference in 1850, and had been stationed at Waupaca, Dartford, Metomon, Berlin, Wausau, and Sheboygan. He then served as Presiding Elder on the Waupaca District a full term, and was subsequently stationed at Vinland and Omro. In all these fields he had acquitted himself creditably, and was now doing a good work at Brandon. After leaving Brandon, he has served North Oshkosh, Clemensville, Menasha, Utica and Zion. At the last named he is now hard at work for the Master.

Rev. A.A. Reed, who had just completed a three years' term at Brandon, was now at Sheboygan Falls. This charge was continuing to hold a fair rank in the Conference, and during Brother Reed's Pastorate received many accessions, and also improved the Church property.

Brother Reed entered the Conference in 1859. His appointments had been Empire, Lamartine, Byron, Greenbush, and Brandon. At the close of a three years' term at Sheboygan Falls, he was sent to Beaver Dam, where he succeeded, as before stated, in erecting a fine Church, and greatly multiplying the membership. His present field, the Agency of the Lawrence University, is one of great labor. But in this work, as well as in whatever may be assigned him, Brother Reed is a grand success, and will accomplish his task.

The General Conference met in the month of May of this year in Chicago. During the session I was entertained by an old Milwaukee friend, Capt. J.C. Henderson, long known on the Lakes as the Sabbath keeping Captain. The two great questions that came before the body were Lay Delegation, and the admission of the Delegates from the newly formed Conferences in the South. Both measures received the approval of the General Conference, but as they were brought to the attention of the reader through the periodicals of the Church, I need not burden these pages with a further reference to them.

The Conference of 1868 was held Oct. 1st at Racine, Bishop Ames presiding. The term of Rev. Joseph Anderson on the Waupaca District having expired, one of the young, men of the Conference was appointed as his successor. I refer to Rev. T.C. Wilson.

This promising brother graduated from the Lawrence University in 1859, and was admitted to the Conference in 1862. Before being appointed to the District he had been stationed at East Troy, Clinton, and Neenah. His labors on the District were highly appreciated, and, at the close of his term in 1872, he was appointed Presiding Elder of the Appleton District, where he is, at this writing, still employed in the good work. He is recognized as a man of thorough scholarship, a good Preacher, and a successful laborer in the vineyard.

At the close of the Conference, the writer was returned to the Fond du Lac District for a fourth year. On the District there were but few changes, but among them was the bringing of two new men to Fond du Lac.

Rev. H.C. Tilton, appointed to Division Street, entered the Maine Conference July 21st, 1841. His appointments in that Conference were Mount Desert, Deer Island, Steuben, North Penobscot and North Bucksport. At the division of the Conference he fell into East Maine, and, before coming West, was stationed at Frankfort, Hampden, Bangor, Rockland and Damariscotta.

Brother Tilton came to the Wisconsin Conference by transfer in 1857. His appointments have been Summerfield, Janesville, Janesville District, Racine District, Asbury, Division Street. Court Street, Janesville, and Appleton.

Brother Tilton is a veteran in the work, having been in the Itinerancy nearly thirty-four years. Having possessed a vigorous constitution and firm health, he has taken his full share of privation and hard work. His services have always been in special demand, and he has not spared himself. He is a man of vigorous intellect and a ready delivery, his pulpit efforts always commanding the attention of the people. At this writing he is building in Appleton one of the best Churches in the Conference.

Rev. John Hill entered the North Indiana Conference in 1855. His appointments were Elkhart, La Grange, La Grove, Indianapolis, Anderson, Greenfield and Fort Wayne. He came to the Wisconsin Conference by transfer this year, and Cotton Street was his first charge. His next appointment was Summerfield, Milwaukee, and the last was Bay View. Here he was thrown from a wagon by the sudden starting of the horse, and, falling upon his head, received a severe injury, from which he died in twenty-four hours.

Brother Hill was a man of small frame, but a large brain and a generous heart. His style of speech was clear, distinct and rapid. He could reason a question with great force, and could fringe the most commonplace subjects with wit and humor. He was a true man, a good Preacher, and a faithful Pastor.

Rev. Isaac Searles was this year stationed at Brandon. He entered the Rock River Conference in 1841, and was appointed to Indian Creek Circuit. His subsequent appointments in that Conference were Sycamore, Cedar

Rapids, Rock Island, Union Grove, and Hazel Green. In 1848, at the division, he fell into the Wisconsin Conference. In Wisconsin his appointments were Dodgeville, Lindon, Platteville, Madison District, Fox Lake, Fall River, Dartford, Beaver Dam District, Watertown, Waukesha, East Troy, and now Brandon. At this place his health failed, and, after lingering; until December 8th, 1870, he was called to the Father's house: above. His death was triumphant. His last words were, "Jesus is mine, Jesus is mine." "He saves me to the uttermost." "I am standing on the Rock." Thus passed away a. noble man, a true friend, and a veteran Minister.

Rev. J.B. Cooper was this year employed to supply Byron charge. This excellent brother entered the traveling connection in the State of New York, where he filled several appointments, but, his health failing, he took a superannuated relation in 1854, and came to Janesville. In 1857 he rendered special service, as before stated, in the great revival of that year, and in 1860 re-entered the regular work in the Wisconsin Conference. His charges have been Evansville, Delavan, Hart Prairie, Byron, Randolph and Rosendale, where he is stationed at the present writing.

Brother Cooper is a good specimen of the Itinerant Preacher. His manner is affable, his spirit genial, and his hand diligent. In all his charges he is deservedly popular.

At one of the Quarterly Meetings of this charge, I was approached, at the close of the morning services, by a gentleman who enquired whether I came from the State of New York. On learning that I did, he further enquired whether I attended, when a boy, Prof. McLaren's Academy at Gallupville. I informed him that I was there several years. "Well," said he, "are you the one who measured the shote?" I replied, "Tell me about it, and we will see." He then related the following incident: "At the time to which I refer there was a boy about thirteen years old who was very proficient in figures, and the Professor took great pleasure in giving him difficult problems to solve during the dinner hour. On one of these occasions, as the Professor was going across the green for his dinner, the boy met him and asked for a problem. Looking up, he saw a half grown hog near by, and quickly replied, 'Give me the cubic inches of that shote.' And, supposing he had got a good joke on the boy, he passed on. But as soon as he was fairly out of sight, the boy called together several other boys, and stated the case to them, adding, 'Now, boys, if you will help me to catch that shote, we will show the Professor a thing that they have never done in Edinburgh.' The boys consented, and his hogship was soon made a prisoner. Under a vigorous vocal protest, he was then dragged to the back end of the Academy building, and plunged into a half hogshead of water. After his release, of course, the vacant space in the hogshead, caused by the displacing of the water, represented the actual size of the shote. In five minutes more, the cubic inches were obtained, and on the return of the Professor the answer was ready for him." The story was well told, and I was obliged to confess to the impeachment.

During this, the last year of my second term on the Fond du Lac District, my strength was taxed to its utmost. Besides the regular Quarterly Meetings, I had made it my earnest concern to aid all the Preachers on the District in their work as far as possible. During the winter this service was largely rendered in protracted meetings, and during the summer in Church enterprises. In fact, the latter branch of labor had been made a specialty during the entire term. And as a result, two Churches had been dedicated in Fond du Lac, three on the Chilton charge, three on the Hingham work, one on the Byron, two on the Markesan, one on the Brandon, one on the Rosendale, one on the Fox Lake, one on the Empire, and one on the Horicon and Juneau, besides quite a number that were remodeled and largely improved. Including both classes, we had had on the District during the term twenty-two Church enterprises. Extensive revivals had occurred, and we were now able to report an increase of eight hundred and seventy-seven members.

CHAPTER XXIV

The Conference of 1869 was held September 23d at Appleton, Bishop Scott presiding. My term on the District had now expired, and a new appointment must follow. Several of the strongest charges opened their doors, but for reasons that were quite satisfactory both to myself and the good people, I was stationed at Ripon.

The following week I started for my new field of labor. As before stated, I had visited this locality in 1845, it then being known as Ceresco. But, besides a casual visit and a week's stay during the session of the Conference, I had enjoyed limited opportunities to maintain an acquaintance with the people or the charge. I reached the city Saturday afternoon, and immediately, satchel in hand, started down Main Street to find some one who might invite me to lodgings. I had not gone far when I saw a gentleman hastily crossing the street to intercept me. On approaching I found it to be Rev. E.J. Smith, a Local Preacher, to whom reference has been made in former chapters in connection with Fall River. I had learned of his removal to Ripon, but was hardly prepared to meet my old friend so suddenly, and receive such a hearty greeting. An invitation to lodgings immediately followed, and I joyfully accepted, remembering the kind hospitality this noble family had given me in other days.

After chatting over the past, and taking some refreshments, my old friend took me out to a multitude of introductions among the brethren. I found them all cordial, and began to feel quite at home among them. Passing down Main Street, we visited the Church, a building of respectable size and comparatively new, and passing down still further into the borders of what was formerly known as Ceresco proper, we found the Parsonage. This little walk of Saturday gave me an outline of the lay of things, and helped me to poise my head and arrange my thoughts for the Sabbath.

The Sabbath gave me a fair congregation, and at the close of the service we enjoyed a good Class Meeting, Led by my old friend, E.J. Smith. And as one of the living members of the class, I found also an old acquaintance of my boyhood and later years, Albert Cook. There were also a few friends of other days still residing in Ripon, and several who had come from other places to reside in the city, to join in the cordial greeting that was given me. The Sunday School, under the charge of Rev. Byron Kingsbury, so well known throughout the State in the Sunday School work, met also at the close of the morning service. It was in a flourishing condition, as it could not well be otherwise with such a Superintendent. The Superintendent introduced the new Pastor to the school, and playfully asked them if they thought the new Pastor was as good-looking as the old. Quite to my surprise, they answered in the affirmative. In the few remarks that followed I accounted for the good looks of both the former Pastor and the present on the score that I was the Father and the former Pastor was one of my boys, as I had introduced him to the Conference some years before. This little sally reconciled the children to the new state of things, and secured me a kindly greeting from all of them.

Since my Pastorate in 1845, a variety of changes had passed over the place and the Church. I found Ripon no longer a small settlement, nestled in the little valley between the bluffs, but a veritable city, now largely perched on the brow of the prairie, with its numerous business houses, its Churches, and its College. The Church, instead of being a small class with its meetings first in the dining hall and afterwards in the small school house, was now a large Society, and comfortably quartered in a respectable Church edifice.

But all these changes had not come in a day. The Circuit of twenty-four appointments, of which Ripon was only one, had been divided and subdivided until they had become nearly a score of charges. To trace these changes in detail would weary the reader, and hence I have only referred to them incidentally, as they have fallen into the line of my subsequent labors. In this connection, I must confine myself to Ripon and its immediate vicinity.

The first Quarterly Meeting of which I can find a record was held in Ceresco by Rev. J.M. Walker, Oct. 15th, 1855, Rev. William Stevens was then the Preacher in charge. The official members were: George Limbert, Local Preacher, Z. Pedrick, Recording Steward, Thos. P. Smith, Steward, and David S. Shepherd, Class Leader. There were at this time four classes connected with the charge, and these were located at Ripon, Ceresco. Rush Lake, and Utica. At the fourth Quarterly Meeting of this year there were two Sunday Schools reported. One at Ceresco, with thirty-three scholars, and one at Ripon, with twenty-one.

The following year, 1856, Rev. R. Moffat was sent to the charge. Utica was now put into another charge, and Democrat Prairie attached to Ceresco. During this year, a small frame Church was built in Ceresco, on the east side of the street, and about forty rods south of the Ceresco mill. The pioneer Church was used until 1860, when it was sold to Mr. W.H. Demming, who removed it to its present location for a cooper-shop. From 1856 to 1860, while the services in Ceresco were thus held in the small Church, the meetings in Ripon were held in the City Hall, which was rented for the purpose. When the new Church was built, the congregations were united.

The new Church, under the Pastorate of Rev. William Morse, was commenced in May, 1860, and the lecture-room was ready for use in March, 1861. The audience room was not completed until the Pastorate of Rev. J.T. Woodhead in 1862. Brother Woodhead was succeeded by Rev. Joseph Anderson.

Brother Morse had entered the traveling connection in the State of New York, had located, and had come West, seeking health for his wife. The death of Brother Maxson, of which mention is made in a former chapter, had left Ripon without a Pastor, and Brother Morse was employed to fill the vacancy.

Besides filling out the unexpired year, he remained two years on the charge, and during his Pastorate there were many accessions. He filled several other appointments subsequently in the Conference with great acceptability, but on account of family affliction, he was finally compelled to retire from active labor. At this writing he is in Western Iowa, where he does what he can to help on the good cause. He is a man of sweet spirit, and is highly esteemed by all his brethren.

Brother Anderson entered the Wisconsin Conference in 1852, and was stationed at South Grove, in Racine District. His subsequent appointments had been Milton, Geneva, Sheboygan Falls, Fond du Lac District, and Appleton. On the stations, and during his four years on the District, he had done efficient work, and was now brought to Ripon as the successor of Brother Woodhead, where he was well received. After leaving Ripon, his appointments have been, Presiding Elder on the Waupaca District four years, Waupaca Station, Second Church, Oshkosh, and Omro, his present field.

Brother Anderson is a man of large frame, and gives evidence of unusual physical strength. He has a strong head, a kind heart, and is inclined to the humorous. He can tell a good story in a social circle, and can relate a good anecdote in the pulpit. In the latter he is gifted in the line of similes, which often in his hands make the sermon interesting and profitable. He gives promise of many more years of usefulness.

At Ripon, the Sabbath having passed, steps were taken to place the Parsonage in readiness to receive the Pastor's family. Those noble women, Mrs. Kingsbury, Mrs. Smith, and others, not only aided in the necessary provision, but actually gave their personal superintendence to the arrangement of the furniture. A new carpet was put down in the parlor;

a new stove in the sitting room, and such other measures taken as were deemed necessary to render the coming and stay of the Pastor's family agreeable to them. And when the family came on Thursday, they found the rooms warm, the table spread, and the house filled with happy faces, warm hearts and ready hands, to give them a cordial greeting. Such a reception, given by such a people, robs the Itinerancy of half its burdens, and gives to the relations of Pastor and people an exquisite setting.

The preliminaries settled, I took up my work in the order I had been accustomed to follow whenever assigned to station work. Knowing the importance of the pastoral as well as the pulpit labor, I had always been accustomed to adhere strictly to a division of labor, giving the forenoons to my study, and the afternoons to pastoral visits. By this arrangement I found I could give to the study all the time necessary to fully employ a healthy brain, and yet find time to pass over in consecutive order the entire list of families in regular attendance upon the Church, three or four times a year. The prosecution of this plan in Ripon soon filled the house with people, and also added greatly to the spiritual prosperity of the membership.

During the winter considerable revival interest pervaded the congregation, which had now come to fill the Church to suffocation, and not less than seventy-five persons professed conversion. The students from the College came to the Church in great numbers, and several of them were found among the converts.

During the winter, a lecture course was instituted, under the auspices of the Literary Society connected with the College, and I was requested to give the first lecture. The flattering manner in which the effort was spoken of by the press brought other invitations, and I yielded to several of them, though my time was too much occupied with my regular work to indulge myself far in this direction. At this time I was also employed to do considerable work in connection with the press. Besides becoming one of the corresponding editors of the Index and the N.W. Advance, two papers published in Milwaukee, I accepted the position of a Local Editor on the Fond du Lac Commonwealth, and in this capacity represented Ripon and its vicinity in its columns.

During the winter, I was called to Onion River to dedicate the new brick Church that had been built on the Hingham charge, and in the following summer I was called to Oshkosh to re-open the First Church, which had been enlarged and greatly improved by the Rev. Wm. P. Stowe. Frequent calls were also made upon me for addresses on Temperance and other subjects. I yielded as far as consistent with my other obligations, but made in these cases, as ever in the course of my labors, all such calls yield to the pressing demands of my regular Ministerial work.

But at this stage of our work, another enterprise lay immediately before the good people of Ripon. The Church could no longer accommodate the crowds of people that thronged it, and an extension became necessary. A united and generous effort, however, soon rendered this necessary improvement a fixed fact. By an extension of the length and reconstruction of the basement, and suitable refitting, the Ripon Church became not only commodious, but, in size, the second Church in the northern portion of the Conference.

On one of the beautiful days of June, I concluded to make a visit to Berlin. Taking my family in a carriage, we passed over a delightful country and along pleasant roads, wondering at the change that had come over that region since I made my wild excursion in this direction in 1845, to find Strong's Landing. I now found Berlin a pleasant city and the home of many valued friends, whom I had known elsewhere.

Berlin, though now aspiring to be a charge of respectable standing, had its beginning, like all others, in "the day of small things." The first Methodist sermon was preached by Rev. Mr. Bassinger in September, 1850. The services were held in the office of a warehouse. Berlin was now connected with Dartford, and became a regular appointment. Brother Bassinger formed a class in connection with the first service in the warehouse. The members were Reuben Tompkins, his wife, and two daughters, Mrs. Kellogg and Mrs. McElroy.

Until a Church was built the meetings were held, after leaving the warehouse, first over Mr. Bartlett's store, and afterwards over Mr. Alexander's clothing store. The first Church was built under the Pastorate of Rev. J. Pearsall in 1851. It did good service for several years, and was then sold. It is now used as a blacksmith shop. The second church, the present respectable edifice, was built in 1858 by Rev. D. Stansbury, and was dedicated by the late Dr. T.M. Eddy. The Parsonage was built by Rev. D.O. Jones in 1862.

Rev. Isaac Wiltse, the Pastor at Berlin at this time entered the Wisconsin Conference at its April session in 1859. His charges before coming to Berlin were Wautoma, Kingston, Door Creek, Lowell, Liberty Prairie, and Dartford. Since leaving Berlin, his appointment has been Beaver Dam, where he is now doing a good work for the Master.

Brother Wiltse is one of those men who usually remain on a charge as long as the law of the Church will permit. He is a young man of a clear understanding and genuine piety. As a Preacher he holds an excellent position in the Conference, and he is not less esteemed as a Pastor. Avoiding all effort to make a show in the world, he furnishes a large stock of Gospel truth in his sermons, and puts into his administration an equal share of common sense.

The next session of the Conference was held Oct. 12, in Janesville. We were returned to Ripon, as expected by all. But the year opened with another of those occasions which strangely unite both joy and sorrow. On the third day of November, a happy group were met at the Parsonage, to celebrate the marriage of our second daughter, Laura Eunice, and Mr. Jesse Smith, of Fond du Lac. This event took to Fond du Lac our second and only remaining daughter, leaving us alone with our son, now twelve years of age, as the only representative of young life in the household. Those only who have thus felt the shadows one after another creeping around the home hearth, can realize the desolation of feeling that broods over the parental heart on such occasions. But there is no time in this life to estimate its losses. The duties of the day are ever upon us, and we must away at their call.

The Church enlargement had been completed, and every indication gave promise of a successful year. Our associations were exceedingly pleasant, and the Church, at peace in all her borders, was in a healthy spiritual condition. During the winter a revival again blessed the labors of Pastor and people. The following summer was one of great comfort. The two years spent at Ripon were among the most happy of all our Itinerant life. Not a jar had disturbed the fair fabric of our dreams, not a ripple had disturbed the happy flow of feeling. And, strongly entrenched in the confidence and good feeling of all the people, we closed the year in full expectation of a return and another successful term.

CHAPTER XXV

The Conference of 1871 was held in the Summerfield Church, Milwaukee, Oct. 11, and was presided over by Bishop Simpson. At this session the election of Delegates to the General Conference again occurred. The Conference was entitled to five clerical Delegates, and the Laymen to two. The Conference elected G.M. Steele, C.D. Pillsbury, Henry Bannister, P.R. Pease, and W.G. Miller. The Laymen's Convention elected Hon. Wm. P. Lyon, of the Supreme Court of the State, and R.P. Elmore, Esq., of Milwaukee. Judge Lyon being unable to attend, his place was filled by Prof. H.A. Jones, of Lawrence University.

At this session provision was made to hold a Methodist State Convention at Madison during the following summer. Able reports were also adopted on the subject of Temperance and the observance of the Christian Sabbath, showing that the members of the body kept abreast with the demands of the times.

This year the Conference was called to make a record of the death of two of its members, Rev. Isaac Searles, and Rev. Thomas Hughes. As reference has been made to the first named in a former chapter, it need not be repeated in this connection.

Brother Hughes was a native of Wales, and had been connected with our Welsh work. Alter serving two years in the Welsh Mission in Oneida Conference he came to Wisconsin in 1857. He settled in Fond du Lac county, and for several years supplied the Welsh Mission in Nekimi, preaching also at times to the English population in that neighborhood. His death occurred in Utica, N.Y. He was a man of strong mind, amiable spirit, and thoroughly versed in the doctrines of the Bible and the standards of the Church.

Besides this depletion of the Itinerant ranks, three of our brethren had been called during the year to go down into the deep shadows of domestic affliction, in the loss of their companions, Revs. William Teal, Warren Woodruff and H.H. Jones. The obituaries of these devoted co-laborers were inserted in the Conference Minutes.

During the session of the Conference, Mrs. Miller and myself were entertained by the Misses Curry, whose generous hospitality made our stay with them exceedingly pleasant. We also visited many of our old friends in the city as opportunity permitted, little dreaming of the surprise that was awaiting us.

The Conference closed in the usual manner by the reading of the appointments. But judge of our surprise to find ourselves assigned for a third time to the Pastorate of Spring Street Station, Milwaukee. To say we were surprised indeed would be but to state the truth, and yet to say we were pained we could not, for who that has ever known the good people of Old Spring Street, could ever deem it an affliction to be stationed among them. However, when we looked upon the weeping eyes of several of our dear Ripon friends in the congregation, and thought of the many others at home, we would have been other than human if our eyes had not also filled with tears. Nor is it too much to say, that we did not know how much we were attached to the good people of Ripon and our work there, until we found ourselves so suddenly separated from them. But on the other hand, what could we say? We came first to Milwaukee when in our youth. We came again to the Milwaukee District in 1859, and to the station in 1862, giving to the first four years of severe labor, and to the last three of the most successful years of our Itinerant life. We had known this people as it seldom falls to the lot of Itinerants to know a people. With not a few we had knelt at the Altar of God, when they passed into the spiritual kingdom. The names of very many of them had been entered by the writer's hand on the records of the Church. With many we had bowed our heads in recognition of their deep sorrow, and with many had clasped hands in the day of their rejoicing. And now, to be sent back to a third Pastorate within a period of twenty years, could not be deemed less than a great privilege.

But to our work. Following my life-long custom, the first Sabbath of the new Conference year found me at my post of labor. I was happy to find the charge in a good spiritual condition, and hence I was able to take up the work in its ordinary line of service. My first care was to arrange a complete system of pastoral labor, still entertaining the conviction that upon the faithful prosecution of this branch of the Ministerial work depended, in a good degree, the success of the pastoral function. And in this branch of service Spring Street Station imposes a vast amount of labor. As the mother Church of the city, her membership is widely scattered, and her congregations large. Yet the Pastor, with a careful husbanding of time, and an earnest effort, can pass over the field as often as the exigencies of the work require. He may not always visit each family as often as they desire, for there are many in every Church who have a very limited idea of the amount of labor, care and thought the pastoral office imposes, but he will be able to meet all reasonable demands.

The new Church had been completed during the preceding year, and had been dedicated by Rev. Drs. Eddy and Ives on the Sabbath before Conference, Oct. 8th, 1871. The building is a fine brick structure, one hundred feet in length by eighty in width at the transepts. Besides the auditorium, it has a large lecture-room, three parlors, a Pastor's study, a library room, and a convenient kitchen. The entire cost of buildings and grounds, including the Parsonage, was sixty thousand dollars. At the dedication subscriptions were obtained to meet the indebtedness of twenty thousand dollars with a satisfactory margin.

The new year opened with all the Church appliances in vigorous operation. The class and prayer meetings were well attended, and the intervening evenings were occupied by the meetings of the Ladies' Aid, the Literary and other Church societies. The Sunday School, under the superintendence of Rev. Edwin Hyde, was in a flourishing condition, ranking, doubtless, as one of the most numerous and successful schools of the city.

The Milwaukee District was now in charge of Rev. C.D. Pillsbury, who entered the Maine Conference in 1843. He filled the following appointments in that Conference: Dover, Atkinson, Sagerville, and Exeter. At the division in 1848, he fell into the East Maine Conference, where his appointments were Machias, Summer Street, Bangor, Agent of East Maine Seminary, and Presiding Elder of Bangor District. He was transferred to the Wisconsin Conference in 1857, and stationed at Racine as the writer's successor. His subsequent appointments have been Racine District, Chaplain of the Twenty-Second Regiment, Beloit, Agent of the Freedmen's Aid Commission, Janesville District, and Milwaukee District.

After leaving the District Brother Pillsbury has been stationed at Bay View and Menasha, but, his health failing, he took a supernumerary relation at the last Conference, and at this writing is residing at Minneapolis. He has done considerable literary work, in connection with his Ministerial labors. Brother Pillsbury has a well balanced mind, and is thoroughly versed in the great questions of the day. He is sound in theology and faithful in administration; a good, strong Preacher, and is universally respected, both as a man and a Minister.

Asbury Church was greatly delighted with the return of Rev. W.W. Case to its pastorate. He entered the Erie Conference in 1859, and in that Conference he had been stationed at Ellington, Cattaraugus, and Little Valley. He was transferred to the Wisconsin Conference in 1864, and had now been stationed three years each at Edgerton and Beloit. During his year at Asbury, he had gathered a fine congregation, and was now in great esteem among the people. He remained three years at Asbury, and was then stationed at Division Street, Fond du Lac, where he is at the present writing, serving the second year.

Brother Case is still a young man, and is blessed with a pleasant countenance, agreeable manners, and an affable spirit. In social life he is a great favorite. He is well read, and has an entertaining delivery. In the selection of his pulpit topics, and in the manner of their treatment, he dwells more in the sunshine than in the storm. He has already reached a position among his brethren that gives promise of great usefulness in the Master's work.

It has not been my purpose to embody in these pages a record of the exceedingly interesting and prosperous work among our German brethren, as their branch of Methodistic labor in the State has developed an Annual Conference of its own, and richly deserves a volume for its proper presentation. But as our Norwegian brethren are connected with our own Conference, a brief reference to their work will not be out of place.

It will be recollected that in a former chapter reference was made to the beginning of the work in our State. We will now refer to the opening of the good work in Milwaukee.

In the spring of 1864, the writer was holding a protracted meeting in the Spring Street Methodist Episcopal Church. At one of the meetings there came to the Altar as seekers, two Norwegians. As the meetings progressed, others came with them, until there were some twelve persons on probation and in full membership, who used the Scandinavian language. During the following summer, it was deemed advisable to form them into a class by themselves, and as they resided in the vicinity of the Asbury Church, put them in connection with that charge. Rev. P.K. Rye, then stationed at Racine, came down a few times and furnished them services in their own language.

At the ensuing session of the West Wisconsin Conference, in which the Scandinavian work was then placed, Milwaukee was connected with Racine charge, and placed under the care of Rev. A. Haagenson. The society was duly organized by the new Pastor on the 25th day of March, 1865. Brother Haagenson was greatly blessed in his labors, and before the end of the year purchased the German Baptist Church, located on Walker Street, between Hanover and Greenbush. The cost of the building and lots was eight hundred dollars. Brother Haagenson remained until 1868, when he was succeeded on the Milwaukee and Racine Mission by Rev. N. Christopherson, who remained until the close of 1870.

In 1871, Milwaukee and Ashipun were put together, with Rev. C.O. Trider as Pastor. The erection of a new Church, twenty-eight by forty-five feet in size, was commenced in December, and in May, 1872, the lecture-room was dedicated by Rev. A. Haagenson. At the present writing, Brother Haagenson is the Presiding Elder of the Norwegian District, and has also charge of the Station, having in the latter portion of his work Rev. O. Hanson as an Assistant.

Brother Haagenson is a man of deep piety and earnest purpose. Studious and laborious, he furnishes an excellent type of a Methodist Preacher. His labors are onerous, but his work is in a highly prosperous state, and is making a record of many conversions.

On the fourth of January, 1872, we celebrated our silver wedding. We had made a note of our wedding anniversary with considerable regularity from year to year, but had never until now celebrated any of the epochs which are so often made to divide the years of married life. In this instance we deemed it advisable to depart from our usual custom, since twenty-five years seems to be a point from which both the past and future may be seen ordinarily with considerable distinctness of outline. And further, it was now probable that the whole family could be brought together, an event which could not be looked upon with any great degree of assurance as probable at any future time.

The entertainment was given in the evening in the Parsonage, and was attended by about one hundred persons. Spring Street and the other Churches of the city were well represented. But in addition to these, there were delegations present from all the charges we had served in the Conference, each bringing the hand of greeting from our old friends to cheer us. A record of the occasion, however, would be incomplete if I were not to state that the silver ware of the house was increased by an addition valued at nearly five hundred dollars. But every rose has its thorn. Never before were we obliged to sleep with one eye open to guard our treasures.

The year now drew to a close, and, counting up the results, we found that fifty-one members had been received, the Pastor's salary, amounting to twenty-three hundred dollars, had been paid, the Church debt had been reduced to ten thousand dollars, and that to meet the balance there were subscriptions, including organ fund, of fifteen thousand dollars.

CHAPTER XXVI

The Conference of 1872 was held Oct. 9th, at Division Street Church, Fond du Lac, Bishop Haven presiding. The Woman's Foreign Missionary Society, having been fully recognized by the General Conference, was made the subject of a highly appreciative report, in which the Conference extended to the ladies of the Church a cordial welcome to this new field of effort, and pledged them a helping hand in the good work.

At this session Rev. A.P. Mead was appointed Presiding Elder of Waupaca District. Brother Mead graduated from the Garrett Biblical Institute in 1861, and was the same year admitted into the Conference. His appointments had been Sharon, Elkhorn, Kenosha, Bay View, and Lyons, when he was sent to the District. He remained only two years on the Waupaca District, and was then appointed to the Fond du Lac District. Brother Mead is a man of genial spirit and large practical sense. His sermons are replete with Evangelical truth, and produce an abiding impression. His intercourse with the people and Preachers is instructive, and his administration cannot fail to prove a blessing to the District.

At this session of the Conference, the decease of Rev. Aurora Callender, among others, was announced. Brother Callender entered the Pittsburg Conference in 1828, and was first stationed at Franklin, a circuit located on the slope of the Alleghany Mountains, and in the neighborhood of the Oil Regions. Before coming to Wisconsin, his appointments were Meadville Circuit, Meadville, Springfield, Cuyahoga Falls, Chardon and Middleburgh. Coming to Wisconsin, he was stationed, in 1850, at Sylvania. His subsequent appointments were Geneva and Elkhorn, Union, Hazel Green, Dodgeville, Mineral Point District, Norwegian Mission District, Clinton, and Agent of American Colonization Society, Subsequently he filled several charges as a supply, and departed this life in the midst of his work at Pickneyville, Ill., Oct. 23d, 1871.

Brother Callender was a veteran pioneer. Capable of great physical endurance, possessing a vigorous intellect, well skilled in theology and Methodist law, his labors were abundant and of a substantial character. In his earlier years, especially, his Ministry led many souls to the Cross.

At this Conference I was returned to Spring Street Station, and, Brother Pillsbury's term on the District having expired, Rev. Wm. P. Stowe was appointed Presiding Elder.

Brother Stowe, it will be remembered, was converted in his boyhood in his father's chapel. When grown to man's estate, he took up the trowel and thereby procured funds to secure his education. He graduated from the Lawrence University as a member of the Second Class, in 1858. He entered the Conference the same year, and was stationed at Sheboygan. The following two years he was stationed at Port Washington, but before the close of the second year his health failed, and he retired from the work. In 1862 he accepted the Chaplaincy of the Twenty-Seventh Regiment, but the year following he was re-admitted and stationed at Sharon. His subsequent appointments were Beloit, Racine, Oshkosh, and Summerfield, Milwaukee, in all of which charges he has left the fragrance of a good name and the legacy of substantial fruit. As a Presiding Elder, he is deservedly popular.

Brother Stowe has a large frame, tends to corpulency, and shows great physical vigor. With large perception, he reads men and surroundings aptly. In the pulpit, he puts ideas in logical relations, and aims at an object. His sermons abound in illustrations, strung on a strong cord of Evangelical truth.

Rev. O.B. Thayer was stationed at Summerfield Church, having become a member of the Conference in 1870. He had been stationed at Court Street Church, Janesville, and at Appleton. In both these charges he had developed a high standard of pulpit talent. He remained at Summerfield two years, and was then appointed to Kenosha, where, at the present writing, he is preaching to fine congregations.

Rev. S. Reynolds, State Agent of the American Bible Society, was also a member of the Ministerial fraternity of Milwaukee. This good brother came to the Conference by transfer from Iowa. He has been engaged for many years in his present work, and has gained a reputation, second to none, in the management of the laborious and manifold responsibilities of his position. In his addresses he deals in stubborn facts, and never fails to interest the audience. He is vigilant in looking after the details of his trust, but he needs a word of caution as to his health. His great labor is evidently overtaxing his strength.

My salary was again fixed at two thousand three hundred dollars. A new system of finance was now adopted, called the "Envelope System." In its principal features, it was similar to the "Card System," introduced during my former term, but contained several additional provisions to render it more effective. The new plan succeeded admirably, giving to the station, at the end of the first quarter of the year, the extraordinary record of having fully paid the Pastor's salary, and every other claim for current expenses, besides liquidating several bills for improvements on the Church and Parsonage. And it is proper to add that the current year closed with several hundred dollars in the Treasury.

The regular work of the station opened this year encouragingly. A general quickening followed, and by mid-winter there had been half a score of conversions. Mrs. Maggie N. Van Cott, who had been engaged for a year to assist us, now came to our help. The meeting continued five weeks, under this most extraordinary laborer, and resulted in the conversion of near four hundred souls, about two hundred of whom united with the Spring Street Church.

The Conference of 1873 was held Oct. 15, at Whitewater, Bishop Merrill presiding. At this session Rev. Henry Colman, who had repeatedly served as Assistant, was elected Secretary of the Conference.

Brother Colman graduated from the Lawrence University as a member of the First Class in 1856. He entered the West Wisconsin Conference in 1858, and filled one appointment in that Conference, when, in 1859, he was transferred to the Wisconsin Conference and stationed at Columbus. In 1860 he was stationed at Green Bay, and the following year at Asbury, Milwaukee. In 1863 he was appointed Principal of the Evansville Seminary, where he remained four years. After leaving the Seminary, he has held a respectable class of appointments, and is now doing effective work at Fort Atkinson. He is a man of clear head and honorable, Christian impulses. Having a thorough knowledge of Biblical criticism, he has for several years rendered the Sunday Schools of the State a good service by furnishing in the Christian Statesman a weekly exposition of the Lesson.

In keeping with the provision of the Discipline, adopted at the recent session of the General Conference, for the Trial of Appeals, the Conference elected her quota as follows: W.G. Miller, O.J. Cowles, Joseph Anderson, J.W. Carhart, P.B. Pease, P.S. Bennett, and W.P. Stowe. But as there were no cases to be tried, the brethren elected were compelled to wear empty honors.

At this Conference, the writer again returned to Spring Street, it being the third year of the third term of my Pastorate among this people, and the thirtieth Conference year of my itinerent labors. Brother Stowe was also returned to the District, and Rev. A.A. Hoskin was appointed to Asbury, and Rev. Stephen Smith to Bay View.

Brother Hoskin entered the Conference in 1867, and before coming to the city had been stationed at Milton, Shopiere, and Menomonee Falls. He is a young man of fine culture, genial spirit, and great industry. His sermons embody the fundamental truths of the Gospel, and their manifold relations to practical life, and are highly appreciated by the people.

Besides being a good Preacher, he is also a poet of considerable reputation.

Brother Smith entered the Conference in 1856, and his first appointment was Sylvania. His subsequent appointments have been Elkhorn, Sharon, Geneva, Manitowoc, Fort Atkinson, Delavan, First Church, Janesville, and Bay View. On all these charges he has left the evidences of earnest and devoted work for the Master. At Bay View, the present year has been one of extraordinary success. The revival that transpired under his labors swept through the entire community, and gave an accession of more than one hundred members, a majority of whom were heads of families.

Brother Smith is a good Preacher, filling his sermons with a clear exposition of Evangelical truth. And his Ministry has ever been a benediction to the people of his respective charges.

The year opened in Spring Street Station with unusual promise. The social meetings were well attended, the congregations were large and attentive, the Sunday School, the largest in the city, prosperous, the several societies were doing effective work, and the finances were in an excellent condition. With this outlook, we were anticipating a glorious year, but how uncertain are all human expectations!

During the delivery of the morning sermon on Sabbath, April 26th, 1874, the writer was taken violently ill. The attack proved to be the prostration of the nervous system, resulting from overworking the brain, a difficulty that had been foreshadowed by several premonitions during the preceding year. My condition at the first was perilous, but after four hours of skillful medical treatment and careful nursing, the crisis passed. Then followed weary weeks of watching and waiting. Meantime, I received the earnest sympathy of my people, and the kind assistance of my brethren in the Ministry, who generously proposed to supply my pulpit.

The Conference of 1874 was held at Oshkosh, Bishop Foster presiding. I was able to attend and answer to my name, but could spend but little time in the Conference room. Whenever present I seemed to myself, as I must have seemed to others, like a dismantled ship, stranded on the beach. I was most kindly treated by all the brethren, being relieved of every burden, and assured of abiding sympathy.

At this Conference Rev. J.W. Carhart, D.D., was stationed, by request of the people, at Oshkosh. Brother Carhart entered the traveling connection in the Troy Conference, and came to the Wisconsin Conference by transfer in 1871, being stationed at Racine. He had just completed a full term, and hence Oshkosh is his second appointment in the Conference. He is a man of superior culture, fine preaching ability, and cannot fail to give character to the pulpit, wherever he may be stationed.

Rev. George A. Smith was stationed at Spring Street as my successor. Brother Smith entered the Conference in April 1859, his first appointment being Principal of the Evansville Seminary. His subsequent appointments were Milton, Emerald Grove, Lyons and Spring Prairie. In his last field his health failed through intense mental application, and he was compelled to retire from the work. After five years of rest he was again able to resume his labors, being stationed first at Pleasant Prairie, and next at Kenosha.

Brother Smith is in the strength of his manhood, has a vigorous mind, is a fine thinker, uses clear-cut and well selected language, has a most amiable spirit, and his Ministry cannot fail to be a grand success anywhere.

Brother Stowers came to the Conference by transfer in 1867, and first served as Professor in the Lawrence University. In 1869, having been elected President of the Upper Iowa University, he was transferred to the Upper Iowa Conference. He returned, however, to the Wisconsin Conference the following year, and was stationed at Janesville. His next charge was Whitewater, where, during his three years' Pastorate, he achieved great success in the erection of a fine brick Church, and in securing large accessions to the membership.

Brother Stowers is a man of great energy and decided talent. He has an excellent voice, a ready utterance, and abundant illustrations, which render his pulpit labors attractive. He is an able and successful Minister.

At the adjournment of the Conference, the Preachers hastened to their new fields of labor, perhaps hardly thinking, in their eagerness to be at their work, of the tearful eyes that were looking after them, and the aching hearts of those brethren who, no longer able to go out with them to the battle, were compelled to languish in hospitals, or linger by the wayside.

As for myself, I returned to Milwaukee, and retired to the quiet home a few personal friends in the city and elsewhere had assisted me to build, and where I now write this, the last line of